Into the
Suffersphere
Cycling and the Art of Pain

In Loving Memory of Richard Malnick,

1937–2015.

Into the Suffersphere

Cycling and the Art of Pain

Jon Malnick

ROBERT HALE

First published in 2016 by Robert Hale,
an imprint of The Crowood Press Ltd,
Ramsbury, Marlborough Wiltshire SN8 2HR

www. crowood.com

www.halebooks.com

© Jon Malnick 2016

All rights reserved. No part of this publication may be reproduced
or transmitted in any form or by any means, electronic or
mechanical, including photocopy, recording or any information
storage and retrieval system, without permission in writing
from the publishers.

British Library Cataloguing-in-Publication Data
A catalogue record for this book is available from the British Library.

ISBN 978 0 7198 2000 7

The right of Jon Malnick to be identified as author of this work has
been asserted by him in accordance with the Copyright, Designs and
Patents Act 1988.

Typeset by Jean Cussons Typesetting, Diss, Norfolk

Printed and bound in India by Replika Press Pvt Ltd

Contents

CHAPTER 1

From Marx to Merckx

'The only antidote to mental suffering is physical pain.'

Karl Marx

I rolled to a halt and staggered off my bike, letting it clatter expensively on to the road. A race vehicle pulled up behind me, headlights ablaze. As I first kneeled, then prostrated myself on the slick cobblestones, I noticed the rain finally had stopped. Then everything faded softly, soundlessly, to black.

I came around a while later, this time laid out in the back of the race ambulance, foggy headed, wondering how long I'd been there and why I wasn't still on my bike. From the front passenger seat, a uniformed young woman asked me, in what I guessed was Flemish – and, after getting no response, once more in perfect English – how I was feeling. As it happened, I wasn't feeling too terrible and probably more chipper than anyone who'd just collapsed sideways off his bike in a rain-sodden, Belgian *kermesse* had any right to feel. Suffering in a bike race was not a big deal. Daily doses of pain and discomfort were par for the course, business as usual. I'd lost count of the times I'd crossed a finish line on the verge of throwing up. If I instead climbed off the bike with a few breaths to spare, with my heart *not* about to explode out of my chest, I'd berate myself for not having suffered enough. During training rides I often hammered up hills so hard that upon reaching the top my vision tunnelled and I came close to passing out. But this was the first time I'd succeeded in rendering myself completely out for the count.

The longest and toughest bike race in the world, the Tour de France, was founded in 1903 by Henri Desgrange, a bicycle racer turned newspaper editor, who, during his racing career, had claimed a dozen track cycling world records, including the world hour record in 1893. In Desgrange's estimation, 'The ideal Tour was a Tour which only one rider would have the necessary power and endeavour to complete.' For him, simple metrics such as speed or power were not the main concern. Exploring the limits of the human body and pitting man against man and against nature were what got his competitive juices flowing.

Desgrange, a lifelong advocate of strenuous exertion to the point of exhaustion, had witnessed France's humiliation in the Franco-Prussian war, and believed that his countrymen were 'tired, without muscle, without character and without willpower'. In the words of a more recent Tour *directeur*, Jacques Goddet, 'Desgrange imposed on himself a life of submitting to daily physical exercises. They had to demand, according to his draconian theories, a violent effort, prolonged, repeated, sometimes going as far as pain, demanding tenacity and even a certain stoicism.' American historian Eugen Weber, the author of a number of well-acclaimed articles on the cultural impact of French sport, believed that the Tour de France played a significant role in early twentieth-century French society. 'It put flesh on the dry bones of values taught in school but seldom internalized: effort, courage, determination, stoic endurance of pain and even fair play,' he wrote.[1] But if most of the above should be self-evident to anyone with a passing interest in the race, then the issue of fair play has always been more contentious.

Renowned French journalist Albert Londres covered the 1924 Tour for his newspaper *Le Petit Parisien*, dubbing the fifteen-day race '*Le Tour de Souffrance*'. During the 371km (230-mile) second stage, the previous year's champion, Henri Pélissier, was penalized for a jersey infraction. Pélissier had ridden off in the pre-dawn chill wearing an extra layer or two, but at some point during the fourteen-hour stage, he discarded a jersey. This contravened race rule no.48, which stated that a rider must finish each stage with everything he had with him at the start. During the next day's stage, a fraction longer at 405km (252 miles), Pélissier, already not in the sunniest of moods, was accosted by a race official who demanded to know how many jerseys he was wearing. A furious Pélissier then abandoned the Tour as it passed through the town of Coutances, with his brother Francis and another teammate, Maurice Ville, also withdrawing in support. Reporter Albert Londres, himself a keen cyclist and writing for *Le Petit Parisien*, later tracked down the three riders in a Coutances café, huddled over mugs of hot chocolate. He asked them what had happened.

'It's the rules. We not only have to ride like animals, we either freeze or suffocate,' Pélissier told him. 'You have no conception what this Tour de France is.' He went on:

It's a Calvary. Worse. The road to The Cross has only fourteen stations; ours has fifteen. We suffer from start to finish. You haven't seen us in the bath after the finish ... when we've got the mud off, we're white as a funeral shroud, drained empty by diarrhoea; we pass out in the water. At night, in the bedroom, we can't sleep, we twitch and dance and jig about like St Vitus.

'There's less flesh on our bodies than you'd see on a skeleton,' offered Francis Pélissier.

'And our toenails,' said Henri. 'I've lost six out of ten, they get worn away bit by bit every stage.'

In recounting the suffering of the 1924 Tour de France, Albert Londres coined the phrase '*Les Forçats de la Route*' (The Convicts of the Road), his choice of words most likely influenced by his visit to the French penal colony in Guyana the previous year – a place he had denounced as a 'factory churning out misery without rhyme or reason'. A true pioneer of investigative journalism, he also exposed systematic abuse in French lunatic asylums and exploitation of African workers in the colonies of Senegal and the French Congo. For Albert Londres, a man committed to unearthing injustice and suffering wherever he found it, the 1924 Tour offered up a rich vein of opportunity and in the two Pélissier brothers he found himself a pair of willing accomplices. Indeed, Londres' field reports on the suffering of the Pélissiers, framed in the language of workers' rights and amplified by France's communist press, sparked a national debate about the harrowing nature of the race that went on for many years.

'The day will come when they'll put lead in our pockets because someone reckons that God made men too light,' Henri Pélissier told Londres. 'It's all going down the chute – soon there'll only be tramps left, no more artists. The sport has gone haywire, out of control.'

Italian Ottavio Bottecchia eventually prevailed in the 1924 Tour, completing the 5,425km (3,370 miles) wearing an approved number of jerseys and taking over 226 hours to complete the anti-clockwise lap of Western Europe's largest nation. Most likely to Desgrange's dismay, another 59 of the 157 starters also managed to finish the race. The 2013 edition of the Tour, one week longer in duration but shorter by 2,000km (1,240 miles), was won by Chris Froome in a fraction under 84 hours.

The modern day *Tour de Souffrance* may be a somewhat truncated version of its pre-war incarnation, but that's no guarantee that it's any less painful. In the 1970 Tour, the great Eddy Merckx briefly lost consciousness after pulverizing his rivals on the torturous climb of Mont Ventoux. Three years prior, Tom Simpson had spent the last agonizing moments of his life grinding his way up the same barren slopes before sliding off his bike and tragically expiring in an amphetamine-fuelled stupor. Irishman Stephen Roche, the 1987 Tour winner, needed emergency oxygen after his legendary fight back against Pedro Delgado on the steep ramps up to La Plagne. As Roche later explained: 'The doctor puts the oxygen mask on me straight away. "Stephen, move your legs in …" and I can't move my legs. I can move nothing. He's trying to put a survival blanket on me, and I can't move my arms.'[2] Television commentator Phil Liggett, for reasons that remain unclear, informs us that 'Steven Roche is sitting calmly on the floor, he's okay.'[3] At this point, the TV camera zooms in on a fully horizontal, ashen-faced Roche, who appears some way off any generally accepted definition of okay.

At the most rarified levels of cycling, it is this uncommon ability to push beyond run of the mill, race-day suffering, past the quotidian aches, pains and twinges – and occasionally into a state of hypoxic near-oblivion – that suggests winning something like the Tour de France might require not only vastly superior physical attributes, but also an almost superhuman capacity for hurting oneself. It is these world champions and Grand Tour winners, the likes of Merckx and Roche, those who continue to hammer mercilessly where others might ease off the pace, who constitute the revered inner circle of The Great Pantheon of Sufferers.

By definition, only a select few sufferers ever make it into The Great Pantheon. My own less than epic blackout had taken place in light drizzle on top of a smallish bump in Flanders, not at the top of a windswept Alpine peak. And, unlike a Merckx or a Roche, I had not displayed any monumental ability to withstand extreme suffering. Instead, I'd shown the typically wilful stupidity of a nineteen-year-old – a skinny nineteen-year-old attempting to race while under the effects of a chest infection. And attempting to race, it should be said, against the express wishes of my coach, a former national team adviser who had coached top 1980s British professionals such as Paul Sherwen and John Herety. It is by no means easy to fathom the thought processes of my younger self, this aspiring two-wheeled genius, who, upon finding himself fortunate enough to work with a top-tier cycling coach, then proceeded to ignore more or less everything he was told. In hindsight, I'm surprised I ever managed to ride to my local bike shop and back without undergoing a serious health mishap, let alone finish any races.

Yet, week after week, in the glossy pages of the cycling magazines, in the sharply etched details of this or that rider's pain-wracked race-face, I saw that hurting was part of the game, that there was no glory without suffering and so more suffering surely meant I was more in the game. If I did not return from a ride bedevilled by a certain degree of physical malaise, then I obviously had not *trained*. Of course, training techniques were much less advanced in those days: no power meters on offer, nor any heart-rate monitors to gauge and record one's efforts. A simple odometer on the handlebars was considered fairly cutting edge at the time. My taciturn bike coach, Harold 'H' Nelson, who had been the Great Britain team masseur at a handful of Olympics and World Championships, and was later awarded the British Empire Medal for services to the sport, would offer the same gruff words of advice after each twenty-minute session on the indoor rollers: 'Don't ride home without your hat on.' By which of course he meant something woolly to keep my head warm. Hard-shell cycling helmets had not been invented yet and the traditional, padded 'hairnet' models were rightly viewed with derision. In any case, this woolly hat counsel made excellent sense for anyone braving a wintry Manchester evening and would probably merit inclusion in a modern coaching tome under the heading of 'marginal gains', and yet a little more in-depth guidance would not have gone amiss. Perhaps there was, after all, a subtly coded message from 'H', one that at least hinted at the importance of measured efforts, at a controlled build-up of intensity, because during the regular roller sessions at his Wythenshawe house, none of his protégés was ever allowed to ride above a steady, mid-tempo pace. But since training over at H's place never felt much like what I'd convinced myself was *proper* training, I compensated by thrashing myself like a lunatic for the remainder of the time I was on my bike.

Michael Hutchinson is Britain's most successful time-trial racer to date, amassing an astonishing fifty-six national titles over two decades of riding extremely fast. He's also held competition records at every distance between 10 and 100 miles. In his book *Faster*, Hutchinson writes: 'The instinct of most athletes is to train, and train, and train. The single most important job a coach has is to tell you to stop, to take a rest, to recover.'[4] Which, in hindsight, and in so many words, is exactly what my coach was telling me, but for some unknown reason I believed I already knew what I was doing. As in fact did the younger Hutchinson, who recalls that before becoming a world-class cyclist, his self-designed training sessions 'were selected primarily for their unpleasantness and stuffed into an unrelenting weekly schedule until the days bulged at the seams. It may as well have been deliberately designed to blunt as effectively as possible whatever natural ability I'd started with.'[5]

All of which sounds strangely familiar. After several months of barely registering my coach's understated yet solid training advice, I finished third in my first race of the season, a hilly circuit race around the Peak District. I was fairly beside myself with this unexpected result. But 'H', with typical Mancunian bluntness, seemed less than impressed by my race report. 'Of course you made it into the breakaway,' he grunted. 'But you were in a break of three, and yet you only finished third. Explain what went wrong.' 'H', of course, had reason enough to question my less than stellar tactical nous, to wonder why I'd led my two breakaway companions all the way up the final hill, only for both of them to sprint past me just metres from the line. On reflection I saw how I might have played it better. How I could have played my hand a little closer, instead of excitedly waving my cards at my opponents like a blind-drunk poker player. But developing a decent tactical brain, an ability to read the cat and mouse endgame of a race: this would surely require more experience.

In 1972, the superlative career of Edouard Louis Joseph Merckx reached its glorious zenith. He won the Tour de France, the Giro d'Italia, Milan–San Remo, Liège–Bastogne–Liège, the Giro di Lombardia and a handful of other major events. In August that year he told a journalist he would try to beat the world hour record the following winter. At the Giro del Piemonte in early September, he made a solo attack 60km (37 miles) from the finish; his aim not to win the race, but to practise riding at full power in the same low-profile riding position he would use for the hour record attempt. (But in doing so, he also won the race.) Merckx then embarked on a specific training programme for his record attempt, under the guidance of Dr Ceretelli, an Italian academic considered a leading expert on the body's adaptation to altitude – where air resistance is lower and straight-line speed is higher. Mexico City was eventually chosen as the preferred location, but the great champion was forced to train at home, in his garage, for the six-week build-up, using a facemask to replicate the effects of Mexico City's rarified air. As William Fotheringham detailed in *Half Man, Half Bike*, Merckx took delivery of:

> thirty canisters of air with a reduced oxygen content and trained six times a day on static rollers while breathing in the thin air, and with four doctors looking on as he rode. The only glitch came when one of the canisters exploded, injuring one of the doctors and making Merckx believe, for a moment, that his house had blown up.[6]

Six times a day? I typically managed five or six training sessions per week, all entirely unmonitored by doctors, and I had no idea where I could find oxygen canisters. In my student halls of residence there was a drugged-out first-year student doctor living downstairs from me, who would complain vociferously about the noise whenever I took a spin on my indoor rollers. But in the meantime, with my tactical skills evidently in serious deficit, there was nothing to stop me ramping up my training in preparation for the next race. More suffering surely meant that I was more in the game.

More recently, and during a rare hiatus from road cycling, I would occasionally join a regular weekend mountain-bike ride. A handful of us would flag down a pickup truck taxi to ferry us to the trailhead at the summit of Doi Suthep, the densely forested peak that overlooks my adopted home city of Chiang Mai in northern Thailand. The motorized assistance seemed reasonable enough. Pedalling a heavy mountain bike uphill for well over an hour, along an ever-ascending tarmac ribbon, holds little appeal for the average, sensible cyclist. After quaffing an energizing, locally brewed espresso near the summit, we'd be well primed to plunge back down to the valley floor 1,220m (4,000ft) below, weaving a precarious path through all the rocks, ruts and other obstacles the Trail Gods could throw at us.

All good, dirty fun for this group of certified adrenalin junkies, but there was one small problem. As we stopped to refuel afterwards at a café, my legs would feel absolutely fine. No aching, no soreness; no sense even that the legs had been used and this disquieting sensation, this *itch*, would linger for the rest of the day. Eventually, I worked out a solution, which was to tackle the route back to front. In my lowest gear, a gear that was never quite low enough, and this time riding solo, I would grind my way methodically up the steep dirt trails, pause briefly at the mountain top for some minor resuscitation, then freewheel down along the graded road back into town. Less fun, more pain, a little lonely and yet somehow more satisfying.

I rarely had any takers to join me on my back to front ride. Which was fair enough, I suppose. Most would prefer that their weekend mornings fit loosely into the general category of 'recreation', which for the *Oxford Dictionary* is an 'activity done for enjoyment when one is not working'. Yet at some point – and it remains a little unclear at exactly which point – some of us seem to foment within ourselves a curious, nagging need for precisely this kind of painful work. We start coveting it, craving it, almost as if a hospital X-ray exam might reveal the existence of a suffer-shaped hole somewhere deep inside. We try to assure ourselves that there's nothing inherently wrong with this, with seeking out bodily suffering for the calming sense of spiritual purification that follows. It all has much in common with scratching a stubborn itch. The more you scratch, the more you itch.

CHAPTER 2

The Wheel of Life

'There are times when I wish I hadn't won the Tour de France.'
Bradley Wiggins[7]

During the final mountain stage of the 1956 Tour de France, Federico Bahamontes, the Spanish rider recently voted the best climber in the race's history, found himself dropped early on by his great rival, Charly Gaul. 'The Angel' had got one over on 'The Eagle', as cycling archivists might have it. During the climb of the Col de Luitel, 'The Eagle' Bahamontes was reportedly 'overcome by bad morale'. Grinding to a halt halfway up the mountain, Bahamontes duly stepped off his bike and tossed it into a handily situated ravine. But the mental fog resulting from Bahamontes' swift onset of anguish evidently prompted him to make a poor choice of ravine, as his team helpers were able to scramble down and retrieve his bike. Bahamontes remounted and finished the stage in fourth place.

Bike racers clearly know a thing or two about the art of suffering. But history reveals that a longish list of non-bike racers, those everyday folk otherwise known as the general public, have also staked claims to authentic experiences of suffering. Many have insisted on having their own say on the matter, all too often with mind-numbing prolixity. The nineteenth-century German philosophers made a decent name for themselves writing impassioned and largely unreadable analyses of suffering and the meaning of existence. As one Friedrich Nietzsche liked to say to his friends, 'To live is to suffer'. But the Germans, despite a laudable collective effort, were by no means the first to get serious on the thorny topic of suffering. The Buddhists got there first.

Their story begins a little over 2,500 years ago with a young Siddhartha Gautama, who whiled away a quiet month or two lounging under a Bodhi tree – a large and sacred fig tree – in northern India. In a possible attempt to justify his anti-social, work-shy behaviour, he then claimed to have become enlightened as to the true causes of existential suffering. Remarkably, his observations were entirely focused on the universal human condition and not on remedies for insect bites or a stiff lower back. These discoveries later became enshrined as the so-called Four Noble Truths, upon which the founding principles of Buddhism are based.

The Noble Truths attempt to explain the essence of our earthly suffering, the various causes of such suffering and how we may ultimately overcome them. The language used in many of the early texts was Pali, a direct descendant of Sanskrit and believed to be a *lingua franca* for the many Indo-Aryan dialects spoken at the time in the Indian subcontinent. While the word 'suffering' is probably the closest English translation to describe what was vexing the Buddha in his pre-enlightened mode, it's actually a little too restrictive. While our prototypical Buddhists also gave serious thought to related themes such as anxiety, frustration and stress, our modern understanding of these all too human conditions inevitably skims over the deeper, essentially metaphysical meaning of the Noble Truths. In illustrating the painful and mostly unreliable nature of wide swathes of human existence, the early Pali transcripts make frequent reference to a state known as *dukkha*, a concept that encompasses not only plain old physical and mental suffering, but also what might be termed the 'basic unsatisfactoriness of all things'.

This gives us a useful reference point, namely that in the approximate period between birth and death, there is considerable scope for disappointment and disaster – which handily sums up our First Noble Truth. Of course, this might all come across as rather gloomy: universal suffering is to be our lot in life, now go away and deal with it. Yet your average Buddhist still prefers to believe that his or her take on existence is one of realism and objectivity, not abject pessimism. Herein lies the Second Truth, which tells us that dissatisfaction is largely a choice, merely the result of an enfeebled state of mind; that our constant craving for satisfaction every step of the way amounts to a base ignorance of the true nature of things. A little more cheerily, the Third Truth explains that only after we fully grasp the complete folly of our human condition, our foolish cravings and aversions, can we then free ourselves from the torment of endless suffering, the repeating cycle of birth, life and death known as *samsara*.

Sir Bradley Wiggins may well look back upon 2013 as the year of his descent into *dukkha*. Certainly it was an *annus horribilis*. Perhaps the loquacious Londoner would more typically sum it up as a 'pile of crap' – which, as any enlightened soul knows, amounts to more or less the same thing. This would have been nigh on impossible to predict a year earlier when Wiggins won the Tour de France – the first Briton ever to do so – and then claimed Olympic time-trial gold, all within the space of a few weeks. With many commentators hailing him as the best British sportsman of all time, Wiggins said: 'I don't think my sporting career will ever top this. That's it. It will never, never get better than that.'[8]

Ah, Bradley. Although not to my knowledge a practising Buddhist, Wiggo here does seem *au fait* with the vicissitudes of life, the suffering of impermanence, of what Buddhists call *viparinama-dukkha*. As regal and imposing as he'd looked on his Hampton Court throne following his 2012 Olympic time-trial victory, Wiggins' *annus mirabilis* had come dangerously close to collapse just a few weeks earlier. On stage eleven of the Tour de France, Wiggins, already resplendent in yellow and with a two-minute lead overall, was so incensed by an unscripted mountain-top attack from his teammate, Chris Froome, that he later sent the Team Sky managers a text message that read: 'I think it would be better for everyone if I went home.'[9]

When even the triumph of a Grand Tour win comes bundled with frustration and irritation, it's then not hard to understand the appeal of the Buddhists' all-revealing Fourth Truth, 'The Path to the Cessation of *Dukkha*'. Imagine if you will a set of detailed instructions on how best to achieve a more suffer-free existence, a kind of antiquarian self-help manual. This prescriptive tonic, more properly known as 'The Noble Eightfold Path', and which forms the foundation of all Buddhist philosophy, might have even become an early bestseller had it not made its appearance well over a thousand years before the world's first printing press. Buddha & Co. therefore had to make do with word of mouth, offering up their newly found wisdom to all as they strolled around the Indian countryside on what amounted to an ongoing national tour. Tough work for sure, even if the annual monsoon season, which made travel virtually impossible, allowed the monks some well-deserved downtime each year.

Early Buddhists did not have bicycles. After all, the velocipede, the short-lived precursor to the bicycle, did not make its first appearance until the early nineteenth century – an oddly late arrival in evolutionary terms, considering that more complex machines such as steam engines were by then widely in use. But Buddhists certainly had wheels. The Iron Age was in full swing by the time Lord Buddha was wandering around lecturing the public on his Truths. Iron smelting was widespread in India as early as 1,000BC and so during the Buddha's lifetime several centuries later, the Iron Age would have been well into its high-tech phase. Wrought-iron wheels were hammered into shape for all manner of carts, wagons and chariots. The idea of fitting spokes to wheels, usually made from wood to produce lighter and faster vehicles, had been around since as early as 2,000BC. Basic wheel design in fact did not change much over the next couple of millennia, not until the advent of the rubber tyre opened up a new realm of possibilities.

The ancient Aryans who brought the Sanskrit language to India were a nomadic tribe who did most of their travelling in ox-drawn vehicles. In classical Sanskrit, *du* is a prefix that denotes 'bad', while *kha* was originally the term for an aperture, or a hole, and specifically an axle hole for a vehicle. Many scholars believe the correct etymology of *dukkha* is that of a poor-fitting axle hole, one that causes discomfort for the vehicle's occupants. Another variant of *dukkha* in Sanskrit was that of a potter's wheel that would not turn smoothly. Various other Buddhist cultures have used similar terminology; in China, *dukkha* goes by the name of *k*, signifying a broken or irregular wheel that gives the rider a jolt on each revolution – a sensation not unfamiliar to many amateur racers who have unwisely splashed their hard-earned cash on a pair of cut-price carbon wheels, most probably made in China, and probably not built to last. Similarly, we have *ku* in Japanese, *ko* in Korean and *kh* in Vietnamese.

On a winter training ride in early 2013, the newly knighted Sir Wiggins sustained a nasty jolt in the form of several broken ribs when possibly the UK's most hapless van driver unwittingly knocked him off his bike. Wiggins recovered well enough to start the 2013 Giro d'Italia as the pre-race favorite, but then came down with a heavy head cold, a chest infection, and – following a crash early in the race – a serious loss of confidence on the descents, admittedly on roads that were often slick from atrocious, unseasonal weather. To add insult to *dukkha*, Wiggins suffered a slow puncture during the Giro's individual time trial, a stage he was under some pressure to win. Television coverage showed him hurling his Pinarello time-trial machine off the road (no handy ravine this time), his frustration all too evident as he awaited a spare bike.

After abandoning the Giro on stage twelve, Wiggins then pulled out of the 2013 Tour de France a week before the start in Corsica. Whatever narratives were offered up to explain Wiggins' non-participation, the plain truth was that Chris Froome, teammate if not exactly best mate, was a stronger candidate to challenge for the 2013 Tour. Froome duly obliged by reaching Paris in yellow and with the biggest winning margin for sixteen years. After Froome's triumph, Wiggins explained to reporters: 'I didn't watch it – I couldn't watch it. ... I followed it from afar, but it was too painful to watch.'[10]

A year earlier, Wiggins had spoken at length about the extreme sacrifices involved in preparing for the Tour de France – the six-hour training rides each day, then bedding down for the night in a hermetically sealed oxygen tent; the monotony of living on top of a volcano in the middle of nowhere and the long months away from his wife and kids. Training for the Tour involves suffering. Winning the Tour calls for more of the same. But despite putting in the graft, all the *pre-suffering*, Wiggins then found himself, at the eleventh hour, demoted to the role of race spectator for the 2013 Tour. While he could have followed the race from the comfort of home, he chose not to, admitting he would have become 'depressed' if he had. The last time Wiggins had watched the race from the sidelines had been back in 2011, after he'd crashed out on stage seven with a broken collarbone. But was Wiggins' devastation at missing out on the 2013 Tour a still more painful experience, an unwelcome, supersize serving of *dukkha*?

Bradley's calamitous 2013 might have taken him by surprise, but it's worth noting that in the Eastern Hemisphere at least, this powerful association between wheels and suffering, between rotational mass and dissatisfaction, dates back more than two millennia. Buddhist philosophy likewise attaches strong symbolism to the simple wheel. The *Dharmachakra*, or 'Wheel of Life', is recognized globally as a symbol of Buddhism. It also happens to be the emblem at the centre of the Indian flag. In 1921, Mahatma Gandhi proposed a flag with a traditional spinning wheel at its centre, to symbolize his desire that Indians become self-sufficient by making their own clothing. But only days before the country's independence in 1947, India's National Assembly instead decided that the flag's emblem should be the *Ashoka Chakra*, a variant of the *Dharmachakra*.

The Wheel of Life is widely depicted in Buddhist art and iconography. It appears in many sizes and with different spoke options, as of course do bicycle wheels. Typically, the *Dharmachakra*'s hub denotes discipline, the essential core of meditation practice. The wheel's rim, holding all the laws (spokes) together, signifies mindfulness. *Dharma* wheels variously appear with twelve spokes or twenty-four spokes. There's even an asymmetric option consisting of thirty-one spokes. But the eight-spoke wheel representing The Noble Eightfold Path is the most common configuration. Whereas an eight-spoke bicycle wheel would be a fairly specialized, race-specific affair and certainly not one recommended for everyday use, the wheel denoting The Noble Eightfold Path – the path to self-awakening and liberation from endless *dukkha* – is a must-have item in any Buddhist kitbag.

For those of us who like to believe we've achieved at least a modicum of self-awakening, there is always the possibility that bike rides can be enjoyable on occasion, not merely a litany of disappointment and disaster – or nothing but unadulterated *dukkha*, in short. Riding a bike can be fun. *Should* be fun. While many have made a decent living out of despairing of the future of the human race, it's the Buddhists, with their time-honoured formulae for micro-managing despair, for minimizing suffering, who will tell you that most aspects of life can in fact be joyful if approached with the right mindset. That once we've accepted the general unsatisfactoriness of just about everything, there is plenty of satisfaction to be found, if only we knew where to look. Of course, the Buddhists' deadly simple solution to this exhausting quest for satisfaction, or happiness, or joy, or call it what you will, is to not go looking for it in the first place. 'Ask yourself whether you are happy, and you cease to be so,' John Stuart Mill concluded some years ago.[11] He was surely barking up the right tree, even barking up a Bodhi tree, but for us blithely to avoid asking the question altogether seems a pretty big ask in itself.

Buddhist gurus also stress the critical importance of a healthy sense of humour as we fumble our way through life and three-week bicycle races.

The Dalai Lama himself has an infectious giggle and a well-documented fondness for practical jokes. But the biggest Buddhist joke of all is that most of us seem trapped in endless pursuit of something that's right in front us of. It's like ransacking the entire house in search of the car keys already stuffed inside your pocket. 'Our state of mind is crucial in determining whether or not we gain joy and happiness,' the Dalai Lama says. 'So leaving aside the perspective of *Dharma* practice, even in worldly terms, in terms of our enjoying a happy day-to-day existence, the greater the level of calmness of our mind, the greater our peace of mind, and the greater our ability to enjoy a happy and joyful life.'[12]

The quest for a happy and joyful life is a task perhaps best left to the professionals. But a happy and joyful hour or two on a bicycle: this is surely something well within our grasp. 'Just mount a bicycle and go out for a spin down the road, without thought on anything but the ride you are taking,' as Sir Arthur Conan Doyle waxed. Yes indeed. Surely that's why any of us hop on a bike in the first instance? We learn to ride as kids. It's the uncomplicated, unalloyed joy of trundling around the garden or the local park on your first toddler tricycle. And, really, what a life it is, to be three years old and on the move, travelling under your own steam. Here's yet another liberating, enfranchising form of self-propelled forward motion, and coming so soon after the frankly miraculous discovery that you can use your wobbly little legs for walking around. True, your miniature contraption probably doesn't have pedals, or a chain, and certainly no gears. In technical terms it's actually not even a bike, it's merely a stripped-down imitation of a bicycle. But over time we graduate to a bike proper and to the challenge of learning to stay upright on only two wheels – which as anyone who's ever spent time in the middle of a peloton will be well aware, is a technique that some never quite master.

George Hincapie, Lance Armstrong's most trusted lieutenant over the years, had his signature way of announcing when feeling especially happy and joyful on the bike. He'd ride up alongside a teammate, a wide grin on his face, and declare: 'I don't feel a chain. Is there a chain on my bike?' Hincapie was alluding to the sense of sublime ease and serenity we feel on those days when bike and body are in perfect sync: when both are well tuned and oiled, when the cranks spin freely and the legs are supple. In French, *la souplesse* refers to the act of executing any physical movement as smoothly as possible. In cycle sport, it remains the gold standard, a means of judging whether riders exhibit a decent style, if their form on the bike is pleasing to the eye. Some appear to be blessed with natural *souplesse*: the likes of present-day champions Alberto Contador and Vincenzo Nibali, for example. Other professionals habitually come across as if they're trying to strangle their handlebars: Tommy Voeckler and Chris Anker Sørenson spring to mind here. What Mr Hincapie was not alluding to of course was the fact that much of his apparent *chainlessness*, his low-friction aura of feel-good, might have had to do with a few 'supplements' administered earlier by his team doctor, but at this point that's neither here nor there.

The point is that those splendid, gently backlit, tail-winded days on the bike do occur from time to time – interspersed of course between extended spells of *dukkha* – and whenever they do, there's really nowhere else you'd rather be. The Buddhists have long recognized this. For as much as we are unable to escape the general pervasiveness of *dukkha*, when the alternative does present itself, why indeed not bask and wallow – like a hippo in a low veldt mud pool – in some joy, in pleasure, in a sense of satisfaction and ease? In the ancient Pali language, the antonym of *dukkha* is *sukha*. The etymology is essentially the same: by simply changing the prefix from *du* to *su* – by substituting 'good' for 'bad' – our previously stiff, jammed-up wheel axle changes into one that 'runs easily or swiftly', according to the *Rig Veda*, one of the canonical texts of Hinduism. In the Pali literature, the term *sukha* denotes the idea of ease and flow and, by association, a sense of pleasure, happiness or bliss.

Cycle-specific *sukha* may lack a precise dictionary definition, but we know it well enough when we feel it. When wheel rims run smooth and true. Saddles and backsides remain in good accord, in an *entente cordiale*. Brakes engage without squeak or squeal. Gear shifts become effortless and precise. The recent introduction of electronic gear shifting has been even hailed as a step towards cycling *nirvana*. And it can be, most of the time, at least until you forget to charge the shifters' onboard battery. In this instance, you will find yourself stuck in a horribly overgeared *samsara* all the way home. A rebirth as a more enlightened being that better appreciates the importance of battery charging is, however, always possible.

A chain is indeed present on these *sukha*-filled halcyon days, but it remains unsung and unassuming. Bicycle chains, like small children, are best seen and not heard. Cranks and pedals spin away merrily with no creak or click. It turns out this last point is actually fairly crucial. Because however wonderful a time you're having on the bike, however joyful your ride may be, the first hint of any irregularity, of the slightest commotion or disturbance from the vicinity of the drivetrain, and it's basically all over. Nothing deflates a sense of bike-bound bliss faster than the sound of components feuding with each other – especially a sound that repeats itself on each pedal stroke. It is the bicycling equivalent of Chinese water torture. And here I could outpour an entire chapter on the unadulterated, misery-inducing *dukkha* of the new press-fit bottom bracket assemblies, but I'll restrain myself.

For Bradley Wiggins, as 2014 rolled around, it seemed that his unbidden bout of *dukkha* had not quite run its course. He appeared somehow adrift, in a curious state of limbo. He had a crack at the Paris–Roubaix classic, finishing a creditable ninth. But Christopher Froome was by now established as Sky's preferred leader for stage races, with team boss Dave Brailsford clearly intent on scheduling separate race programmes for his two feuding team members. Wiggins took a comfortable victory at the Tour of California, but despite stating his willingness to ride in support of Froome at the 2014 Tour, he was omitted from the ten-man selection and consigned to once again spending much of the month of July on his sofa, semi-submerged under a stack of cushions and stealing sidelong glances at the television.

As sporting dethronements go, this was fairly grim. While British cyclists such as Chris Hoy or Mark Cavendish have garnered more outright race wins, the breadth of Wiggins' achievements on the bike is unparalleled. To win a Tour de France, on top of Olympic gold in the individual pursuit and the road time trial, requires dominance at events lasting variously four minutes, one hour and three weeks. Not even Merckx managed this. An equivalent achievement in athletics might be to win the 100m, the 1,500m and the marathon. When double Olympic champion Mo Farah recently switched to the marathon after proving almost unbeatable at 5,000m and 10,000m, many felt it was a risky move and Farah has struggled thus far at the longer distance.

But here was brave Sir Wiggo, one of the world's most accomplished bike riders, and yet all of a sudden only semi-employed – certainly a highly lucrative form of part-time employment, one that the rest of us would jump at, but still. Further Grand Tour exploits appeared unlikely. A return to his track roots seemed probable and a move to a new team was even mooted, preferably one without a gangly, balding Anglo-Kenyan at the helm. But this is *dukkha*. This is the naked truth of impermanence. This is exactly what the Buddhists are on about. One minute you're on top of the world, perched splendidly upon your Olympic throne, or at the very least on a swivel chair in a large corner office, then before you've even had a chance to take it all in, the *viparinama* viper rears up and nips you on the backside.

And for a wistful Sir Wiggo, it was not simply a case of grappling with the truth of impermanence, but also with the inevitable dissatisfaction of things – even those things we'd thought would most satisfy us:

> You can plan physically to try to win the Tour but I could never plan for what was going to happen after it. It just went mad for a bit. Looking back now you don't fully appreciate it at the time, you just try to take it in your stride ... and drinking and stuff to try to ease your way through it. It was massive really. I can't really put it into words how much it changed everything.[13]

To Wiggins' credit, he managed to refocus his efforts back on to the track – the source of his early success – and within weeks had grabbed a silver medal in the 2014 Commonwealth Games team pursuit. He confirmed that further Grand Tour exploits were off the agenda, with the 2016 Rio Olympics now the principal target. 'The last six or seven weeks since I've been back on the track have just been really refreshing and a good distraction from all of that Tour de France nonsense,' a newly bearded and bulkier Wiggins told the *Guardian*. In early 2015, he confirmed his forthcoming retirement from the road scene, targeting one final attempt at Paris–Roubaix. With Rio 2016 locked in the sights, the former Tour winner will be the spearhead for the eponymous 'Team Wiggins', a new, Sky-funded elite squad. 'It's given me another focus rather than just lolling about at home feeling miserable.'[14]

Of course, had sofa-bound Bradley peered above his cushions for long enough to catch the early stages of the 2014 Tour, he would have watched an upended Chris Froome crash painfully on various sections of France's northernmost highways – not once, not twice, but three times, all within a 24-hour period. If the first cut wasn't the deepest, it still shredded the left side of Froome's shorts and stripped away several layers of his skin. Froome at least managed to fall to his right for the second *chute*, but after sliding off his bike a third time barely an hour later – and this before even reaching the stage's treacherous cobbled sections – enough was clearly enough. A soggy Froome, face set to impassive, handed over his bike to a Sky helper and folded his lacerated limbs into the backseat of the team Jaguar. A hospital X-ray scan found he'd broken bones in his left wrist and right hand.

Only hours before Froome abandoned the 2014 Tour somewhere outside of a rain-sodden Ypres, his much anticipated title defence over before even turning a pedal in anger, millions – or more accurately billions – had watched Germany trounce Brazil 7–1 in the FIFA World Cup semi-final. This amounted to a truly shocking fall from grace for the *Seleção Brasileira*, a collapse that had journalists worldwide scratching their heads, wondering if we'd witnessed the greatest single sporting surrender of all time. It felt entirely reasonable to believe that whichever karmic deity was on duty that week for major sports events, cranking those weighty, cast-iron levers of fate and fortune, he was certainly having great fun on the job.

CHAPTER 3

Talent, Transcendence and the Suffersphere

'What is talent, really? Is it the fact that your heart pumps more volume than the average person's or that your blood turns less acidic when exercising? No, talent has to do with your capacity for suffering.'

Eddy Merckx

A twelve-year-old Bradley Wiggins informed his art teacher that he planned to win the Tour de France one day. 'My art teacher at school, St Augustine's in Kilburn, dragged me to one side and asked me: "What are you going to do with the rest of your life Bradley? You can't go through it like this,"' Wiggins told the BBC. 'I said "I want to wear the yellow jersey and win an Olympic gold medal" and she said "that's crazy", because how many kids from Kilburn did that?'[15]

At the age of fifteen – around the same time that a two-year-old Bradley was learning to walk – I'd certainly heard of the Tour de France, but had no great desire to take part in it, or any other bicycle race for that matter. I had though just completed my first ever long-distance ride, 60 miles from London to Brighton, aboard my new twelve-speed Raleigh. For reasons I can no longer recall, I'd convinced myself that tennis shoes and a pair of bootleg Levi jeans were perfectly functional items of cycle wear and that a packet of crisps every 5 miles or so represented optimal nutrition for endurance events.

My pale green Raleigh Rapide was much admired and ogled; she was for a short while the pouting starlet of the school bike shed. But almost overnight there appeared a usurper, a thoroughbred race machine with far more sumptuous lines and curves: Columbus superlight tubing; metallic blue with chromed forks and stays; full Campagnolo accoutrements; and dark grey anodized Mavic rims. This was ultimate bike porn, circa 1983. The bike's owner, a pint-sized, bespectacled Singaporean called Andrew Lim, was even a member of a local cycling club. There's a scene in many a Hollywood movie where decent but average kid first espies the shimmering beauty of the leader of the school cheerleading squad: aching, unconsummated desire. But at our school there were sadly no girls to espy, let alone cheerleaders. Andrew's bike was by far the loveliest thing I'd ever seen. It left me weak at the knees. In comparison, my bike was just a heap of metal.

With somewhat Machiavellian motives I befriended Andrew and soon became privy to his major plans for the coming season. 'Must train. Train hard every day,' said Andrew. Would it be possible, I asked, to maybe join him on a ride? Andrew cautioned that not all of us were cut out for hard training, but he nodded his assent and on a wintry morning, both of us wrapped in several layers of wool and lycra, we threaded our way through the high streets of suburban North London towards the quieter lanes of Hertfordshire. But barely 5 miles into the ride, at the foot of Barnet Hill, Andrew was wavering. 'Actually is quite cold today,' he said. 'And windy.' I signalled my agreement. 'Actually not good to ride in condition such like this one. We must turn back.' Turn back we did. Follow-up training rides with Andrew never quite materialized: it wasn't always the weather, but it was always something. I soon worked out it was feasible to train alone and that it might be worth searching for a new mentor. Andrew later agreed to sell me his gorgeous bike, but then mysteriously returned to Singapore before a deal could be struck.

With his homewards U-turn, the owner of north London's sexiest bike was ignoring the plain fact that the current incumbents over at The Great Pantheon – Hinault, Fignon, Kelly – were out on their bikes in all conditions, even cold, windy ones. Irishman Kelly typically thrived in atrocious weather. And besides which, training – hard training in single-digit temperatures – while a prerequisite for success, is not in itself sufficient. Had the diminutive Lim managed to train as hard on the road as he'd planned inside his own head, he was still never going to win the Tour de France, nor even gain selection to carry water bottles for a Tour de France winner. Nor was I of course. Barring the way stands the minor issue of exceptionality.

Only a very small percentage of athletes, by definition, can be considered exceptional. In bike racing as with many other sports, it is not always obvious just how much exceptionality is required at the uppermost levels. As an example, a decent club cyclist might be able to average 40km/h (25mph) over a one-hour time trial. At first glance, that might look within acceptable range of world time-trial champion Wiggins, who typically averages 48km/h (30mph) or so on a flat course. After all, what's a mere 8km/h (5mph)? That's barely the pace of a leisurely weekend jogger, shuffling his way around the local park. But an alarmingly non-linear relationship between speed and power output means that travelling at warp factor, Wiggins requires around 80 per cent more lung and leg power than even a reasonably well-conditioned club rider puts out. Or suppose instead that three untrained but otherwise able-bodied blokes turn up on a triple tandem for a head(s)-to-head against Sir Wiggo. Their combined power output might just about match that of Wiggins, but due to all the extra weight and wind resistance, they still won't go as fast. Put another way, an amateur who improves his power output by only 10 per cent can transform himself from mid-peloton finisher to outright winner. Any pro rider who conjures up a similar improvement in performance will find himself fielding tricky questions from the doping agencies.

How you get to be exceptional is an area of endless debate. There's author Malcolm Gladwell's popular 10,000-hour maxim, 10,000 being the approximate hours of practice believed necessary to become world class in almost any discipline, whether it's pro sports, brain surgery or the performing arts. In a similar vein, Matthew Syed's recent book *Bounce* espouses the power of practice over the 'myth' of talent.[16] Syed argues that with enough determination and dedication, almost anyone can reach the top of their chosen field. But this theory works better for, say, table tennis – Syed is an ex-England international – than for an endurance sport like cycling. For table tennis players, the critical skill of hand–eye coordination is honed through years of daily practice. And while they undoubtedly need to be in decent physical shape, few, if any, table tennis champs have ever needed extra oxygen in the aftermath of a gruelling finale.

In contrast, cycling performance from a purely physiological standpoint is highly dependent upon a few key markers. Five times Tour de France winner Miguel Indurain had a reported maximal oxygen uptake (VO_2 max) of 88ml/kg. More simply, his lung capacity was about double that of an average, non-athletic male. While training can increase VO_2 max to a limited extent, a less naturally gifted rider might train diligently for years and still not score a VO_2 max much above 60ml/kg. Another important metric is that of lactate threshold, the point at which lactic acid and other waste products start to accumulate in the bloodstream during intense exercise. Two of the highest lactate thresholds ever recorded in up and coming riders? Lance Armstrong and Alberto Contador.

Raw talent, however defined, may not be the only component for success, but it certainly helps. Two times Tour de France winner Laurent Fignon switched from football to cycling at the age of fifteen and was promptly told that he had left it too late to succeed on the bike. His parents also disapproved of cycling, so he would sneak out of the house to go for training rides. All of which mattered little: talent will out. In Fignon's first race, he attacked alone from a field of sixty or so and won by almost a minute. Indeed, most pros can recount similarly gilded tales of their initiation into racing. George Hincapie, who completed seventeen Tours de France, was wiping the floor at his local under-sixteen races at the tender age of twelve.

At roughly the same age as Fignon, I finished ninety-eighth in my first bicycle race, over ten minutes behind the winner. My parents did not exactly disapprove of bike racing; I think they assumed that wearing colourful lycra was a strange form of teenage rebellion. My mother's puzzled indifference to my chosen sport switched to mild concern when, a few months later, I started shaving my legs. The cool factor, the overall hip quotient of cycling, may have increased exponentially in recent years, but in early 1980s Britain, it barely even registered as a recognized sporting activity. I would have been no further from the mainstream if I'd taken up curling or clay pigeon shooting. As one of my mother's friends told me recently: 'We always wondered if there was something wrong with you.'

Since claiming that coveted top 100 spot in my first event, I've raced bikes on and off over several decades across several different continents. I've won my fair share of races, have come within a shout of winning a few more and finished well down the field in countless others – almost always with a sense that I could have, *should* have, done better. And yet, as a neophyte rider with a few decent results tucked away, it's all too easy to start entertaining delusions of cycling grandeur. But it is a fragile, precarious delusion and one that is unlikely to withstand a close encounter with genuine talent. I can recall my slack-jawed astonishment as a junior rider when the existing national champion came thundering past me in a time trial – astonishment not so much that I was being overtaken, but that any human being could propel a bike forwards with such violent force and intensity. But if natural talent on a bike is a slippery concept to define, identifying talent is comparatively straightforward, particularly when it comes hurtling past you at full tilt, or, in a marginally less humbling scenario, when you're busting a lung trying to hang on to its back wheel.

These days, I occasionally join a weekend group ride comprised mainly of other middle-aged men in Lycra, also known affectionately by their acronym, MAMIL. Market-research company Mintel coined the now ubiquitous phrase back in 2010. Its report found that the MAMIL demographic was mostly comprised of socioeconomic groups A and B, earned decent incomes and read broadsheet newspapers. Said purchasing power would buy them their choice of high-end bicycle (or bicycles), pro-level machines typically priced at several thousand pounds apiece. And MAMILs are, by definition, exclusively male. As a BBC report noted: 'Flashy sports cars are out, now no mid-life crisis is complete without a souped-up road bike.'[17] It does appear that no self-respecting MAMIL (here the BBC declares the correct collective noun to be a 'girth') wants to be seen out on a bike worth less than three grand. Today's ultimate MAMIL mount, an all-black carbon Pinarello, virtually identical to those raced across Europe by Team Sky, will lighten MAMIL wallets by at least twice that amount. As self-confessed MAMIL Matt Seaton wrote in the *Guardian*, there are of course many far worse temptations waiting to ensnare Britain's middle-aged males: 'Despite appearances to the contrary (rendezvous with strangers, an empty bed in the early morning, unaccountable foreign travel), there is no infidelity involved.'[18]

Certainly, if the Wiggo-inspired coolness factor weren't now such a big element of cycling, it would be much harder for companies to sell 150-quid pairs of sunglasses than it actually is. Not to mention the £5,000 bikes. The distinction to make here is that while pro riders, with a few exceptions, do look unfailingly cool on the bike, there are essentially two kinds of ageing amateurs. Firstly, those who make it a matter of principle to replicate down to the very last detail that insouciant, wind-cheating professional look: the slammed-down stem; the saddle set back just so; sock height carefully calibrated; and brake hoods micro-aligned with respect to the Earth's core. These aspirational MAMILs might have to endure a certain amount of lumbar discomfort in their super low-slung position, but they at least look the part.

The second kind of not-so-youthful amateur simply gets on the bike and rides, often with an unwarranted confidence that no critical parts of his machine will fall off or self-destruct before he arrives back at home. Dress code is ultra-casual, meaning that old running shorts will suffice if the only pair of cycling bibs happens to be in the wash. Last year, I arrived at a ride meeting point to find a hirsute, fifty-something Australian sporting a pair of pro-team replica bib shorts. 'Fair dinkum,' I might have thought, if it weren't for the fact that apart from his shoes, he was wearing nothing but bib shorts.

'No jersey today?' I asked. 'Nah, mate. Far too hot for jerseys,' he replied. Nor was it as if he had the kind of torso that warranted being on such public display. This was a torso that had spent more hours in the pub than on the bike. Averting my eyes from the saggy pair of 'moobs' that bulged against his bib straps, I wondered if he might have got lost en route to a wrestling match.

At 8 o'clock on Saturday and Sunday mornings, a dozen or so mostly shirted MAMILs roll up to our local ride's designated rendezvous in ones and twos, in a colourful hodgepodge of shapes and sizes, as well as in various states of aerobic conditioning. Despite all of the state of the art, featherweight equipment on display, none of us will ever be mistaken for professionals. Well, none of us except Maurizio.

Maurizio Ponchiroli is one of those elegant, perfectly turned-out Italian riders who give the impression of having been born on a bike. And perhaps he was; I've never got around to asking him, nor have I been introduced to *mamma* Ponchiroli. A contemporary of the late Marco Pantani, Maurizio rose up through the Italian junior squads alongside the ill-fated *Pirata* and claims he actually would have won some of the climbs on national team training rides were it not for the constant presence of the diminutive Pantani. Having ridden up many hills with, or more accurately, behind Maurizio, I see no reason to doubt his claim. The infuriating part is that Maurizio only recently got back on his bike after a lay-off of some twenty years. Against all known rules of human physiology, his fitness and conditioning seemed to reappear magically after about twenty days. Now he enjoys sitting on the front of the motley peloton for an hour or two at a time and anyone brave or foolish enough to challenge him on a climb gets swatted away like an annoying mosquito. And each time Mauri's graceful form vanishes over the crest of another hill, it gets that much harder not to believe in divine talent.

The generally accepted explanation of why Maurizio has to wait around patiently at the top of climbs is that the rest of us – we wheezing, gasping, cursing mortals – are coming up against our physiological limits, while Maurizio's own limits, assuming he has any, remain untested: his limits remain off limits, if you will. Various early twentieth-century studies of endurance athletes supported the theory that while an individual's oxygen consumption steadily increases in line with exertion during exercise, it eventually reaches a plateau where the body's cardiovascular system can no longer supply the muscles with more oxygen. This plateau is known as the lactic threshold. Pushing through this threshold quickly forces the muscles to start working anaerobically, which causes lactic acid and other waste products to accumulate in the bloodstream. Chronic muscle fatigue as a direct consequence of elevated blood lactate levels remains a contentious area of sports science, but is nevertheless easily identifiable to most cyclists as the point where, depending on your objectives for the day, you either stop pedalling as hard, or you jab a finger at the big red pain button and resign yourself to some serious suffering.

But as we depart the oxygen-rich environment of steady tempo riding and push up into the hypoxic strata of the suffersphere, what exactly is it that delineates our physical limits; where is the absolute ceiling of our pain altitude? Tim Noakes, a professor of exercise and sports science at the University of Cape Town, has suggested that our ability to go beyond a certain perceived level of pain and fatigue is constrained not so much by aching legs or bursting lungs, but by the old noggin itself. The fact that we humans and other mammals (note: not MAMILs) function as well as we do is largely down to the principle of homeostasis, whereby the body's internal processes are designed to operate within controlled limits, for example the maintenance of a constant body temperature or a neutral pH balance. But there's still fierce debate about whether extreme, exercise-induced fatigue is in fact caused by peripheral muscle failure ('uh-oh, the damn legs have gone again') or, alternatively, the result of a more centralized process, of something known as a 'homeostatic regulator'.

Noakes has argued the latter, proposing that: 'physical activity is controlled by a central governor in the brain … the extent of skeletal muscle recruitment is controlled as part of a continuously altering pacing strategy, with the sensation of fatigue being the conscious interpretation of these homeostatic, central governor control mechanisms.'[19] This sensitive mechanism factors in an athlete's prior experience of intense exercise, the expected duration of the exercise and the current metabolic state of the body. According to Noakes: 'the rising perception of discomfort produced by exhausting exercise progressively reduces the conscious desire to over-ride this control mechanism, which, if it were to be reduced, would lead to the recruitment of more motor units'.[20]

In this situation, recruiting more motor units – or muscle fibres – would threaten homeostasis in the body, with potentially dangerous consequences. But it turns out that under normal circumstances, we're not actually able to do this, however brave or reckless we may be feeling. Noakes explains that the reason why we can't literally ride or run ourselves to death is essentially due to this nanny-like central governor – an eternally vigilant nanny to boot, one that's always on the lookout for our best interests. The central governor's function appears to become even more critical in extremely hot weather, with numerous studies showing that athletes' performances start to taper off well before body temperature reaches 40°C (104°F), the point at which heatstroke sets in. Yet the paradoxical part of this entire process is that although it's all taking place inside our own brains, we don't have any control over it.

Under extreme conditions, however, it is unfortunately possible to ride oneself into the ground: poor old Tommy Simpson, for example. Simpson's official cause of death was heart failure due to dehydration and heat exhaustion. But in Noakesian terms, the amphetamine pills swilling around Simpson's system as he toiled up the ramps of Mont Ventoux in the Tour de France in 1967 simply caused his central governor progressively to shut down. Similarly, the spate of cyclist deaths relating to the performance-enhancing drug EPO in the late 1990s and early 2000s were a consequence of what happens when central governors are forced to operate outside normal parameters, rather like when you fill up your car's petrol tank with several gallons of diesel.

While cyclists should be thankful to their delicate brains for generally intervening in time to prevent catastrophic overexertion, it seems we're mostly an ungrateful bunch. Instead, we try to trick our brains, to cajole them into allowing us to go faster. As any cycling coach will tell you, a rider can typically put out 5 per cent or so more power in a race setting than he can during training, a statistic that suggests our nanny-governor imposed limits are at least partly negotiable. Cycling coaches also like to focus on a variable known as 'relative perceived exertion', or, in blunter terms, how much pain is experienced during a particular effort. But it is this sketchy quality of perception that makes things problematic. Come race day, with your freshly washed bike sparkling in the sunshine, your shoes shined and with a handful of roadside spectators to cheer you along, a steep hill climb might not feel quite as painful as it did during a cold, wet training session the previous week. Bill Gifford, writing in *Bicycle Magazine*, highlights a study that found 'cyclists who merely taste a sweet energy drink, but don't swallow it, will ride faster because the brain expects a shot of carbohydrate fuel'.[21]

Any analysis of physical pain remains subjective, of course, since it is impossible to ever know exactly how or what anyone else is feeling. For that matter, it is probably also impossible to know with any empirical certainty how *you're* feeling at any given moment. Because although you or I might feel as if we suffered more in yesterday's race than we did a couple of weeks ago in a different race, to what extent can we count on our own memories as reliable narrators? These days, my memory only grudgingly allows me to remember basic tasks like collecting my laundry and even then it needs frequent prompting. And, given enough time, all feelings and memories will, like old Polaroid snaps, lose their definition and intensity, fading away eventually into a blurry splodge.

We also tend not to do our most lucid thinking while in considerable pain. As our levels of discomfort rise, our sense of rationality goes the opposite way. Above a certain intensity of pain, most of us will be unable to think about anything else. Milan Kundera, a several times nominee for the Nobel Prize for Literature, notes that 'in intense suffering the world disappears and each of us is alone with his self. Suffering is the university of egocentrism'.[22] In the broadest sense, to wallow in the suffering of our own egos is to become oblivious to the suffering of others. And in the specific context of a bike race, this is never a particularly helpful strategy. 'On a climb, especially if it is an hour long, and you're hurting, you have to think that this poor sod behind me is going to be hurting, too,' explained Bradley Wiggins recently. 'You're thinking logically. When you look at the sacrifices you have made, that's when you start thinking rationally.'[23]

Elite riders are typically on familiar terms with this law of comparative hurt and they now have the additional benefit of real-time power data that all but confirms their current coordinates within the suffersphere. But, as an amateur racer, especially an inexperienced one, it is too easy to fall into the trap of thinking that you are about to slip into a coma while those around you are casually taking in the scenery. I've flummoxed myself this way on many occasions, only to find myself a minute or so later riding alone, metres ahead of my rivals. Rational explanation: the other poor sods were indeed hurting more.

There is little doubt that elite racers are more proficient at suffering than the rest of us. They've put more time into it, which, as Malcolm Gladwell has emphasized, is typically how you get to improve at anything. So will encountering pain as part of your daily routine alter your relationship with it over time? Or is the ability to withstand suffering somehow a more innate attribute? 'I'm good at pain,' confessed Tyler Hamilton in his recent autobiography. 'I have a secret: you can't block out the pain. You have to embrace it.' Hamilton here gives due credit to his family for his impressive tolerance: 'Hamiltons are tough; we always have been. My ancestors were rebellious Scots from a warring clan.'[24]

Likewise Federico Bahamontes, the first Spaniard to win the Tour de France and whose impoverished family struggled to make ends meet during the Spanish civil war. 'I became a cyclist at the age of ten because I would have starved otherwise,' he told the *Independent*. 'I used to nab fruit off the lorries in the local market and sell that, and with the money I made I bought my first bike in order to sell more fruit faster.' He went on: 'I'd ride around with up to 150 kilos of fruit and vegetable on the back on the bike. But all that extra weight, I think, helped me become a better mountain climber. Once I shed it all, I could fly.'[25]

To be fair, the pros are much better rewarded for their suffering than the teeming masses of weekend racers. But this still only partly explains the pain principle. If the great Eddy Merckx's assertion is correct, that talent ultimately 'has to do with your capacity for suffering', then from whence exactly did he acquire his prodigious tolerance for pain? Merckx's non-warrior parents ran a grocery on the outskirts of Brussels. Their son certainly trained hard enough and long enough, but so did his contemporaries. Merckx, as many have noted, may also have been relentlessly driven by an overwhelming fear of failure. But it seems disingenuous for Merckx to completely dismiss out of hand the matter of natural talent. His grand assertion seems to stack up only within the confines of The Great Pantheon: when a handful of the world's top riders slug it out in the closing stages of a classic, then – ignoring a dozen other factors – the eventual winner might be whoever can dig deepest into their pain reserves on that day. But as US cycling coach Rob Muller points out, 'I know my wife has a higher "pain threshold" than I do. But I can't see her ever beating me in a race regardless of how much pain she can endure or how much she suffers.' On this topic, Muller takes care to distance himself from the views of Merckx and from the likes of Gladwell and Syed: 'What wins races is talent: talent that is normally God-given,' he says. 'And that God-given talent is in the form of your genetic makeup. If you don't believe in God, then it's parent-given; it's good genes.'[26]

If talent is a tricky number to pin down, then pain remains even more of a mystery, even to some of the sharpest, most inquisitive minds. Since what we subjectively experience as suffering stems from a highly complex, labyrinthine process, the result of a convoluted bundle of interactions between multiple brain areas and neurochemical systems, the scientific community can be forgiven for not yet getting to the bottom of pain. But there is strong evidence to show that our response to pain – whatever the precise definition of pain actually is – will adapt over time. Specifically, it appears that the more often we suffer on the bike, the more we're able to suffer on the bike. A 2012 study from the University of Heidelberg found that athletes had significantly higher pain tolerances than non-athletes, even though their pain thresholds – the point at which discomfort is first discernible – were statistically no different to the average.

Another study, this time from California State University, examined how ex-Olympic cyclists dealt with pain during both training and competition. It found that elite cyclists typically employ various coping mechanisms such as visualization and deep breathing techniques to confront pain actively, as opposed to ignoring it and hoping it will go away. As they well know from experience, such hope is futile: the pain does not go away. In an event like the 4,000m team pursuit, the pain counter needle hits maximum well inside the first minute and remains jammed at the far end of the dial for the next three minutes. But as the CSU study noted:

> There's a philosophical view built on the premise that one's perception is one's reality. In this investigation, the participant could have been putting forth the same amount of exertion, under similar circumstances, yet the pain could be perceived as different. The amount of pain perceived was inversely proportional to the enjoyment of the experience.[27]

It also turns out that there's good reason to doubt whether, as individuals, our physical experiences of pain are even that closely correlated, irrespective of our different psychological or philosophical interpretations. A 2003 study published in *Science* magazine found that its test subjects metabolized certain key neurotransmitters such as dopamine and epinephrine at varying rates in response to a sustained onset of pain. A subset of this sample 'showed diminished regional μ-opioid system responses to pain … These effects were accompanied by higher sensory and affective ratings of pain and a more negative internal affective state.' The study essentially claims to identify a genetic marker that 'influences the human experience of pain and may underlie individual differences in the adaptation and responses to pain and other stressful stimuli'.[28]

If observable genetic differences in athletes' adaptations and responses to physical pain indeed do exist, is it not then simply a case of '*chapeau*' (or as non-Francophones like to say, 'hats off') to those who adapt quickest and respond best; to those supermen topped up with their premium-grade neurochemical mix; to those optimally configured to scorn and sneer in the face of pain? It's not that they don't suffer. They most certainly do. But the true champions, those most esteemed members of The Great Pantheon, tend to do their suffering only after they've left all others reeling in their wake, faltering in the midst of what pro rider turned commentator Paul Sherwen enjoys describing as a 'world of pain'. Of course, the catchy, colloquial phrase favoured by Sherwen is simply another way of stating what the lab boffins prefer to classify as 'a more negative internal affective state'.

CHAPTER 4

Passion and Flogging

'Some days I would weep on my bike.'

Eddy Merckx[29]

'Jesus took his first spill at the third turn. His mother, who was in the stands, became alarmed.'
Alfred Jarry, 'The Crucifixion Considered as an Uphill Bicycle Race'[30]

For a young cyclist aiming to transform himself into a deadly, single-minded racing machine, the club time trial was the traditional English rite of passage. On Saturday afternoons during what we hoped were the summer months, a small congregation from the Barnet Cycling Club would gather in a lay-by on a quiet Hertfordshire 'B' road and begin discarding various outer layers of clothing. The most advanced chronometry on display would have been the timekeeper's push-button stopwatch. Steel toe-clips and leather straps ensured feet remained securely attached to pedals. Helmets, aero or otherwise, hadn't yet been invented, or at least were not anywhere in evidence, and sunglasses were something you might wear once a year on a foreign holiday. One blustery Saturday in May, my schoolmate Vik rode out with me to have a crack at the club's weekly 10-mile event. Vik, a talented footballer and annoyingly proficient at other school-sanctioned games, was intrigued at my sudden departure into the alien world of cycling. He wanted to come and see what all the fuss was about.

A few other club members rolled up and down the lane, loosening their legs in preparation for the effort ahead, their lightweight tubular tyres humming on the tarmac as they rode past. A sharp whiff of muscle liniment wafted on the stiff breeze. And the bikes themselves: not the stealth carbon machines of today, but gleaming, metallic beasts. From time to time stray shards of sunlight burst through the low cloud, bouncing off chromed hubs, aluminium rims and whirring spokes.

'What exactly is the strategy for this kind of race?' Vik asked, as we went about our warm-up in the prescribed manner.

'Fairly simple,' I replied, eager to pass on the wisdom of my six months as a club cyclist. 'Basically, you start as fast as you can, and then keep it going until the roundabout at halfway.'

Vik nodded solemnly, his eyes fixed on the road ahead.

'Then, on the way back, you'll need to push a bit harder. And give it absolutely everything for the last mile or so,' I added.

Vik, perhaps lacking the confidence to question my logic, nodded again. Before hi-tech wizardry and its limitless flow of metrics transformed virtually every facet of our lives, bicycle racing, like so much else, was much more straightforward. As the club's seasoned old boys would explain, you could go *hard*, or you could go *easy*. There may have been an intermediate setting between hard and easy, but I'm not too certain about that – and if there was, I don't believe I ever attempted it. These days, of course, the average club cyclist is no more likely to ride a time trial without at minimum a heart-rate monitor to gauge his efforts than he would start a bike race minus his shorts. And any halfway-serious racer is now almost obliged to invest in the latest must-have bike gadget, a power meter. But if someone had asked me back then about my wattage on the bike, I'd probably have assumed the question was to do with the unwieldy Eveready lights we used for riding on dark winter nights.

Some thirty years on, Vik still clearly recalls my race strategy that day. He gleefully quotes it back to me at every opportunity, which is all the more remarkable since after that initial foray he never again showed even a glimmer of interest in bike racing. It is feasible, I suppose, that the nature of my pre-race advice had something to do with his rapid and total loss of enthusiasm, the instant deflation of his hopes. Perhaps it is the case that some of us can get along perfectly well without the pain. But for those that cannot, the exquisite suffering often seems to take the maddening form of a lover whom we know is difficult to live with, yet fear we cannot live without.

Senseless suffering – any form of misdirected, superfluous suffering – most would agree is best avoided. War and conflict rarely produce any outright winners and neither do solo breakaways into a headwind. But if suffering for no good reason is wasteful and silly, then suffering in the name of a worthy cause can be a different story altogether. The Latin word *passio*, the etymology of which essentially means 'to suffer', forms the root of the English word 'passion'. In the Gospels, 'The Passion' refers to the suffering of Jesus on the Cross. Even if for most laypeople the word is nowadays more synonymous with pleasure than pain, the truth is that passion and suffering remain closely entwined. As James Shelley explains in 'Passion Over Pleasure':

> To be passionate, truly passionate, demands a willingness to suffer for the object or cause of your passion. It is unswerving commitment in spite of pain and loss ... There can be no passion without the experience of personal loss: until one suffers, one's passion is not exposed. Your passion is *not* what makes you feel *comfortable* – the things you are passionate about will probably make your life less comfortable. Potentially *miserable*, actually.[31]

Dedicated athletes at all levels will have come across this particular dichotomy: self-inflicted misery as a proxy for passion; suffering as a surrogate for satisfaction. Californian Bob Krogh took up competitive running in his early forties. After a comfortable career in banking had evaporated in the aftermath of the 2008 financial crash, Bob found himself with a decent redundancy package and plenty of time on his hands. Freed from the corporate shackles, Bob upped his running mileage and was soon training several times a week with his local race crew. Within months, he'd finished sixth in his first 10km race. 'It was hell, but it was exciting,' he told me. Soon he was winning everything in his age category and then scoring race victories outright. So far so good, but Bob was hurtling headlong into the classic training trap: 'I thought if I run harder, I'll get faster. And I did for a while, but then it all kind of fell apart.' Instead of tackling his training intervals at a high but controlled tempo as recommended, Bob blithely assumed that running each interval flat out would make him even faster. 'The way I am, I don't listen to people,' he confessed.

Months of consistent overtraining resulted in serious damage to the plantar ligaments in Bob's feet, leaving him in excruciating pain. Several doctors advised him to stop running altogether, but he reasoned that attempting to run longer distances at a reduced intensity would be a fair compromise. 'I guess it just defined me. Running was who I was. Looking back, it's almost embarrassing,' he explained. 'When it was taken away from me I felt like a loser.'

When high-profile cycling coach Joe Friel noted that it is possible to be extremely fit, but not necessarily healthy, he was most likely thinking of athletes much like Bob – and much like myself. Having discovered that running on an indoor treadmill was far easier on the feet than concrete or tarmac, Bob was soon ramping up the intensity again. 'I was taking a lot of painkillers, I wasn't sleeping well. My stress level was through the roof,' Bob told me. 'I was in the best shape of my life … and I was a mess. It was the worst period of my life. I almost destroyed my relationship with my family.'

When physical overload starts to have emotional repercussions, the overzealous athlete can find himself entering a dangerous feedback loop, where more physical pain still seems a viable way to stave off the accumulative mental stress. Bob consigned himself to even longer daily sessions on the treadmill – 'I can't even describe how painful, how intense it was. I would kill myself for hours' – while at the same time believing that 'everyone was out to get me. I lost all my confidence. I was extremely depressed.'

Bob eventually weaned himself off his torturous treadmill programme after hopping on his mountain bike one afternoon and discovering he could give himself a decently draining workout without shredding his feet in the process. He has since become a fearsome competitor on a road bike, yet as he approaches his fiftieth birthday, he claims to have finally made peace with himself. Although he admits that he does miss the purity and simplicity of running flat-out intervals, his regular efforts on the bike – usually up the side of a mountain and at a mere 90 per cent or so of maximum – nowadays provide optimal doses of passion, misery and satisfaction.

A bicycle certainly can be as good a place as any other for working through one's inner demons. According to former schoolteacher Claudine Merckx, who's been married to the world's greatest ever cyclist for the past forty-eight years: 'Eddy never looked for glory. He just wanted to be at peace with himself.' But for the latter-day disciples of Merckx, the so-called 'Cannibal', who would consume his competition on a regular basis and who during his career won the equivalent of one race a week for six years, it's sobering to think that even he did not fulfil his potential. In 1969, soon after his first Tour de France victory – where he made a clean sweep of the overall, points and mountain jerseys – he crashed heavily during an exhibition race in the Blois velodrome. The motorbike rider who was pacing Merckx also crashed and was killed instantly. Merckx was knocked unconscious and was later found to have cracked a vertebra and twisted his pelvis. Merckx claimed he was never again able to ride without some degree of pain, especially while climbing. 'I was never as strong again in the mountains. Without the crash I could have won more Tours,' was the frank assessment from the man himself. An obsession with tweaking his saddle position then became a Merckx trademark as he attempted, in vain, to find a perfect, pain-free set-up on the bike.[32]

One of the more unfortunate things about suffering is that, through the years, it has often suffered a bad press. Maybe we should be less harsh on poor, misunderstood suffering. After all, acute physical suffering as a lifestyle choice has at certain points in history actually been quite popular, faddish even, before again falling out of favour, much in the way of flared trousers or waxed moustaches. Long before pro cyclists started conking out from oxygen debt on top of European mountain passes, public acts of self-flagellation were much in vogue among the more God-fearing citizens of Ancient Greece and Rome. When these empires eventually fizzled out, as empires are wont to do, the Catholic Church was more than willing to take up the running in the flogging department. Northern Italy turned into a stronghold of self-harm, notably Perugia, where, following a major epidemic in 1259, thousands of residents marched through the city whipping themselves. Although the Pope, in a rare moment of clarity, then issued a decree banning this sort of behaviour, it popped up again in Austria and Germany shortly after. Self-flagellation as a form of penitence remains popular even today in a few scattered corners of the Mediterranean and notably in the Catholic-dominated Philippines.

While religious self-flagellation may have some merit as a form of spiritual salvation – or, alternatively, an inexpensive outdoor hobby – to investigate why apparently sane individuals would actively seek out suffering of the sporting kind, to make more sense of the why of competitive suffering, we need to take another look inside The Great Pantheon of Sufferers. A cursory study of these elite pain junkies might be illuminating. Who knows, it could even offer us a glimpse of the brighter side of suffering.

In terms of pure physical hardship, distance running is one of the few sports that can stake its claim alongside cycling; ultra-marathon running, sometimes covering distances up to 160km (100 miles) and occasionally further, is seen as the ultimate test for those who find themselves lacking the motivation to get out of bed for a mere single marathon. The ultra-marathon concept itself is absurdly unhinged, especially when you consider that the standard 42.2km (26.2 miles) marathon was not so long ago thought to represent the upper limits of human endurance. Ultra-marathoner Dean Karnazes has run fifty marathons in fifty days. He can also knock off 160km (100 miles) in a day in much the same way as normal folk jog around the local park. Here's Dean's alternative worldview:

> People think I'm crazy to put myself through such torture, though I would argue otherwise. Somewhere along the line we seem to have confused comfort with happiness. Dostoyevsky had it right: 'Suffering is the sole origin of consciousness.' Never are my senses more engaged than when the pain sets in. There is a magic in misery.[33]

Erstwhile bike racer and charity fundraiser Lance Armstrong echoed similar sentiments in his 2002 interview with *Time* magazine. 'I'm not happy if I'm not doing some physical suffering,' he said. Armstrong went on to recount moments in his racing career when 'the suffering is so intense that it's absolutely cleansing. The pain is so deep and strong that a curtain descends over your brain.' A journalist once asked Armstrong what pleasure he derived from undertaking such long, hard training rides. '"Pleasure?" I said. "I don't understand the question." I didn't do it for the pleasure, I did it for the pain.'[34]

Alfred Jarry, an early twentieth-century French writer cited as a forerunner to the Surrealist movement, is the author of a work entitled 'The Crucifixion Considered as an Uphill Bicycle Race'. His brief article focuses on the travails of just one competitor, Jesus Christ, who arrives at the event with a 'bicycle frame constructed of two tubes soldered together at right angles'. Christ gets off to a promising start, but soon suffers a puncture, after which he 'climbed the slope on foot, carrying on his shoulder the bike frame, or, if you will, the cross'. Jarry, a keen cyclist himself, continues his commentary: 'There are fourteen turns in the difficult Golgotha course. Jesus took his first spill at the third turn. His mother, who was in the stands, became alarmed.' After remarking on the many Israelites along the course, all of them cheering and waving handkerchiefs, the author ends his report thus: 'The deplorable accident familiar to us all took place at the twelfth turn.'[35] Alfred Jarry published his crucifixion story in 1903, the year of the inaugural Tour de France. Considered at the time as a pioneering work in the field of absurdist literature, it seems likely that many of the riders who then flogged their way through the insane demands of the Tour's early renditions would not have considered it quite so absurd.

My own mother, in sharp contrast to Mary of Nazareth, preferred not to watch her son compete. I suppose she was fairly busy working part-time and bringing up three kids – plus, as she liked to remind everyone, one husband. Besides which, only tennis and figure skating ever made it on to her list of approved sports, an odd combination perhaps, but this list patently was not up for review. Yet in a similar manner to Jesus's old lady, my mother was alarmed at the idea of her precious son com-peting in bicycle races, particularly those races in which I'd contrive to fall off my bike at high speed. Following my first serious racing spill, it was my dad who came to collect me – and my dramatically splin-tered collarbone – from the outpatients' ward of a local hospital. By the time Mum returned home later that afternoon, I was flat out in bed and feeling pleasantly woozy from the painkillers. 'What's happened? What's wrong with him?' she demanded. 'Tell me. Please tell me the truth.' Dad told her the truth. It was only a minor bone fracture. And I would have told her too, but the drugs were making everything feel strangely far off. A while later, and after Mum had been gently reassured that her eldest son was not in any sort of coma, or noticeably brain-damaged, she brought me up a mug of hot tea. 'Well then. I imag-ine you won't want to do any more bike racing after this, will you?' she asked.

What? Excuse me? What did the woman just say? The pleasant, soft-focus ambience provided by my earlier Pethidine jab had mostly faded; I could feel a sharp throb in my left shoulder. *Won't want to race any more?* What kind of defeatist talk was this? Was it even possible to conceive of *la mère* Merckx ever putting such a question to a young, post-chute Edouard? I strongly doubted it. Over the previous twelve months I'd found myself engaged in a futile struggle to convince my mother that whenever I was out on my bike, if I was not racing, I was training. I emphatically was not, as she'd insist on calling it, *prac-tising* – which was something figure skaters and concert violinists might do to pass the time. I felt convinced that *la mère* Merckx must have made a better hash of understanding the basics, of getting to grips with the gist of cycle sport. In any case, with my left arm wrapped in a sling, I was back on my indoor rollers a week after the accident – *training* mother, *training* – and competing again just a few weeks after that, where, boosted by my unscheduled but restorative lay-off, I rode surprisingly well.

For a sport in which suffering is not only inevitable but is also worn proudly as a badge of honour, there can be intense competition over who gets to wear the biggest, shiniest badge. Perhaps less so among the ranks of the pros, who have to do what they do to make any kind of living, but for a specific breed of amateur – which naturally includes myself and most cyclists I've ever ridden with – their sense of self-worth is to some extent predicated on how much self-imposed hurt can be endured on a daily basis. True, there always will be those who claim to have triumphed without any training at all, those who glibly ace their race without appearing to even break sweat – much like the cocky straight-A kids at school who insist they never so much as opened a textbook. But equally there will be those who like to toss around their saddle-borne suffering with much bravado. And for those cyclists who fervently believe that their suffering should be a source of great pride and honour, the world of sporting endeavour in 2011 made a sudden turn for the better. Previously, all estimates of competitive suffering were by default highly subjective – subject primarily to the inherent distortions of one's own mind. This was all to change drastically.

In 2011, Strava, the online geo-tracking application that allows cyclists (and runners, walkers, swimmers and skiers) to record and analyze their workouts in the most intricate detail imaginable, introduced its 'suffer score' feature. This attempt to quantify precisely our exercise-induced suffering, to put a definitive number on it, was in hindsight such an obvious thing to do that it seemed odd no one had thought of it before. It turns out, however, that they had, as long ago as the 1990s, but then ensued a lengthy wait for the technology to catch up; in particular, the military-bequeathed Global Positioning System that we now all carry around in our pockets, or attach to our handlebars. In times past, tales of improbable pedalling prowess were annoyingly commonplace. (You say that you climbed Mont Ventoux six times in one afternoon? Great ride mate, well done.) Fast forward to 2015, and if your ride's not posted up there on Strava, you'll have a hard time convincing anyone you were even out on your bike. Indeed, as writer and cyclist Tom Vanderbilt observes, the advent of Strava has 'raised a new kind of philosophical inquiry: Is the unexamined ride worth riding?'[36]

Strava means 'to strive' in Swedish. Of course it does: Michael Horvath, the company's founding CEO, is of Swedish descent. And it would be a neat trick indeed if a simple three-digit suffer score could represent with pinpoint accuracy our individual experiences of sport-induced striving, of any particular trip into the suffersphere. But this is where it gets complicated. Strava's suffer score is a composite, a function of both ride intensity (measured by the proxy of heart rate) and ride duration (logged by onboard GPS). All of which sounds logical enough and a number of numerically savvy Strava users claim to have reverse-engineered the actual algorithm used by the company. But a frequent user complaint is that the formula is overly skewed towards ride duration, which in turn inspires its own grand philosophical debate – namely whether, say, a seven-hour ride at moderate speed involves greater total suffering than a seven-minute time-trial ridden at scorching, lung-shattering pace. And as with all philosophical debates, there is no right answer. Nor wrong answer. We all have our own individual aversions and preferences. It is worth noting, though, that while the 'moderate' seven-hour ride can be in theory completed without ever once venturing inside the *de facto* suffersphere, a seven-minute test at near VO_2 max evidently cannot. Yet any seven-hour slog will earn you a bumper suffer score on the Strava website: behold, your name up in lights, to be appraised by the global community of pedalling peers.

There are, of course, endless debates in the online forums as to the highest Strava suffer score ever recorded. One apparently still-alive subscriber in California has claimed a suffer score of almost 1,200 for an 800km (500 miles) ride, completed in thirty-nine hours and with over 13,000 calories burned. By way of comparison, Strava's website classifies scores of 100–150 as 'tough', 151–250 as 'extreme' and 250+ as 'epic.' While the pros are often protective of their data, understandably so, it would make for great entertainment to see some Tour de France suffer scores. We'll never know what kind of monstrous aggregate scores Eddy Merckx would have logged during his most cannibalistic exploits.

But since the vast majority of Strava's enormous and still expanding user base consists of highly motivated recreational riders, it is reasonable to assume that the company does know its algorithms from its elbows. After all, no cyclist in the world wants to slump through his front door after a long day in the saddle, only to have his smartphone or laptop duly inform him that, according to available data, he did not really suffer all that much. Former CEO Michael Horvath believes that Strava's target market is not so much those individuals levering themselves off the couch each weekend in the quest to lose a few pounds, but more what he terms the 'avids', or 'people who have defined their lives around their sport'.[37] And this term is very familiar to us in a different guise: Strava and MAMILs were evidently made for each other, a love match forged in a sweatier version of heaven, as Tom Vanderbilt testified recently in *Outside* magazine:

I became one of Horvath's premium users a little over a year ago, just as I was getting into an early-middle-age cycling kick – right on schedule. Expensive carbon bike? Check. Lactic-threshold test? Affirmative. Sprocket-shaped grease smear on right calf? Testify! At this point in life, with most career goals met, here was a new place to find a sense of raw, if vaguely ridiculous, advancement.[38]

Strava and a host of similar applications appeal to a certain type of rider. Roughly 90 per cent of the company's cycling subscribers are male and it is fair to say that many of those are tech-minded, deriving their kicks from crunching numbers, not to mention obsessing over them. As Vanderbilt says, 'Strava may be a home for repressed Walter Mittys clad in the yellow jersey of the mind, but it can also unlock a kind of inner frontier of exploration.'[39] Runner turned cyclist Bob Krogh confesses to being a passionate Stravaphile, often preferring to train alone and then heading home to pore over reams of fresh data. I was not too surprised to discover that Bob was on more familiar terms with my own Strava numbers than I was. And while sizing up the competition can be an inherently useful activity, it nevertheless might behove all incipient Stravaholics – as with any addictive personality type – to heed the early warning signs.

Vanderbilt goes on to highlight another archetypal Strava devotee who enjoys participating in their regular online challenges: epic feats of exertion that usually include hellish amounts of climbing. Robin Squire, a cyclist aged forty-eight from south-west England, climbed over 30,000m (98,425ft) in seven days for one such challenge – a vertical gain on a par with the toughest week of any Grand Tour. Strava meanwhile had allocated a more reasonable six weeks to contestants. Squire noted that while he 'wouldn't not be on Strava', he still wonders if the new technology has fundamentally altered his approach to the sport. 'I've kind of lost the small pleasure of going out on my bike for the sake of going out,' he admitted.[40]

The redoubtable sufferings of Eddy Merckx were recorded and analysed in the entirely analogue formats of the era: the breathless radio commentaries; the flickering newscast footage; and not least those originating from the encrypted pathways of his own mind. In addition to the likely unprecedented (if sadly unrecorded) suffer scores he would have notched up on his bike, Eddy Merckx crashed over seventy-five times during the course of his racing career, a handful of which were deemed to be serious. It's still unknown to what extent this alarmed Merckx's mother; whether it caused her to suffer undue anxiety. While it's eminently reasonable to assume that she did suffer at times, I imagine at some point – perhaps with a resigned Gallic shrug and a muttered '*ouf*' – she had to reconcile herself to the fact that her young boy was *Le Cannibale*, and that was that. And it's not as if *le fils* Merckx, even while competing towards the end of his imperious reign, ever considered the possibility of resting on his laurels. He rode the last six days of the 1975 Tour de France with a double fracture of his cheekbone, unable to eat and sustained only by fluids. He finished the race second overall, almost three minutes down on Bernard Thévenet and missed out on his sixth Tour victory. Yet he continued to attack his rival all the way to Paris, causing Thévenet to later admit he could not be completely sure of victory until the last two laps on the Champs-Élysées.

In William Fotheringham's biography of Merckx, he poses the question of how the rider was able to withstand such intense suffering, concluding that Merckx was primarily motivated by fear of failure. But as Henry Sheen, writing in the *New Statesman*, counters:

> Any successful sportsman must endure a fear of failure. Suffering, and the moral dimension it offers, is perhaps the most fascinating aspect of racing cycling. This is the moral futility that the French find so ennobling. When Merckx speaks of his 'passion' for cycling, Fotheringham underestimates the significance of the term. 'Passion' has deep Christian resonances, and is almost synonymous with suffering. Did Merckx consider it ennobling to suffer as he did? Was it through such suffering that he became more than human – until, at the age of 30, his body could endure no more?[41]

CHAPTER 5

Blood, Sweat and Fears

'I think I pretty much had tears in my eyes before I even hit the floor.'

Dan Martin[42]

If the Tour de France is legendary for the sheer volume of blood, sweat and tears left on the road to Paris every summer, in more recent years, it's been the blood – usually chilled, calibrated and centrifuged, then smuggled into a team bus or a hotel room – that's grabbed more than its share of headlines. And of course no one's grabbed bigger headlines over the past decade or so than Lance Armstrong, with the alleged and eventually admitted contents of Mr Armstrong's fridge and bathroom cabinet coming in a close second.

Even now, following Armstrong's carefully choreographed confession on prime-time TV, it's hard to know exactly what to make of the man. Few sportsmen have polarized public opinion in the way he has. But if Armstrong's complex psychopathology might offer sufficient material for an entire psychiatric conference – and this would have the makings of a truly fascinating, sold-out event – it's worth noting that over the years he has waxed more lyrically and insightfully than most on the grand theme of suffering. 'Suffering, I was beginning to think, was essential to a good life, and as inextricable from such a life as bliss,' he claimed in his biography *Every Second Counts*. He went on:

> It's a great enhancer. It might last a minute, but eventually it subsides, and when it does, something else takes its place, and maybe that thing is a great space … Each time I encountered suffering, I believed that I grew, and further defined my capacities – not just my physical ones, but my interior ones as well, for contentment, friendship, or any other human experience.[43]

If Armstrong's earlier bravado and motivational babble now ring hollow in our ears (recall the infamous advert for Nike: 'Everyone wants to know what I'm on. What am I *on*? I'm on my *bike*, busting my ass six hours a day'), there's still little doubt he's spent more time getting up close and personal with suffering than would be the norm for a man his age. After doctors gave the younger Armstrong only a 30 per cent chance of survival, he then suffered on the operating table just as he suffered on the bike. If ability to endure physical pain is to some extent an acquired trait, then there's every reason to believe that what Armstrong had to endure as a cancer victim enabled him in turn, as an against-the-odds survivor, to punish and hurt himself even more on the bike.

The question of whether copious quantities of hurt off the bike have the potential to make you quicker *on* it remains an intriguing one. Canadian Nic Magnan had shown promise as a young rider and continued to notch up impressive results into his twenties. Although his brother made it to the fringes of the national squad, Nic eventually came to accept that a career in pro cycling wasn't going to happen for him. Instead he decided to join the army, in the reasonable belief that a spell in the Canadian military would entail a period of relatively stress-free employment with a guaranteed pension. Which for a while was precisely how things were working out, right up until the morning of 11 September 2001. Shortly after, Nic was informed that he'd been selected for transfer to Canada's combat forces in Afghanistan. A month into his second tour of duty in the war-torn state, and while on a patrol in Kandahar, the armoured vehicle in which Nic was travelling took a direct hit from a Taliban IED, or Improvised Explosive Device. Two other soldiers in the vehicle were killed instantly. Nic, still conscious but gravely injured, was trapped in the wreckage for over an hour ('by far the worst moments of my life'), before being evacuated to a nearby field hospital and later airlifted to a military hospital in Germany.

Nic's legs had been completely shattered by the explosion. Amputation was narrowly avoided, but multiple operations and skin grafts were needed to restore his legs to a rough approximation of their previous form. I met Nic for the first time on a Sunday morning group ride in our adopted home city of Chiang Mai. We chatted as we rode along, loitering at the back of the group as we meandered out of town and headed for the mountains. When Nic he told me he'd served time in the Canadian military, I believe I made a flippant comment about the grave importance of warding off any potential US invasion. But as Nic recounted his story, I glanced down at his distinctly war-torn legs and immediately swallowed my tongue. I decided it might be better if I finished the ride in respectful silence.

During seemingly endless months of intensive rehab, Nic's under-reconstruction legs would not yet support his body weight, so walking unaided remained out of the question. But there was another option. There's an astonishing clip from a Canadian television news broadcast that shows Nic literally crawling along the hallway of his apartment, teeth gritted, then using his arms to haul himself up on to his indoor bike trainer. His legs clearly were not up to the task of walking, but it turned out they could still spin the pedals.

There have been moments during bike races – usually somewhere near

the top of a climb – when I become convinced that the pain I'm experiencing (the aching, lactic-heavy legs, the seared, rasping lungs) is absolutely the worst I've ever felt. The urge to stop pedalling, to dismount,
to rest – and even to sneak a restorative roadside nap – is always overwhelming and yet, oddly, almost always unheeded. But if the physical
pain of racing easily makes the top of my personal hurt list, it's just not
so for the likes of Nic. However tough it may feel on the bike, however
agonizing it might be to close down a gap in a race's latter stages, or
to desperately try to hold on to a breakaway gap you've created, Nic
remains mindful, remains acutely aware that it could always be worse.
Has been worse, much worse. 'Ain't so bad, ain't so bad' were the words
Rocky Balboa muttered over and over to himself while being pummelled
completely senseless by Clubber Lang in *Rocky III*. I've started to suspect
that Nic, who over the past couple of years has rediscovered his old form
to become one of the top amateur riders in the region, might be using a
similar mantra.

Whether or not his recent string of impressive race wins has been aided
by the use of performance-enhancing trauma is perhaps something the
sport's governing body, The Union Cycliste Internationale, should investigate.

That the UCI haven't yet got around to regulating this potentially
unfair advantage is most likely because they're still much preoccupied with rooting out the baffling and ever-expanding array of banned
substances, the minefield of therapeutic use exemptions and the fact that
too much professional cycling blood still finds itself discreetly siphoned
off into high-tech, biocompatible plastic bags, to be later re-transfused
for a welcome rest-day pick-me-up, a bracing red-cell booster shot. Poor
Henri Desgrange would be at his wits' end, no doubt, even apoplectic.
This is not at all what he envisaged. Suffering should be taken on the
chin, not wafted away with a syringe and a bottle of pills. But he might
take a crumb of comfort from the knowledge that a decent quantity
of riders' blood still ends up at more traditional destinations: in other
words, smeared and pooled by the side of the road.

In a typical Tour de France, one-fifth of starting riders will fail to reach
Paris and most of these will have abandoned the race after crashing.
For those who have never parted company with a bicycle at high speed,
consider this analogy from David Millar: 'The next time you are in a car
travelling at 40mph think about jumping out – naked. That's what it's
like when we crash.'[44] And fellow professional Ted King succinctly sums
up the key differences between riding and racing: 'Bike riding is a beautiful thing. Peaceful and serene, flowing and artistic, freeing and blissful,
pedalling a bike over hill and dale is ethereal. Tack a number on your
back, though, and bike racing is a bizarrely unnatural sport hinging so
much on luck.'[45]

Irishman Dan Martin has several major victories under his belt, including the Liège–Bastogne–Liège one-day classic, but during the 2014 season he put in a strong claim for what might be termed the Hamlet Prize, where cycle sport's 'slings and arrows of outrageous fortune' receive due recognition. Defending his Liège–Bastogne–Liège title – one of the toughest events in the one-day calendar – and perfectly placed in second position with 200m (660ft) left to race, the Garmin climber slid off his bike on the final corner:

> It's one thing to make a mistake or know what you've done but we figure that there's a patch of oil or something. I think I had tears in my eyes before I even hit the floor. There aren't really words for it. To race for seven hours and for that to happen on the last corner ... It's poetry.[46]

The Ode to Dan Martin turned out to be something of a threnody – with a familiar refrain – when twelve days later he crashed out of the team time-trial first stage of the Giro d'Italia in Belfast. Intermittent showers and slippery conditions affected the stage and nearing the technical finish one of Martin's Garmin-Sharp teammates appeared to lose control of his front wheel on a manhole cover. In a team time trial, up to nine riders hurtle along in a tight phalanx, only centimetres apart and at speeds often in excess of 60km/h (37mph). Several riders came down in a heap and Martin was suddenly out of the 2014 Giro, stranded by the kerbside nursing his right arm, the telltale sign of a broken collarbone. 'Nothing to be done. Professional bike racing is cruel,' was the blunt verdict from his team manager, Jonathan Vaughters.[47]

While oil-slicked roads and manhole covers are known occupational hazards, misfortune can strike from almost any angle. In the 2011 Tour de France, breakaway riders Johnny Hoogerland and Juan Antonio Flecha were sideswiped by an official vehicle covering the race for the French TV2 channel. Hoogerland, who was flung at high speed into a barbed wire fence, was somehow able to finish the stage, albeit bandaged and dripping copious amounts of blood. 'I will be marked for the rest of my life,' he claimed.[48]

Former world pursuit champion Taylor Phinney, hammering down a descent in the 2014 US road championships, had to swerve suddenly to avoid a race motorcycle that cut across in front of him. He ploughed straight into a crash barrier at 70km/h (44mph). Phinney's left leg 'snapped as a toothpick does under a heavy thumb,' according to one report. 'He was screaming like I've never heard anyone scream before. I could see the extent of the injuries rather gruesomely,' said Lucas Euser, who'd been following a few metres behind. Phinney, facing up to nine months of rehab, managed to remain philosophical:

My relationship with the bike itself is completely different now. When you're going through a hard time, it really is a nice escape and it allows you to filter all of the shit that you have built up in your mind. I had the relationship with the bike before, but I never went through anything as difficult or trying as this, and I've learned a lot about myself in the process.[49]

If there are few recorded instances of riders finishing a race with a double-broken leg, the mind still boggles at tales of those who have ploughed onwards with only marginally lesser injuries. Italian Fiorenzo Magni, despite racing in the substantial shadows of Fausto Coppi and Gino Bartali, was one of the grittiest competitors on the post-war scene. 'Cold, wind, rainy or snowy days were music to my ears,' Magni told one interviewer. 'In all three of my Tour of Flanders victories I remember cold, terrible weather. I was in my element!'[50]

At the age of thirty-six and in his final Giro d'Italia, Magni crashed on stage twelve and broke his left collarbone. For racing cyclists, a broken collarbone in fact scores relatively low on the suffer scale. Arguably the most commonplace fracture – collarbones being the weakest skeletal link when human strikes tarmac – they're about as much bother to the true hard men of the peloton as a hamstring tweak or a groin strain for today's pampered premier league footballers. While a compound break will put you out of action for a few weeks, a minor displacement or hairline fracture is often shrugged off – at least figuratively, since shrugging is the one thing you definitely will not want to attempt with a broken collar- bone.

Magni managed to finish the stage, in only moderate amounts of pain, and with the race headed for the high mountains, he vowed to continue. Warming up for the uphill time trial of stage fifteen, Magni discovered that he was unable to pull on the bars with his left arm, so his mechanic fixed a length of inner tube to his stem. To help him up the steep gradi- ents – and to help him focus on something other than pain – Magni gripped the other end of the rubber in his teeth. But the downhill sections were much trickier, as anyone who's ever tried to descend a mountain using only one arm and his teeth can probably testify. On the next stage, he lost control of his bike and fell again on his left side. 'I fainted from the pain,' he said. Ignoring race officials who wanted to ferry him to hospital, Magni instead remounted his bike, finishing the stage with a broken elbow now added to his quota of injuries. On the now legendary twentieth stage, over four snowbound mountain passes and on a day when sixty riders abandoned, Magni finished second – and went on to claim an astonishing third place overall.

Tyler Hamilton was more prone than most to close encounters with tarmac. In 2002, he crashed early in the Giro d'Italia, fracturing his shoulder. He rode through the pain and eventually finished second, but not before grinding several of his teeth down to the roots – which later required surgery. 'In 48 years of practising I have never seen a man who could handle as much pain as he can,' said Hamilton's physical therapist, Ole Kåre Føli.[51] In the 2003 Tour de France Hamilton crashed again, once again on the first stage, this time fracturing a collarbone. By now more or less accustomed to one-armed racing, he continued, even winning one stage and finishing a remarkable fourth overall. Hamilton even waxes a little mystical on how he managed to overcome the suffering:

> You get into a place where the pain increases so much that you disappear completely. I know that sounds kind of Zen, but that's what it feels like. To me the whole point is to go out of yourself, to push over and over until you arrive somewhere new, somewhere you could barely imagine before.[52]

'This too shall pass,' said the Persians. The ancient Sufi poets told the tale of a ring inscribed with these words – words that could make a sad man happier, but also a happy man sad. The same words are now a staple of Jewish folklore. Indeed, the Jews took such a shine to them that they merit their own acronym in modern Hebrew, consisting of the letters *gimel*, *zayin*, *yodh*. President Abraham Lincoln borrowed the phrase for an 1859 speech. 'How much it expresses! How chastening in the hour of pride! How consoling in the depths of affliction!' Pain is temporary, said Lance Armstrong, continuing the theme. Everything is temporary say those veritable experts on impermanence, the Buddhists – but which would also include, unfortunately, the absence of pain. 'That which does not kill us makes us stronger,' insisted Friedrich Nietzsche, who, after seeing a horse being whipped on the streets of Turin, suffered a massive mental breakdown that put him in an asylum for the rest of his life.

As tempting as it is to believe in superhuman feats of heroism and bravery, another more prosaic explanation should also be given some airtime. The chemicals that give us our blissful exercise-induced buzz, a family of neurotransmitters known as endorphins, were only discovered as recently as 1974. Released by the body in response to prolonged, continuous exercise, these endorphins then interact with the opiate receptors in the brain to reduce our overall perception of pain. Morpheus, the Greek god of sleep, provides us with the etymology of endorphin – along with *endo*, meaning 'from within'. In addition to reduced feelings of pain, secretion of endorphins leads to euphoria, release of sex hormones and enhancement of the immune response. Although there's still some debate over the precise role of endorphins – proxy measurements typically must be taken from blood plasma, not directly from the nervous system – there's little argument over the existence of a 'runners' high.' Bikers talk of similar pleasant sensations, even if 'cyclists' high' hasn't entered the vernacular in the same way.

But it is now well established that physical injury also releases its own flood of endorphins. In a study entitled 'Pain Perception and Serum Beta-Endorphin in Trauma Patients', its authors noted that 'acute traumatic injury engenders the production of beta-endorphin and other endogenous opioids'.[53]

Cortisol, known also as the 'stress hormone', is released by the adrenal glands as part of the fight or flight mechanism, in which the body becomes mobilized and ready for action. Any cyclist who's had to drop out of a race in its early stages (weather, mechanical problems and so on) knows this can be a pretty uncomfortable feeling: muscles ready and primed – primed for a fight, in strictly biochemical terms – and yet denied the opportunity. It's a kind of athletic *coitus interruptus*. But as endurance coach Christopher Bergland explains, without the physical release of fight or flight, elevated cortisol levels can wreak havoc on mind and body. Author of *The Athlete's Way: Sweat and the Biology of Bliss*,[54] Bergland is himself no stranger to acute physical stress: he once ran over 240km (150 miles) in twenty-four hours (a world record) and is the three-time champion of the Triple Ironman, which entails an 11km (7-mile) swim and a 540km (336-mile) bike ride, followed by a 125km (78-mile) run.

Bergland notes also that stress is not always counterproductive: while negative stress (distress) has no obvious benefits for performance, there is also positive stress (eustress) that 'creates a "seize-the-day" heightened state of arousal, which is invigorating and often linked with tangible goals'.[55] In this instance, cortisol levels rise and then gradually return to normal upon completion of the task. When the likes of Magni, Hamilton and Hoogerland defied all odds by continuing to pedal rather than accept the more comfortable option of the back of an ambulance, their battered bodies were at the same time being peppered with cluster bombs of fight or flight hormones. Endorphin and cortisol levels, already elevated from the intense effort and physical stress and further boosted by random busted limbs and lacerations, then conspire to convince these unfortunate accident victims that quitting, as goes the current parlance, is not an option. Seen from this perspective, a devil's advocate might even argue that a well-timed accident or injury will make you ride faster. There's really nothing like coming to a sudden, dazed halt upside down in a ditch to really get the bit (or inner tube) between your teeth – especially if you're then chasing down the sorry excuse for a bike handler who put you into the ditch. In *Monty Python and the Holy Grail*, when the swaggering Black Knight, despite having lost both arms and legs, refuses to surrender during his swordfight with King Arthur – and claims he's merely suffering from a flesh wound – it's clearly the endorphins and cortisol doing the talking. Our unruly stress hormones like to big it up whenever they get the chance.

There's certainly no shortage of cases where those suffering acute mental and physical stress have pulled off highly improbable feats. In 2003, trekker Aron Ralston found himself pinned to a Utah canyon wall by a large boulder that rolled on to him as he attempted to manoeuvre around it. After six days, dangerously dehydrated, hypothermic and facing eventual death, Ralston amputated his right hand with a multitool. 'It was strange. I kind of entered a flow state,' he said. 'I was so engrossed that I had to catch myself when I got to the arteries so that I didn't sever those without a tourniquet on.' In answer to how much pain he endured, he explained:

> Well, I didn't have any sensation in my right hand from the time of the accident onward. When I amputated, I felt every bit of it. It hurt to break the bone, and it certainly hurt to cut the nerve. Overall, it was a hundred times worse than any pain I've felt before. It recalibrated what I'd understood pain to be. At the same time, it was also the most beautiful thing I've ever felt.[56]

Racing cyclists cannot avoid crashes and the ensuing suffering, but the more skilled at least know how to crash properly, if not always stylishly. They tend to get plenty of practice, after all. In the half-second or so between accepting the inevitability of a crash and the finality of the act itself, a stoically resigned racer will weigh up his immediate options, in particular his choice of destination. Crash-management protocol usually dictates that, for example, grass verge beats concrete barrier, but concrete barrier might appeal more than the sheer drop on the other side. It's a game reminiscent of rock–paper–scissors, although one understandably played out in a highly compressed time frame.

The first time I played the game, in a time trial many moons ago, I selected grassy undergrowth over gravel-strewn corner. Truth be told, I'd rather impressed myself with this rapid-fire calculation, if not so much with my bike handling skills, where I'd neglected to modify my entry into the corner in any way despite a raging tailwind. And it was no one's fault in particular that after vaulting over my handlebars, the presumed grassy undergrowth turned out to be a dense thatch of stinging nettles – to which my Lycra skin suit presented as much of a protective barrier as a layer of skin does to an X-ray machine. Rather than persevere to the finish, Johnny Hoogerland style, I headed back to the windswept car park and then home to spend the afternoon in bed with a bottle of Calamine Lotion. To the best of my knowledge, my family lineage contains no warrior types.

Before becoming a pro team manager, Coloradan Jonathan Vaughters rode four times in the Tour de France, but failed to finish on each occasion. With something of a knack for being in the wrong place at the wrong time, Vaughters earned himself the nickname *El Gato* (The Cat) after managing to land on his feet after a headfirst crash in the 1999 Tour. After also crashing out of the 2000 Tour, his 2001 season got off to a more promising start with victory in the Dauphiné Libéré time trial. But in the 2001 Tour, Vaughters, out on a rest-day recovery ride, took a wasp sting just above the right eye. Seeking treatment at a local hospital, a doctor informed Vaughters that a cortisone injection to reduce the swelling would be in breach of UCI regulations. Thus untreated, he attempted to contest the next stage as a visually impaired rider. Within fifteen minutes he knew his Tour was over: 'They started going fast, it started going technical and I couldn't see out of one eye.'[57]

On the same day of Vaughters' untimely sting, an increasingly hostile press, fuelled by persistent rumours of widespread doping, launched a barrage of questions at his higher-profile teammate, Lance Armstrong. Another case of wrong place, wrong time for *El Gato*, without a doubt: 'Everyone in cycling has become absolutely obsessed with doping. People need to stop thinking that that's the only thing that's going on in the race,' said Vaughters, not so prophetically.[58]

No great shortage, clearly, of creative and interesting ways in which to suffer on the bike. 'Nothing is pleasant that is not spiced with variety,' said sixteenth-century essayist and philosopher Francis Bacon and even serial unpleasantness can be a little easier to digest if it's garnished with a dash of spice. Snapping a bone or two doesn't have to be a race-breaker, but be mindful to steer clear of those pesky wasps – and well-camouflaged nettles. Furthermore, Mr Bacon's twentieth-century namesake, many of whose best-known artworks depict the human figure in scenes of violence and suffering, believed that 'an artist must learn to be nourished by his passions and by his despairs'.[59] And surely not just the artists: on the long, hard road to Paris each summer, it's those who find strength and sustenance in the blood, and the sweat, and the tears who go on to claim the biggest spoils.

CHAPTER 6

The Beige Jersey

'Tell your heart that the fear of suffering is worse than the suffering itself.'

Paul Coelho, *The Alchemist*[60]

Footballer Lionel Messi, rated by many as the best player in the world today and maybe the greatest ever, has developed an unfortunate habit of vomiting before and during matches. Messi's national team doctors have failed to come up with a medical explanation, as have the doctors at his club side, Barcelona F.C. But the Argentina head coach, Alejendro Sabella, believes he has identified the cause. 'Nerves,' he said. 'I reckon that in these moments there is anxiety more than anything. It's difficult to remain calm.'[61]

Reading about Messi's nerves made me feel a little anxious. Because – and let's speak frankly here – if a man with the God-like sporting talents of Lionel Messi can't keep his lunch down during a game, how on earth can the rest of us ever expect to remain worry-free? Even the peerless Eddy Merckx was by many accounts a perpetual worrier, a man who, according to rival Raymond Poulidor, who spent much of his own career flailing valiantly some way behind the Belgian, 'always believed he wasn't at his best, that he had some problem or other'.[62] And this of course raises the question of how incredibly worrisome and nerve-wracking it must be to have to compete against the likes of Merckx and Messi.

If bicycle racing is mostly about pain and also about worrying, it's also got a lot to do with the jerseys. Back in those not so distant times when cycling jerseys were fashioned from scratchy wool, they served as a constant reminder of one's corporeal suffering, much like the hair shirts of Biblical times. Ascending an Alpine pass at race pace is not much fun under the best of circumstances, but grinding up a gravelly, unpaved Alpine pass, in heavy rain, on a bike with no gears, while carrying a few extra pounds of damp sheep on your back is really quite beyond the pale. It actually defies belief that anyone ever managed to finish Desgrange's Tour de France during the race's formative years.

Modern fabric technology offers effective relief from this particular form of itchy torture, yet the epic battles – the attacks, defences and skirmishes – that define cycling's Grand Tours are still contested in the name of coloured jerseys. Even though these jerseys will nowadays earn their recipients sizeable piles of cash, in the form of race bonuses and the promise of upgraded contracts from team sponsors, it's still remarkable how many riders manage to conjure up performances far beyond their usual abilities while in possession of a race leader's jersey. The jersey classifications are also negotiable. For example, since the overall stand- ard of racing in Asian countries lags behind that of the more established cycling nations, UCI-sanctioned events on the Asia Tour often include a local rider classification – in other words, a dedicated jersey for the speediest Asian. So while it's usually a European, Australian or North American rider perched atop the podium at a major Asia Tour event like China's Tour of Qinqhai Lake or Malaysia's Tour of Langkawi, the up and coming Asian teams at least get some recognition for their efforts, while gaining valuable experience of racing against a world-class field.

In a similar vein, I've made numerous clean sweeps of the unoffi- cial and largely unrecognized 'Fastest Jew' classification since resum- ing my racing career in Thailand several years ago. I freely admit this has been against minimal competition. Bicycle racing has never been a hugely popular pastime for Jews anywhere and the Jewish population of Thailand is not so large. There was a brief window some years back when it seemed possible that Levi Leipheimer, one of Lance Armstrong's loyal, long-serving lieutenants, might be of the faith (certainly the name and also possibly the looks: balding of dome, aquiline of nose), but this rumour was eventually scotched. To the best of my knowledge, the ranks of pro cycling today remain solidly Jewless. Thus far, I've only come across one other Jewish competitor in Thai bike races and said competi- tor, Jeff, is ten years my senior and poses no serious threat to my title. Jeff does, however, hold the separate distinction of having won an age- category road race on a filth-encrusted clunker of a bike fitted with tour- ing panniers and a bell.

Fastest Jew in Thailand: not quite the heroic stuff of my schoolboy dreams, but I'll take it anyway. Yet a cursory skim through twentieth- century history shows us that European Jewry, all too often preoccupied by other, more pressing issues, has traditionally paid scant attention to bicycle-related affairs. As *Jewish Currents* magazine explains: 'For the Jews of the East European *shtetls*, strenuous physical activity was for goyim – and for those Jews unfortunate enough to have to earn their keep as shleppers, water-carriers, porters, and the like. A Jewish boy was supposed to study.'[63]

So it appears that my Polish ancestors preferred studying to pedalling and in hindsight this was probably the correct choice. In any case, life- long membership of one persecuted minority group is already enough. A bicycling Jew, almost by definition, then exposes himself to the risk of yet further minoritization. A minority of a minority; this is the square root of a minority and begins to sound like a dangerously small number.

In marked contrast, though, suffering, in all of its myriad forms has always been a popular Jewish pastime. Which most likely explains why, in the less tropical and more typically Jewish habitat of New York City – my previous home away from home – it took a pair of Jews to introduce the concept of the 'beige jersey'. Or, to be more exact, one and a half Jews, since the jersey's co-inventor, who goes by the name of Brian Sieger, has always claimed to be half-Jewish. This seemed an authentic enough claim. When I rode with Brian on the same team, it was blindingly obvious that his legs came from the non-Jewish, Germanic side of his family: sturdy, reliable and well engineered. But Brian's frequent bouts of pre-race mental torment left me in no doubt that his head was 100 per cent Jewish.

The beige jersey came into being to correct a glaring omission in the world of cycle sport. In the Tour de France, the overall leader wears yellow, the top sprinter wears green and the highest-placed young rider wears white. The best climber sports a lurid red polka dot number. To complicate matters further, members of the fastest *team* overall wear yellow race numbers (and helmets). The most combative rider – a relatively new category – from the previous stage wears a red number on his back. This 'combativity' prize for the most aggressive performance on a stage is the only subjective jersey-related decision, the only award to require an element of judgment. During the Tour, a panel of eight experts will sit down to analyze each stage and to reach an agreement on the feistiest rider of the day.

The less celebrated beige jersey also embraces this subjective element, bestowing long-overdue recognition to the hitherto unheralded qualities of self-doubt, mental frailty and general malingering. Unlike the other categories, however, outstanding beige-jersey performances often take place *before* the start of an event. In fact, obliterating the competition before a pedal is even turned in anger is the hallmark of the serious beige contender. My teammate Brian's attempts to claim beige typically had him fixating on being wrongly attired: either he didn't have enough layers on, or he had too many layers; he'd brought the wrong pair of sunglasses, or an ominous bank of low cloud was rolling in and he'd forgotten his rain jacket. And so on. Once you've established beyond reasonable doubt that your own clothing has conspired against you, any semblance of a race plan usually self-destructs without much further ado.

The beige jersey is effectively the antithesis of the Tour's combativity award. It seeks to glorify those suffering from a profound lack of self-belief and a bucket list of other neuroses. Yet beige should in no way be confused with a poor performance per se. In the Tour de France, the slowest rider on general classification is known as the *lanterne rouge*, named after a red lamp that – going back a century or so – was hung at the rear of freight train carriages as a means of checking that none of the couplings had worked loose. There is rarely any shame in this distinction; the *lanterne rouge* is typically a valued team player, working flat out for his leader and with no expectations of personal glory.

The beige jersey, let's be absolutely clear, has little to do with *de facto* failure. It has everything to do with the fear of failure. Spare wheels, arm warmers and energy gels might be key items on a rider's pre-race checklist. Nervous jitters, what-ifs and a nagging sense of foreboding really shouldn't be – and yet they often insist on coming along for the ride. To us one and a half Jews there was clearly an urgent, unfulfilled need to codify these various aspects of race-angst. A textbook beige-jersey gambit is to wake up on race day and immediately write off all chances of success, citing illness, lack of training, lack of sleep, or any number of other reasons for guaranteed failure. Despair at this appalling reality means that staying in bed feels by far the best option, but then to grudgingly crawl out of bed, drive to the race, warm up, *start* the race, help initiate the key breakaway and finish with a podium position. This I know. This I've done.

That my teammate Brian was able to boast both German ancestry and an Italian girlfriend (now wife) in no way hampered his aspirations of being the least combative rider in any given race – quite the opposite, in fact. It turns out there's good reason to believe that German and Italian are in fact the spiritual mother tongues of beige. Not that Brian was exactly fluent in either language. He could manage, more or less, offering up a few German phrases here and there, and his Italian did improve dramatically during a year spent working in Rome, where (impressively) he became a training partner and good friend of former world champion Mauritzio Fondriest.

The English language, so expressive in so many aspects, falls short when it comes to matters beige. 'Feeling a bit rough today' is a common enough lament heard on the start line. 'Me bloody legs feel like lead.' A little better this one, yet it still fails to convey truly beige sentiment. We Anglos are still constrained by our longstanding traditions of stiff upper lip and chin up, old boy. It goes without saying that the lips of any serious beige jersey candidate will necessarily flop and quiver with worry and indecision.

Enter the marvellous German lexicon, which according to linguist Arika Okrent is able to describe over a dozen unique illnesses that simply don't exist in other languages.[64] The curious malady of *Föhnkrankheit*, for example: headaches and general unwellness caused by wind that cools air as it draws up the side of a mountain and then warms it as it compresses coming down the other side. *Frühjahrsmüdigkeit* is a debilitating bout of 'early year tiredness', while the more pronounceable *Hörsturz* refers to a sudden loss of hearing, a stress-related condition that apparently affects many Germans. There are plenty more, including *Ostalgie:* an overpowering sense of nostalgia for the old East Germany.

The Italians, though, are not far behind. After more than a decade in Italy, BBC correspondent Dany Mitzman concluded that being Italian is bad for your health. 'As winter draws in, those around me are suffering from a range of distinctly Italian ailments that make our limited British colds and flus sound as bland as our food,' he observed.[65] Mitzman's research revealed that most Italians over the age of thirty live with a condition known as *soffro di cervicale,* which translates approximately as 'cervical suffering', but leaves us not much the wiser. *Colpo d'aria* is a related illness (literally: 'a hit of air') that seems especially dangerous for Italians. It can affect the eyes, ears, other areas of the head, or any part of the abdomen. A precautionary measure is never to leave the house during winter months without first donning a woollen vest, known as a *maglia della salute* ('a shirt of health').

Suffice to say that a smattering of German and Italian language skills will come in most handy for anyone with serious pretensions to the *maglia* beige. Of course, the word 'beige' itself is of French origin, denoting the colour of natural wool, and the French themselves are certainly no slouches in this *département*, what with their endless bouts of *ennui*, their periodic *mal du siècle* and, indeed, the highly unpleasant *maladie Anglaise.* But the fact that beige is spelt identically in English, French, German and Italian (with differing intonations) proves beyond doubt that the condition of 'beigeness' is a genuinely borderless affliction.

Even for the merely monolingual cyclist, it is of no help whatsoever that so many things can and do go horribly wrong during a bike race. Hurtling downhill at speeds above the legal driving limit, on skinny tyres woven from lightweight cotton or silk, where a momentary lapse in concentration from any one of the hundred-odd riders within close proximity can spell instant disaster – this is hardly the right time or place to be feeling apprehensive about the near future. But this apprehension, this generalized sense of dread and unease is something that us Jews, over many generations, have appropriated, refined and claimed as our own. In this sense, the worldwide dearth of Jewish bike racers is no great surprise. Neither is the fact that those who somehow do manage to slip through the net invariably end up as prime contenders for beige.

This is not to say that some measure of apprehension – an ability to evaluate a race's critical moments through a pair of beige-tinted sunglasses – is not a useful attribute in itself. Bradley Wiggins was heavily criticized when he appeared to lose his nerve on the rain-slicked descents of the 2013 Giro, but as he explained to the BBC: 'When it comes to descending down a mountain during a stage race, I always ask myself if it is worth the risk. If it is not, I'll lose 30 seconds and catch it up on the next mountain.'[66] In the same interview, Wiggins then goes so far as to colour himself lightly beige, and dare I say, even a tad Jewish:

> I'm always thinking of the consequences of my actions. Some riders don't do that; they just live in the moment. People say I have no panache, but I'm very calculating in what I do. When we're in the heat of the moment, I'm very businesslike. There are two sides to me: the emotional character who loves sport and the one who is calculating.[67]

Calculating. Businesslike. Oy. While there's no reason to believe Bradley has any Jewish blood in him – no reason at all apart from the substantial *schnozz* – his comments underscore how a healthy dose of apprehension is certainly not out of place in the winning mindset. Rational decision-making may become all but impossible whenever an eminently reasonable sense of caution gets washed away in a turbulent flash flood of beige, but it turns out that a degree of anxiety and stress can actually boost performance for some athletes.

Russian sports psychologist Juri Hanin conducted in-depth studies of athletes' emotions in terms of 'individualized zones of optimal functioning'. Challenging the prevailing belief that most athletes perform best with low underlying amounts of anxiety, he noted that others do better when they 'fire themselves up' before a major event, calling upon their fight or flight response. Hanin worked with Russia's top divers before the Montreal Olympics and observed that while some athletes were successful with relatively high levels of anxiety – those divers with more fight in their flight, presumably – others who were calm and relaxed performed well short of their best. This apparent paradox led him to study more elite athletes and to conclude that any correlation between anxiety and performance was far from straightforward: it all came down to the individual athlete.

If our fear of failure takes the centre stage of beige, then it's the fear of suffering that's found waiting in the wings. Because win or lose, it's always going to hurt. In the words of Greg LeMond, the first American to win the Tour de France: 'It never gets easier, you just go faster.' It's not only about the racing either. Another Greg, New Zealander and former Team Sky member Greg Henderson, likens the intensity of training at pro level to 'fighting with a Gorilla. You don't stop when you're tired. You stop when the Gorilla is tired.'[68] And if the wisdom passed down from The Great Pantheon, from those Higher Powers of Suffering, is that physical pain can be both glorious and edifying, then how to explain, come race day, the fear and loathing lurking in the pit of your stomach?

Of course, it's precisely these unpleasant feelings that have inspired some of the most spectacular beige performances of all time. Shortly after the introduction of *le maillot beige*, my own ambitions shrivelled and dwindled away as it became apparent that Brian's name was written all over it – not only for that particular season but for several seasons to come, as he repeatedly, and with an almost Lance-like intensity, saw off all beige challengers. After due consideration, it was decreed that an actual beige race jersey would be an abomination; certainly such a thing could never be worn anywhere near the bike, conflicting as it did with the strict dress code and colour schemes of cycle-wear etiquette. Instead, a beige cardigan, replete with leather elbow patches, was sourced from a local charity shop and presented to an emotional Brian at the end-of-season team dinner. Approved exclusively for use in the home, the beige cardigan was in fact retired from active service some years ago and can now be found framed and on display at *la casa* Brian, in a manner not dissimilar to those infamous yellow jerseys, all seven of them, that grace Mr Armstrong's expansive living room walls over in Austin, Texas.

The current heir to the beige jersey is another lanky American. Joe, who's a useful masters racer on occasion, is also an extensive depository of cycle sport arcana. While the jersey itself was retired long ago – and in any case the original woollen item would be unwearable in Thailand's heat and humidity – the essence of the jersey, the importance of what it signifies has found a spiritual home inside Joe's head, where it stubbornly remains, despite the best efforts of teammates to exorcise his morale-sapping phantoms. And while Joe isn't Jewish – not even fifty per cent – he's typically the most Jewish-acting member of any group ride, which often includes one or two genuine Jews. Joe brings to mind the Seinfeld character Dr Tim Whatley, who converted to Judaism 'for the jokes'.

Joe and I were out riding some hills one morning, out to the northwest of Chiang Mai, keeping pace with the rolling shadows of our bikes cast by the early morning sun. While we rode along on our bikes, we'd fallen into the habit of debating why we rode our bikes. I knew a few of my reasons. It got me out of the house. It kept me off the streets – or rather, it kept me on them. After a hard ride, and feeling duly pacified and becalmed – deactivated almost, like a piece of unexploded ordnance – I would gracefully metamorphose into a more pleasant, more functional human being. My then girlfriend had taken to booting me out of the front door whenever I was in a dither about whether to ride or not, safe in the knowledge that this guaranteed a more harmonious domestic atmosphere later in the day.

'But I don't actually *like* cycling,' said Joe, as he'd expressed numerous times before. As we crested a small incline, a verdant panorama of terraced rice fields unfurled in front of us. A few minutes up the road was a hillside café with a view, where we would stop for coffee and sit for a while. We'd finish the ride with a low-tempo spin back into town, an hour or so away.

'But what about when you're just out enjoying the ride?' I prompted Joe. I may not have been the beige-jersey elect, but I at least had some form here, some 'previous'. We rolled up at the rustic-themed café and leant our bikes gingerly against a terracotta wall. 'No. Not really,' Joe said, removing his gloves and helmet. 'I only ride because I don't want to get fat.' When Joe did stop riding for a year, he did get fat. He became, in the words of a teammate, 'distinctly pear-shaped'. His principal excuse was that he whiled away a good part of that year in Cambodia, where not only did he not have a bike, but bottled water is more expensive than a can of beer.

Whenever Joe talks about cycling, I'm reminded of what I think of as the 'Agassi Effect'. As Andre Agassi wrote in his autobiography, 'I play tennis for a living even though I hate tennis, hate it with a dark and secret passion and always have.'[69] In an interview with *Spiegel* magazine, shortly before publication of the straight-talking, confessional *Open*, Agassi explained: 'While I was winning Wimbledon, I felt like I would die. I feared to fail; I feared embarrassment.'[70] Asked how he felt upon retirement from the sport, Agassi replied:

> Free. I was liberated. I never missed tennis. I never liked the competition. I never liked the pressure I put on myself. I never liked that I couldn't be perfect at it. It felt like I had been created to never be satisfied. I resented how bad losing felt and how not good winning felt. It was never balanced. I could not escape this.[71]

This crippling fear of failure, this fleeting sense of satisfaction: both at times seem almost obligatory traits within the top echelons of sport. By the time Agassi was six, he was hitting 2,500 balls a day. His father rigged up an automatic ball machine, nicknamed 'The Dragon', estimating that one million balls a year was the magic number that would render his son unbeatable. Steffi Graf, Agassi's wife, suffered similarly as a gifted young player due to 'competitive father syndrome'.

Unlike Mr Agassi, neither Joe nor I were making any kind of living from cycling. My prize money usually covered what I spent on tyres. Most of the time we were racing for nothing more than *toffees*, which was how any native Thai attempt at enunciating trophies usually came across. On our worst days we couldn't even race *for* toffee, which of course meant different things to different people. Possibly we were devoting a bit more time to cycling than was strictly warranted. With both of us well into our forties, our chances of improving, of getting stronger, of going any faster, were slim, to say the least – slimmer even than this latest version of Joe, who, by refusing to ever eat anything, had shed all of his year-off extra bulk and then some. Joe explained that his only other reason for riding – other than remaining skinny – was because riding looked cool.

As a cyclist, Joe does look the part, at least until the starter's gun goes off. He looks pretty fantastic on the bike. He's long and lean and looks like he's going to crush the field. But I'd hazard that his ongoing hunger strike at least partly accounts for why he hardly ever crushes the field. Joe's teammates have put it to him on several occasions that he might have more appetite to race mean and tough if he had more, well, appetite in general. But Joe's body-image dysmorphia most probably now requires professional help. It's my opinion that Tyler Hamilton's recently published account of how after long training rides and as a weight-loss strategy, he would ingest only a sleeping pill and a bottle of mineral water, was a grossly irresponsible act, potentially endangering the physical well-being of countless teenage girls and more than a few middle-aged cyclists. That said, even a reasonably well-fed Joe has been hamstrung on too many occasions by the classic conundrum of beige. In a race with fifty-nine other starters, he always needs to beat sixty riders to win. And it's usually the plus one that's Joe's trickiest opponent of all. But at least he's not fat.

For any rider hoping to eventually overcome his race demons – or, in other words, anyone not planning to contest the beige jersey – then the suggestion from author Paul Coelho, that our fear of suffering might be worse than the suffering itself, is certainly worth bearing in mind. And since, as any good Buddhist will tell you, the mind has a nasty habit of wandering, before your next race it might not be a bad idea to print out Coelho's wise words and tape them securely to your handlebars.

CHAPTER 7

Brits and the Four-Year Itch

'If we have our own why in life, we shall get along with almost any how. Man does not strive for pleasure; only the Englishman does.'

Friedrich Nietzsche

'I no longer wanted to ride around in circles.'

Victoria Pendleton[72]

When a hugely moustached Nietzsche managed to summarize his life's work and in the very same sentence score a quick dig against the English, he most probably earnt himself extra kudos from his German contemporaries. For Nietzsche, the biggest *why* in life – or his 'will to power' – was all to do with achievement and ambition; the striving to do one's absolute best in a chosen field. Hard striving alone should be sufficient in itself, he said, not just as a means towards a desired end – towards something as fluffily insubstantial as pleasure or happiness. Here, Nietzsche pooh-poohed the likes of Jeremy Bentham and John Stuart Mill, the liberal, clean-shaven Englishmen who had earlier been preoccupied with foolish utilitarian ideas such as how to find the 'greatest happiness of the greatest number'.

The hard striving of British cyclists in recent years has at last transformed into regular success, both on the road and on the track, in marked contrast to the paucity of earlier times. But judging by many of the firsthand accounts of the victors, the success does not always feel as good as expected. For Olympic gold medallists in particular, the long, painstaking build-up followed by the split-second supernova of a major victory is often a sure-fire recipe for anticlimax, for a sense of 'Well, that happened, now what?' 'I just knew it was not meant to feel this way,' wrote Victoria Pendleton, summing up her blank emotions while atop the podium at the Beijing Olympics. 'In the end, it was all an act. I just about got away with it. My glazed emptiness could be excused as disbelief or ecstasy.'[73] None of this will come as much of a surprise though to those familiar with the Buddhist concept of the suffering of impermanence. And with greater emphasis on the sacrifice and self-discipline required over years of preparation than on the transient joy of standing on top of a podium, the rigours of modern Olympic training would probably meet with hearty Nietzschean approval.

Sir Bradley Wiggins similarly found that winning his first individual pursuit gold in the 2004 Athens Olympics was not the life-altering experience he'd imagined. 'The reality was quite different,' he said. 'I woke up every Monday morning and we were still overdrawn and I'd think, 'God, I don't feel like riding my bike again.'[74] There was bitterness that nothing had changed after all the hard work but it went deeper than that. I'm not saying I was clinically depressed but there were definite bouts of depression – and lots of drinking.' Wiggins, in his own words, embarked on a 'nine-month bender', arriving for opening time at his local pub every day and knocking back up to a dozen pints before going home to his then pregnant wife, Kathy. 'I was just bored shitless and didn't know what to do.'[75]

For British Olympians, perhaps the only thing worse than a gold medal is two gold medals. After winning both the individual and team sprints in London 2012, Scotsman Jason Kenny also caught a nasty dose of the post-Olympic blues. As he told the *Daily Telegraph*:

> I had no morale, no motivation, I just couldn't face training basically. I went to the tracks and did two laps and just got off and went home. The motivation issue is understandable as London 2012 had been on the horizon for as long as my career. It was always going to be difficult to pick up from there.[76]

Even a lowly amateur competing several rungs down the ladder – racing for nothing more glamorous than another sideboard trophy or a cash prize barely sufficient to cover race expenses – runs the risk of ending up in a similar bind. The journey is the reward, claimed the Taoists. As did Robert Louis Stevenson: 'To travel hopefully is a better thing than to arrive.'

The daily training journey, despite the hardship involved, does provide its own comfortable rhythm, an unwavering point of focus. 'I race therefore I train' – this is what helps get you out of bed on a cold, damp February morning. While the vicissitudes of any individual race will remain forever within the firm grip of the velo-gods, this basic calculus of training – the golden ratio of input effort to output result – will tend to assert itself over time; over the course of an entire season, for example. So we repeat the daily routine, mile after mile, repeat it as a mantra, unwavering, without complaint for the most part and safe in the knowledge that all comes to those who train: a pot of gold at the end of the four-year rainbow for a Wiggins or a Pendleton, and for myself something more akin to twenty-five quid in a crumpled envelope.

But either way, finally arriving at your rainbow can be a distinctly Wizard of Oz moment. Brad Wiggins found a well-stocked pub at the end of his yellow-brick road. Mancunian Graham Jones, a three times Tour de France finisher in the 1980s, had this to say: 'As the Tour progresses, you feel sick and tired of the same routine day after day and you look forward to the end. However, when it comes you have a feeling of anticlimax and you think "God! It's all over." '[77]

When I found my biggest race of the season cancelled one year – an event on which I'd focused several months of training – I slid into a similarly Wiggins-eque slump, if less alcoholic. I was in superb shape and raring to go – raring to suffer for the cause. But with no race and no prospect of suffering, I found myself adrift and rudderless: with this abrupt stymieing of suffering I'd gone and lost my mojo. But this wasn't entirely correct either. I *was* suffering. This was in fact the suffering of suffering denied, an unusual affliction certainly and one that neither Buddhists nor German philosophers have taken much time to consider. I declined all invitations from teammates who wanted to go out and ride regardless. Yes, I told them, the weather was indeed lovely, but really what was the point if there was no race to be raced? The perfect weather could go screw itself. In my mind at least, I'd already tossed my bike into a ravine. Even with more satisfactory season endings, a feeling of hollowness would arrive on cue after the final race of the year: what exactly was I going to do with myself for the next few months? SAD, or Seasonal Affective Disorder, is now a commonly diagnosed condition amongst the general population, brought on by a deficit of natural light, but seasonal ups and downs can take on extra significance for sportspeople.

Psychiatrist Steve Peters, the so-called 'mind mechanic' of British Cycling, has in recent years helped a number of top athletes to navigate a safe path through their mental minefields, to skirt round the edges of the precipitous mental ravine. Before switching to sports psychology, Peters – who played a critical role in Team GB's breakthrough successes at the Beijing Olympics – worked with seriously disturbed patients at Rampton Hospital. This experience then proved handy at Liverpool F.C., who sought out Peters' expert counselling services – and where the impressive, but controversial ear-nibbler Luis Suárez was the standout player. Following Peters' arrival, Liverpool went on to enjoy its best season in decades. In Peters' view, football managers' traditional dressing room tactics of revving players up, getting them 'up for it', is not particularly helpful. 'There's no evidence that approach actually works,' he says. 'When the team are in this state or an individual is, their judgement is impaired. They make errors and they then try to correct that by emotional attacks which result in further errors.'[78]

Peters was later hired by the Football Association to work with the 2014 England World Cup squad. Sadly, Peters, for all his undoubted talents, is still only a psychiatrist, not a magician and the England team surprised almost no one by crashing out of the tournament during the first round. Yet credit is surely due to the FA for finally deeming the issue of mental preparedness worthy of serious consideration. Before the 1998

World Cup finals, then England manager Glenn Hoddle introduced his England squad to a faith healer, who would acquaint herself with each player by placing her hands on his head. At their first meeting, midfielder Ray Parlour reportedly asked for a short back and sides.

If Dr Peters' former high-security patients – those deemed to pose a 'grave and immediate danger' to the public, a label that might include Mr Suarez too – are evidently those in most pressing need of psychiatric intervention, that's not to say that many of us wouldn't benefit from a few sessions on the couch. Similarly, while Peters believes his techniques can help any athlete to improve their performance, he's achieved his most impressive results with those whose 'mindfields' appear most volatile and live-wired.

Snooker player Ronnie O'Sullivan first approached Steve Peters in 2011, midway through a turbulent career. In 2006, Sullivan created a stir when he walked out of the UK championships mid-frame. 'Had enough of it, mate,' he reportedly told his opponent, Stephen Hendry, while heading for the door. Considered by many to be the greatest natural talent in the game's history, O'Sullivan won his first UK championship at the age of seventeen. But he soon became reliant on drugs and alcohol to cope with the pressure of international competition and the sudden disappearance of his father, who had received a life sentence for murder. After a year of counselling with Dr Peters, Sullivan regained the world championship – but then announced an extended break from snooker and an unexpected return to his first love:

> Running is what has helped me to fight my demons, win five world snooker championships and cope with all the crap that life has thrown at me. My running trainers are the most important things I own.[79]

Dr Steve Peters is 'the world expert on common sense', according to Sir Bradley Wiggins. A most handy attribute, no doubt, and yet Wiggins' remark reads as something of a backhanded compliment. Wiggins, a proven world-beater by the time Steve Peters took up a full-time position at British Cycling in 2005, had by then perhaps already worked through his worst demons, many of which – as with Ronnie O'Sullivan – related to an absent father. But for Victoria Pendleton, who remained plagued by self-doubt throughout her cycling career despite winning nine world track titles, Peters was a far more pivotal figure. Win or lose, Pendleton appeared locked in a never-ending battle with her brittle emotions and her post-race interviews were often fraught, tearful events. For many years, she suffered from chronic anxiety, OCD and self-harming tendencies – which first surfaced when she made it into the national squad. 'I was in the midst of an opportunity of a lifetime,' she said. 'What right did I have to feel so bereft?'[80]

A familiar theme lay behind many of Pendleton's issues: a parental theme, a father theme. Lance Armstrong and Bradley Wiggins were both abandoned by their fathers at the age of two. 'The hero who did it without his dad,' ran a *Telegraph* headline after Wiggins' 2012 Tour victory. 'Wiggins does what he does because he doesn't want to end up like his father.'[81] But there was no absent father figure in Victoria's case: Max Pendleton, a former grass track national champion, was a looming presence during his daughter's formative years, portrayed in her recent autobiography as half-accountant, half-tyrant. Mr Pendleton, who presented his youngest daughter with a toolbox for her eighteenth birthday, would insist she accompany him on long weekend training rides, where he'd make a point of dropping her on each climb. Pendleton later describes her thoughts at the Beijing Olympic velodrome, seconds before the start of the individual sprint final: 'It's taken my whole life to reach this point. The little girl trying desperately to stay in sight of her dad.'[82]

What exactly is the foundation of the Peters approach? In his bestselling book *The Chimp Paradox*, Peters contends that our personalities consist of three separate parts: the human, the computer and the chimp. While the human part is mostly rational and the computer is unerringly logical, the chimp is unfortunately neither. Success, sporting or otherwise, says Peters, crucially depends on our taking firm control of our inner chimps – the irrational, hyper-emotional character traits that make our moods unpredictable and often self-destructive. Peters views the chimp as that section of our brain powered by gut instinct and snap judgments. Other, more evidence-based areas of our thinking are better able to discern graduations of grey as opposed to only black and white. MRI scanners that show blood flowing into different parts of the brain when making rational or emotional decisions offer support to Peters' model. While our basic survival instincts remain necessarily under chimp control, to allow it free reign over the rest of our lives is to invite certain disaster. According to Peters:

> You can't kill the chimp but you can manage it. If you don't have a plan, the chimp comes up with one for you. It's about how do you deal with pressure situations and clear thinking. It is about understanding emotion: how the mind works and not rushing in with knee-jerk stuff.[83]

As many have found to their cost, neglecting your inner chimp is potentially to expose yourself to all manner of screeching and poop flinging. For many elite sportspeople, an opportunity to offload worry and self-doubt on to a pair of sympathetic ears is perhaps half the battle won. If the relatively new field of mind mechanics does involve more than basic common sense, it is still a less complicated discipline than, say, the field of quantum mechanics. A few well-chosen words of moral support can make a huge difference, but it still isn't rocket science. Neither does the Peters prescription work for all. 'I never agreed with his chimp theory. I always thought it was a distraction from who you were as a person,' explained Bradley Wiggins in a BBC interview. 'If someone had a go at you, particularly in the track environment, it was like, "just ignore him, it's his chimp talking". I always had a problem with that, I was like, "no it's not. It's Shane Sutton and he's being horrible to me!"'[84]

Double Olympic gold medallist Laura Trott expresses similar sentiments: 'I don't think I'd need Steve because I can sort it myself.' Miss Trott, born with a collapsed lung and who later suffered with asthma, also admits to a desire that most of us have felt at various points in our lives: 'I was thinking on the rollers today that, before a race, if I could just pick my brain up and put it on the side of the track for four minutes it would be perfect.'[85]

An excellent idea from Laura, even if this summary disabling of the chimp is completely at odds with the mind view of Dr Peters. Surreptitious brain removal is in fact something I've long suspected of many of the world's top riders. Certainly for any event against the clock – time trials, pursuits and the like – an ability to switch off the active mind, to not have to *think* about all the suffering, should amount to a definite performance enhancer. To this end, any mental trickery that can coax the mind into a more meditative state – mantras, music, Japanese haikus – and out of its regular, pain-averse consciousness will also put more power through the pedals. Here I would like to offer a belated acknowledgement to 1980s synthpop-crooner Howard Jones for his unwitting role in my first sub-one hour 40km (25-mile) time trial. 'It's as hard to distinguish his music as it is to distinguish it from your carpet,' carped the *NME*.[86] Yet an internal playlist of Jones' vapid electro-drone was remarkably effective in decoying my mind away from thoughts of extreme physical discomfort.

'All he wanted to do was to help people become happier,' is how Victoria Pendleton described Steve Peters' broad remit at British Cycling.[87] And for a raw Pendleton, aged only twenty-two and a new recruit to the national track squad, feeling insecure and isolated as the lone female, perhaps this reassuring, avuncular presence was just what the doctor ordered. 'Steve gave me many profound insights into myself, and life, during our weekly sessions in his office at the velodrome. He calmed and soothed me.'[88]

But while there is no inherent reason why something like Olympic training – and subsequent success – should be an unhappy experience, we are on rather shaky ground if we expect it to make us deliriously happy. Buddhist monks, fully certified mind mechanics in their own right, have a marked tendency to sidestep this thorny question of happiness. During a group meditation session I attended recently, our saffron-robed moderator offered to take questions from the floor. 'Would you say you are happy?' inquired one attendee. The monk paused for a few seconds. He certainly looked serene: quite at ease, in fact. Well grounded. 'No,' he replied eventually, his head tilted a contemplative ten degrees, as a faint murmur echoed around the room. 'I am not especially happy. But I am peaceful.'

If peacefulness is a more realistic, more attainable goal than happiness, how does that then square with the idea of striving? Can one strive peacefully? Yes, certainly, in many fields, but it often seems a tall order within the context of elite sport, and cycling in particular. In the countdown to the Beijing Games, Pendleton's teammate Rebecca Romero told reporters that she would feel satisfied as long as she managed to give her best, all the while appearing neither happy nor peaceful but instead noticeably on edge. Yet the intense focus required to compete at the highest level – or even, as I've discovered, at a more modest level – does turn out to be a remarkably effective way of drowning out almost all other thoughts and concerns, of dampening the incessant naggings of *dukkha*, the general unsatisfactoriness of all things. A four-year Olympic training plan will leave you precious little time to sit around idly fretting about the meaning of life. And if you somehow do find the time, you surely won't have the energy. A gold medal can take on all meaning; all else becomes extraneous. The bigger problems often begin once you've achieved what you were striving for.

If elite cyclists do appear particularly prone to depression, disillusion and demotivation, other professional sports hardly come issue-free. Football has suffered plenty of casualties through the years. George Best provided the original and possibly still not improved-upon template for self-destructive sporting idols: 'In 1969 I gave up women and alcohol – it was the worst twenty minutes of my life,' he famously quipped. More recently, former England international Paul Gascoigne has been repeated front-page tabloid fodder, the sorry tale of a promising career blighted by personality disorders and addiction. Former Arsenal and England star Tony Adams believes that gambling has now replaced alcohol as the most troubling off-pitch problem amongst footballers. Adams and his former Arsenal teammates Kenny Sansom and Paul Merson all received treatment for gambling addictions during their professional careers.

The sport of cricket seems to inspire a different strain of psychic meltdown, particularly amongst its leading batsmen. England top-order batsmen Marcus Trescothick and Jonathan Trott both have seen their international careers curtailed by crippling bouts of anxiety and depression. It could be argued of course that their responses are entirely rational – are in fact a sign of quite robust mental health – given a job description that involves having a small, hard object hurled towards them at high speeds for hours on end. Because, in true *Catch 22* style, if the imminent prospect of this kind of onslaught fails to leave you anxious and stressed, then there may well be something wrong with you. And while base-ball's big hitters might have to cope with similarly intense pressures, it is only for a few minutes at a time, not for endless, unbroken hours at the crease.

If there is a parallel to be drawn between cricket and road cycling, it is that while they are both nominally team sports, they often demand of their participants lengthy periods of individual introspection and concen-tration – periods that can be lonely, desolate and inner-demon channel-ling in a way that simply does not exist in, say, football or basketball. The painstaking test-match century can be regarded as a close analogue of the long solo breakaway in the mountains. A further analogue is perhaps that of the extended cricket tour when compared to spending much of the year on the road at one-day classics, Grand Tours and the like. Jens Voigt, who announced his retirement from pro cycling in 2014, neatly summed up both the stresses of international competition and the poten-tial issues that come bundled with its alternative, the stress of no more stress: 'I'm happy that the sacrificing, the hard training, the travel, the time being away from the family is going to stop. ... But I'm also terrified. Frightened. Because, I mean, in my whole adult life cycling was the most consistent thing I ever did.'[89]

A more sensitive, hands-on approach to the pressures of professional sport is these days to be found in the improbable environs of London Sara-cens rugby club. Long considered the preserve of unreconstructed male aggression and a winner takes all mentality, rugby union seemed a most unlikely candidate for a sport where players are encouraged to express their inner doubts and fears. In 2009, when a South African consortium took over the Saracens, the club's fans were promised a 'revolution', most visibly in the form of a new 80,000-seat stadium. But a more subtle revo-lution was soon under way, as championed by Dr Brendan Venter, the club's new rugby director.

'You can't think about winning all the time,' Venter told journalists. 'I'm far more interested in my players, along with me, improving as people. That's basically the only thing that really matters.'[90] For Venter, it was definitely not all about the rugby. 'If we win everything there is to win but we've broken relationships, we've lost the plot. We've missed our point of being on earth, it's as simple as that.'[91]

To assist in the ongoing revolution, Jules Evans, author of *Philosophy For Life And Other Dangerous Situations*, started hosting a monthly philosophy discussion at the Saracens ground in 2013. Evans, who runs similar projects at a mental-health charity and at a Glasgow prison, was keen to explore how the centuries-old philosophies of the Buddhists, Stoics, Taoists and others might be applied to our lives today. While modern psychotherapy already draws heavily from these ancient value systems, Evans believes that the mental aspects of athletic performance, even at the elite level, are frequently overlooked. According to Evans, professional sports teams who have invested heavily in players' physical fitness should consider their mental well-being as an equal priority. But this is too easily ignored, he notes. Male culture remains characterized by an inbuilt tendency to sweep mental-health issues under the carpet and the ranks of professional sports of course remain predominantly male. The biggest killer of British men under fifty is suicide.[92]

According to Saracens and England full back Alex Goode, who witnessed the revolution at first hand, 'the old Saracens was not a particularly friendly place. There'd be quite brutal banter ... A lot of the players were in it for their own benefit and not the team.'[93] Venter later returned to South Africa, but the revolution, officially known as the Saracens' Personal Development Programme, continued under the stewardship of David Jones, a philosophy graduate, and David Priestly, a sports science PhD. According to Priestly:

> People have an incredibly romantic view of professional sports. But it can be a very brutal world, a machine that squeezes everything out of a person and then tosses them aside. Most of the people in that world are very far from being role-models. Most people in professional sports shy away from anything explicitly about ethics. It's just about winning. Younger players can see people at the top of their sport who are doing very well while still behaving in a questionable manner.[94]

Management concern for the players' mental well-being is not confined only to the psychological impact of the game. In early 2015, Saracens players took to the field wearing plaster-like patches below their right ears. And not just any old patch: the xPatch, created by a Seattle-based company, is a high-tech device designed to monitor the force of blows to the head. A study from the Auckland University of Technology found that its sample of amateur rugby players sustained an average of almost 1,400 head impacts per season. While most were considered low-risk, around 10 per cent were of a force that exceeded the 'risk-injury limit'. 'I don't want to be visiting these players in 20 or 25 years time in a hospital where they are suffering from dementia or some other neurological condition,' said the club's chief executive, Edward Griffiths.[95] Studies of American football players have shown that damage from head injuries is often cumulative, as noted in the *Guardian*: 'It's the series of minor hits that can make a player more susceptible to lasting brain damage; more susceptible to motor function and memory issues; more susceptible to impaired co-ordination, vision and speech; and more susceptible to emotional and behavioural changes, including depression and anxiety.'[96]

Jules Evans, who doesn't play rugby but still admits to being prone to depression and anxiety, has at times questioned the wisdom of his research methods. He recently found himself 'standing in front of a gym full of colossal rugby players at Saracens rugby club, staring at me stony-faced as I discussed how ancient philosophy helped me through panic attacks'.[97] But his workshops at the club have been well attended, and the players receptive, even if some of the club's more ingrained attitudes are proving hard to shift. 'I don't even consider failing,' said one player. 'It's not an option.' But Evans, citing Aristotle, explains to the player how a reasoned, philosophical outlook can still accommodate negative responses to life's tragedies on and off the sports field. It turns out that one Saracen FC core value – even after *La Révolution* – is to 'be relentlessly positive and energized at all times'. This, as Evans duly notes, does sound rather exhausting.

Exhausting physical exercise: not quite Evans' cup of tea, but as Karl Marx, another philosophically minded gent, once said: 'The only antidote to mental suffering is physical pain.' With no recorded instances of Marx on a bicycle, or anywhere near a rugby pitch, it is unclear in precisely which context the grandfather of modern socialism was speaking. But the same fact was also well known to a struggling Victoria Pendleton, a new recruit to the UCI training camp in Aigle and sitting alone in her room with her Swiss army knife. 'The longest blade fills my gaze. I have been here before,' she wrote. 'I know what I need to do to make a new pain which will feel more clean and honest than the knotted mess inside me.'[98]

Not to suggest for a moment that all elite cyclists are bedevilled by a state of deep inner torment, ready to slash forearms, or to drink to oblivion just to experience some brief respite. But for many, the intense physical effort provides substantial relief in itself, soothing and calming the existential backchat just as readily as drugs, alcohol, or a softly spoken sports scientist. A regular diet of elective pain can be good for the soul. On the other hand, those more enamoured of the pleasures of a wholly pain-free lifestyle following the TV–sofa–fridge axis rarely appear all that comfortable in their own skin and often not even particularly alive. It then falls upon us to locate our own sweet spot of suffering, the inflection point of effort, where the next dose of pain is no longer enlivening, but deleterious instead. As with all intense cravings, sometimes we can have too much of a good thing.

Psychotherapist Armand DiMele believes that addiction to pain – or at least to the endorphins, the 'endogenous opioid inhibitory neuropeptides' that course through our bodies during intense exercise – is as real an addiction as any other and can be equally harmful:

> Once you become used to living an endorphin-filled existence, it is hard to give it up. With so much pain-killing substance running through your body, there is a sense of security that makes you feel safer in the world. It's a shield inside the

body that protects you from subtle feelings that are more difficult to block, like tenderness, vulnerability, and love.[99]

Love and tenderness: surely not to be sniffed at, but loss of such subtlety still might seem an acceptable trade-off for some heavy users, those suffering addicts for whom pain functions, paraodoxically, as a pain reliever. But like all addicts, pain junkies require their regular fix, typically an ever-increasing fix, and going cold turkey is rarely for the best. 'To the pain addict, a life without pain is completely unfamiliar,' DiMele continues. 'There are frequent reports of a frightening void that yearns to be filled when pain is no longer dominant. In many ways it is like being without drugs after years of dependency.'[100]

Graeme Obree, the immensely popular but maverick Scotsman, has been on familiar terms with frightening voids. He knows that striving for success can be dangerous; at its very worst a form of madness that carries serious health risks. During a twenty-year career, Obree made his name by riding highly unconventional, home-built bikes in a series of weird and wonderful positions. Obree was diagnosed in 1991 with severe bipolar disorder, two years before breaking the world hour record for the first time and has attempted suicide twice. 'A lot of the positive stuff was driven by negativity,' said Obree in a recent interview. 'I needed that success to feel worthy. My worth was dependent on the next result. When you've reached the highest point with a world record, there's not a rung of the ladder after that, so that's the point when you're thinking: "Oh shit, I've run out of obsessive behaviour." '[101] From this perspective, how much of Obree's two-wheeled striving was merely a form of avoidance coping – of void-avoidance?

In Obree's view, those prone to depressive episodes are also more prone than most to obsessive behaviour. 'There's a higher incidence of depression among elite sport people than the general population,' he says. 'We have a weird level of contentment. Think about it – if you have to win every race then there's something not right about you. It's not a healthy obsession, not the sign of a balanced, self-fulfilled person, happy in their own skin.' As his autobiography, *The Flying Scotsman* – later adapted into a 2006 film – abundantly makes clear, for much of his racing career the Scotsman and his skin were not on the best of terms. Obree has summed up his relationship with the bike as a self-medicating process of survival: 'One day I'd be happy riding, then the next I'd be feeling that I hated it, that there was too much pressure. Then I'd never want to get on a bike again.'[102]

Graham Obree announced his retirement from competitive cycling in 2013, but only after breaking another world record, this time hurtling along the Nevada desert flats inside 'Beastie', a kitchen-table built machine he propelled at speeds up to 90km/h (56mph) from a precarious, prone position – headfirst and belly to the ground. Instead of basking in the glow of a new record, Obree, more or less true to form, grumbled that a number of basic errors in designing the bike's aerodynamic shell had left the project far short of its original target. 'Everyone has been too polite to tell me the shape's a piece of shit,' he said.[103] For his follow-up project, Obree planned to write a survivor's guide to depression, tagging it with a pithy sales pitch: 'The book will cost the same as a bottle of vodka, which we too often turn to in Scotland.'[104]

But this mooted survivor's guide then morphed into a cycling training manual, *The Obree Way*. Conventional wisdom is once again nonchalantly waved aside, in inimitable Obree fashion, as he attempts to reshape the basic building blocks of cycling performance. Breathing, for example: apparently we've all been breathing the wrong way all these years. Thoughts of retirement likewise seemed to fade into the ether as Obree fixed his sights on another tilt at the human-powered vehicle record. This time his twenty-year-old son Jamie would be strapped into an upgraded, but still homebuilt machine, an altogether more slippery contraption, more blatantly wind-cheating; faster, better, stronger. In a 2014 interview with *The Herald*, Obree seemed highly motivated for the next instalment of daredevilry on the desert flats, this latest endeavour in several decades of simply striving for striving's sake, of *self-overcoming*. And it's tempting to think that old bushy-faced Nietzsche would have allowed himself a grudging nod of approval. Obree, a confirmed Scotsman, would recoil from the idea of striving for mere pleasure, just as surely as if he'd been mistaken for an Englishman.

As Armand DiMele points out, there are currently no support groups available for those who suffer from an addiction to suffering, no weekly Pain Addicts Anonymous meetings where habitually heavy strivers can be coaxed gently back into pain sobriety. For those of us not targeting a world record or Olympic gold, to keep both our striving and our suffering within reasonable limits – to prevent striving from shifting into obsession and then into depression – seems no less a revolutionary idea than not downing a bottle of vodka a day and yet it's all too easy to lose sight of those limits.

CHAPTER 8

Rough Ride

'Do not ask things to happen as you wish, but wish them to happen as they do happen, and your life will go smoothly.'

Epictetus

In January 2013, Labour MP John Mann addressed the UK Parliament with an early day motion (EDM):

> This House applauds the outstanding journalism of Paul Kimmage in exposing the drug cheating of cyclist Lance Armstrong and recognises the huge personal and professional stress that the deceitful legal and public relations onslaught from Armstrong and his cronies must have placed on Mr Kimmage; salutes the stoicism and professionalism of Paul Kimmage in the face of such bullying, and further recognises his place as a true champion of the finest traditions of journalism.[105]

Although an EDM in theory calls for a more in-depth debate at an unspecified 'early day', this rarely happens in practice, the main purpose being to draw attention to particular subjects of interest and, on this day in particular, the House was interested in Mr Armstrong.

Irishman Kimmage certainly has better credentials as champion journalist than champion cyclist. After turning professional in 1986 for the French RMO team, he rode three Tours de France, finishing only one of them, in a lowly 131st position. Irish cycling fans at the time were largely preoccupied with titans of the peloton Sean Kelly and Stephen Roche, so Kimmage found his entry into journalism – while still a pro cyclist – by submitting insider articles on the nation's new cycling superstars to an eager Irish press. His own cycling career came to an abrupt end in 1989 after only three years as a professional – and without any wins. Kimmage's kiss-and-tell book *Rough Ride* was published the following year, in which he exposed in telling detail the culture of systematic doping within the pre-EPO 1980s peloton. Just as the heavy drinker refuses to countenance beer or wine as drinking *per se*, Kimmage – who admitted to quaffing a few caffeine pills and the occasional amphetamine – claims never to have touched the hard stuff. But as a neo-pro he soon resigned himself to the fact that a phlegmatic, stoic approach would be needed to survive in such a warped environment. As he wrote of his first Tour: 'For

six months I convinced myself that I could still reach the summit without recourse to a syringe, but everything changed within that first Tour
de France.'[106] Flat-out exhausted after only nine days of the three-week
race, he wrestled with the decision of whether to dope or not – whether
to 'recharge the batteries'. 'Not blessed with any great natural talent, for
me it was always going to be a case of sink or swim,' he wrote. 'On the
Tour's ninth day I shelved my ambition and began to drown.'[107]

After several years with the *Sunday Independent*, journalist Kimmage
joined the Irish *Sunday Times* in 2002. He quickly made a name for
himself as one of the few reporters brave or foolish enough actively to
confront Lance Armstrong – and his powerful entourage – on the persistent rumours of widespread doping within US Postal. The other notable
refusenik was fellow Irishman David Walsh, chief sportswriter for the UK
Sunday Times. Under the headline 'Champ or Cheat?' Walsh revealed as
early as 2001 that Armstrong was working with the controversial Italian
doctor Michele Ferrari. In 2004, Walsh's publication of *L.A. Confiden-
tiel* included damning testimony from US Postal soigneur Emma O'Reilly,
who among other claims stated that Armstrong had asked her for make-
up to cover track marks on his arm. The other principal dissenters at the
time were of course the French, with both *Le Monde* and *L'Équipe* willing to ask much tougher questions than their Anglo-Saxon counterparts.
In 2009, with Armstrong on the comeback trail with the Astana team,
Le Canard Enchainé, sister publication to *Charlie Hebdo*, published a
cartoon showing a cyclist with an assortment of needles sticking out of
his backside. The caption: '*Chez les grands champions, c'est le mental
qui fait la différence.*'

In the aftermath of the recent *Charlie Hebdo* atrocity, Armstrong took
to social media to offer support to the city that hosted his seven Tour
non-wins. 'Paris STRONG,' he tweeted. As Suze Clemitson, author of
100 Tours 100 Tales noted, this was 'a pun as painfully self-referential
and egotistical as he could possibly have made under the circumstances.'
She added: 'But he is forever a cartoon character with a syringe sticking
out of his arse, skewered on his own perfidiousness.'[108]

In 2012, Paul Kimmage achieved the unusual distinction of being
named as one of Britain's ten most influential sportswriters while also
being laid off from his job at the *Sunday Times*, an unfortunate consequence, in Kimmage's view, of so many of his articles having been spiked
by the newspaper's overanxious lawyers. In the same year, Kimmage,
who held the firm belief that the sport's governing body, the UCI, had
been grossly negligent and even complicit in many instances of high-
profile doping, then found himself the target of a defamation lawsuit from
former UCI presidents Pat McQuaid and Hein Verbruggen. The lawsuit
was later dropped in the aftermath of Armstrong's primetime confession, but Kimmage then decided to sue the UCI personally, using money

he'd received from the public to prepare his defence. It feels reasonable to argue that the dogged perseverance and steadfastness he's displayed as a journalist – most notably in 2009 when he stood up in a press conference to call a newly unretired Armstrong the 'cancer of cycling' – is a skill he first honed as a struggling *domestique*, dourly plodding on day after day, against all sensible odds and with no realistic prospects of personal glory. If such determination and stoicism are ultimately what helped to vindicate Kimmage's decade-long quest to bring down Armstrong, then such qualities are surely handy weapons in the arsenal of anyone who finds himself up against the sport's frequent injustices and bias towards capricious misfortune.

Stoicism, a school of Hellenistic philosophy founded in Athens in the early third-century BC and later exported to Rome, quickly established itself as the foremost philosophical doctrine among the educated elite of both empires. Stoics believed all destructive emotions resulted from basic errors in judgment; anyone able to attain 'moral and intellectual perfection' would not suffer such emotions. A fully paid-up Stoic should have complete control over his response to any negative stimulus, thereby rendering himself immune to misfortune and disappointment. Stoicism also tells us that any happiness based upon changeable, destructible elements cannot endure, cannot be considered secure. All of which sounds not hugely different from what was being taught several time zones to the east around the same time. Indeed, a lively philosophical debate rumbles on over what it is exactly that separates a Stoic from a Buddhist. To the confused layman at least, the similarities appear to outweigh the differences. Suffice to say that if Zeno of Citium, the founder of Stoicism, had whiled away a pleasant summer evening in the company of Siddhartha Gautama Buddha, the conversation would have been unlikely to run dry, assuming of course they had a translator on hand. But if Buddhist best practice is simply to observe suffering and other unpleasant phenomena, to let them gently wash over you until they subside, then Stoicism channels a more direct approach, that of countering painful sensations as and when they arise. In the words of Epictetus, the first-century Stoic who viewed philosophy not only as an academic pursuit, but also as a way of life, 'The greater the difficulty, the more glory in surmounting it. Skilful pilots gain their reputation from storms and tempests.'

Epictetus was born into slavery, but later gained his freedom and became the apprentice of Musonius Rufus, a highly regarded Roman Stoic. After ten years of study, Epictetus achieved the status of philosopher in his own right. The early Christian scholar, Origen, told a tale of how a young Epictetus was tortured by his slave master. Observing that his master was forcefully twisting his leg, Epictetus simply smiled back. 'You will break my leg,' he said. A short while later, a disabled, hobbling

Epictetus then observed: 'Did I not tell you that you would break it?' He spent the rest of his life with a crippled leg, or so the story goes.

In recent times, Stoicism has become the unofficial philosophy of the modern US military. In her book *The Stoic Warrior*, Nancy Sherman argues that Stoicism is now the driving force behind the military mind-set, particularly in its emphasis on endurance, self-control and inner strength. A fair amount of the credit for this is surely due to Vice Admiral James Stockdale, author of *The Stoic Warrior's Triad*. During the early 1960s, and as a young navy pilot studying for his masters in International Relations at Stanford University, Stockdale became interested in Stoic philosophy and the teachings of Epictetus in particular. During the Vietnam War, James Stockdale then led US aerial attacks in the notorious 1964 Gulf of Tonkin operation. On Stockdale's next deployment, the A-4 aircraft he was piloting was struck by enemy flak and burst into flames. Stockdale later wrote:

> After ejection, I had about 30 seconds to make my last statement in freedom before I landed in the main street of a little village right ahead. And, so help me, I whispered to myself: 'Five years down there, at least. I'm leaving the world of technology and entering the world of Epictetus.'[109]

Stockdale was held as a prisoner of war for seven and a half years in the notorious Hoa Lo prison, the so-called 'Hanoi Hilton'. More than half of this time was spent in solitary confinement and he was also routinely tortured. Mimicking his Roman mentor, Stockdale suffered a broken leg when his plane crashed, for which he was denied medical treatment. Stockdale was released in 1973, his back broken, his legs shattered and his shoulders torn from their sockets. He later received the Medal of Honour and became one of the most highly decorated US naval officers in history.

'Epictetus was telling his students that there can be no such thing as being the "victim" of another,' Stockdale wrote. 'You can only be a "victim" of yourself. It's all in how you discipline your mind.'[110]

In a conversation with author Jim Collins, Stockdale elaborated: 'I never lost faith in the end of the story, I never doubted not only that I would get out, but also that I would prevail in the end and turn the experience into the defining event of my life, which, in retrospect, I would not trade.'[111] Collins then asked Stockdale about those prisoners who failed to survive their incarceration. 'The optimists,' he replied. 'They were the ones who said, "We're going to be out by Christmas." And Christmas would come, and Christmas would go. Then they'd say, "We're going to be out by Easter." And Easter would come, and Easter would go. And then Thanksgiving, and then it would be Christmas again.'[112] Stockdale added: 'You must never confuse faith that you will prevail in the end –

which you can never afford to lose – with the discipline to confront the most brutal facts of your current reality, whatever they might be.'[113] This duality became known as the Stockdale Paradox.

Bombing the Vietcong and bombing down an Alpine pass in a high-speed breakaway might not be directly comparable, but the rules of the open road are not always that far removed from the conventions of open warfare. As Dutchman Tim Krabbé noted in *The Rider,* his classic account of a bicycle race: 'Road racing imitates life, the way it would be without the corruptive influence of civilization. When you see an enemy lying on the ground, what's your first reaction? To help him to his feet. In road racing, you kick him to death.'[114]

A crippled Epictetus, earning his daily crust as a philosophy teacher in first-century Rome, would have been out of contention for selection to the games of the ancient Olympiad. In any case, following the fall of Greece to the Roman Empire in AD146, the games had entered a period of protracted decline. In *The Pursuit of Excellence: The Olympic Story,* we're offered an explanation why:

> The high ideals of the earlier years were lost sight of. Interest in striving to be perfect, just for the satisfaction of doing one's best, gave way to emphasis on the rewards. Winning became the only concern. Foreign athletes of known prowess were given Greek citizenship so they could enter the Games. Rich men who could not themselves hope to compete began to hire professionals so that they might be sure of winning the bets wagered on the contests.[115]

Some comfort, then, to know that bribery, corruption and rule bending within the ranks of top sporting organizations is not a uniquely modern phenomenon. In AD67, during the reign of Emperor Nero, the Olympic Games arguably hit an all-time low – a lower low even than the three modern Olympiads of the 1980s, which bore witness to the US boycott of the Moscow Games, the retaliatory Eastern Bloc non-appearance in Los Angeles and the Ben Johnson doping fiasco in Seoul.

'Nero appeared at the CCXI Olympiad with a retinue of 5,000, whose primary function was to applaud him,' notes *The Olympic Story.* 'No opponent dared face Nero in the chariot race. When he fell from his chariot, fawning officials put him back, but he could not finish the race. Yet the jury declared him champion.'[116]

Winning at all costs, a large retinue, opponents cowered into silence and fawning officials flexing the rules: this all sounds distressingly familiar to anyone who's followed professional cycling in the twenty-first century, let alone first-century chariot racing. *Plus ça change,* and all that.

'Put me back on my bike,' were the reported final words of Tom Simpson, up on the slopes of a scorched Mont Ventoux; words that his traumatized mechanic, Harry Hall, later wished he had ignored. But there would not have been much argument when Emperor Nero demanded to be put back in his chariot. Nero, the tyrant who famously fiddled while Rome burned, also handed down orders for the murder of his own mother and at least one of his wives.

Amidst such signs of moral decay, Epictetus meanwhile stuck to his philosophical guns. In his concise handbook of Stoic ethical advice, the *Enchiridion*, he treats us to a glimpse of his doctrine as applied to sporting endeavours:

> In every affair consider what precedes and follows, and then undertake it. Otherwise you will begin with spirit; but not having thought of the consequences, when some of them appear you will shamefully desist. 'I would conquer at the Olympic Games.' But consider what precedes and follows, and then, if it is for your advantage, engage in the affair. You must conform to rules, submit to a diet, refrain from dainties; exercise your body, whether you choose it or not, at a stated hour, in heat and cold; you must drink no cold water, nor sometimes even wine. In a word, you must give yourself up to your master, as to a physician.

That a near 2,000-year old training manual remains relevant today is surely great testament to Epictetus, even if modern-day sportsmen will have conflicting views on what 'refraining from dainties' actually entails. 'Something delicious to the taste' is how the Merriam-Webster dictionary would have it, which for Bradley Wiggins could mean shunning the lure of off-season pints at his local. And while these ancient ideals – conforming, submitting, refraining – still today remain prerequisites for anyone hoping to conquer an Olympics or a major tour, notable ex-champions have opted for a more relaxed interpretation of the Stoic rulebook. In his recent autobiography, *We Were Young and Carefree*, two-times Tour de France champion Laurent Fignon spoke candidly about his exploits off the bike, which included an epic drinking session with Bernard Hinault midway through the Tour de L'Armour – a race that ended in victory for Hinault.

Another Stoic-flavoured training manual, this one in French and titled *La Tête et Les Jambes*, was written in 1894 by old stony-face Henri Desgrange. Tour de France founder Desgrange, by all accounts a fervent devotee of both the Stoic and the prudish ways of life, wrote the book as a conversation with an unnamed cyclist believed to be his younger self. Any aspiring pro rider, the manual advised, should have no more need of a woman than an unwashed pair of socks. Desgrange's conviction that the fairer sex offered nothing but distraction from unwavering devotion to *la grand souffrance* would be no doubt considered excessive by current team bosses. But while finish-line clinches with wives and girlfriends

(WAGs) may be *de rigueur* for today's riders, during major races the teams' hotel rooms must remain strictly WAG-free, and so an element of the chaste spirit of Desgrange thus survives intact in modern pro cycling.

Elsewhere in Epictetus' trendsetting manual, he continues to highlight the worthiness of attributes such as commitment and passion, and the dangers of merely posing as a dilettante:

> Then, in combat, you may be thrown into a ditch, dislocate your arm, turn your ankle, swallow dust, be whipped, and, after all, lose the victory. When you have evaluated all this, if your inclination still holds, then go to war. Otherwise, take notice, you will behave like children who sometimes play like wrestlers, sometimes gladiators, sometimes blow a trumpet, and sometimes act a tragedy when they have seen and admired these shows. Thus you too will be at one time a wrestler, at another a gladiator, now a philosopher, then an orator; but with your whole soul, nothing at all.

If your inclination still holds: whether couched in these strictly Stoic terms, or indeed those of the Buddhist Eightfold path – a lightly stirred cocktail of right intention and right concentration – it all amounts to much the same thing. Wobbly inclination won't get you to the podium. Ronnie O'Sullivan's walkout at the 2006 UK national snooker championships was a rather dramatic loss of inclination, a sudden crisis of morale. As was Federico Bahamontes' classic mountainside bike toss. We all have our moments, our hot flushes of non-stoicity: the tennis racquet hurled across centre court; the golf pro's nine-iron snapped in half; the entire baseball dugout charging the mound. And in a sporting event that lasts for three weeks, these moments of vexation, of extreme disgruntlement, are all but inevitable, which in turn helps to explain why those able to transcend them, those able to conjure up sufficient focus, inclination and perseverance are more likely to find their exploits inscribed on the pages of cycling folklore. Riders such as Eugène Christophe, who cracked his front forks in the 1913 Tour de France just as the race entered the Pyrenees, for example. No identically set-up spare machine hoisted off the team car roof for him. Or even a team car, come to think of it. Christophe shouldered his broken bike and jogged several miles to the nearest blacksmith's shop. Since the Tour's (extensive) rulebook stipulated that repairs must be carried out by the rider alone, he duly got to work and was able to hop back on his re-welded bike two hours later. The three-minute time penalty levied post-stage by the ever vigilant Monsieur Desgrange – for the crime of having a young boy operate the forge's bellows – was unlikely to have cost Christophe too much sleep.

Irishman Sean Kelly was possibly the closest approximation to a true Stoic, a modern-day Epictetus, to grace the ranks of the pro peloton. While it would be difficult indeed to prove empirically a strong correlation between a tough upbringing and toughness on the bike, it's still a tempting theory. Kelly left school at thirteen to work on the family farm in Waterford County. 'As a teenager, I grew resentful of the animals, so dumb and needy. I cleaned up their shite, fed them and then there'd be some more shite to clean up,' is how he summed up his teenage years in his recent autobiography, *The Hunger*.[117] French team manager Jean de Gribaldy, who journeyed across to Ireland to offer the young Kelly a professional contract, eventually located him in a muddy field, driving a tractor.

'It is customary to talk of Kelly as quintessentially an Irish rider,' wrote Robin Macgowan, in his book *Kings of the Road*.[118] 'For my part, though, I think it helps to place Kelly better as a cyclist to see him as the last of the Flemish riders,' he then explained. While Macgowan would have been well aware that Kelly hailed from Ireland's south-east, it was his belief that Flemish bike racers, metaphorical or otherwise, 'stood for a certain type of mentality, willing to suffer, narrowly focussed, and hard, hard, hard'. Kelly's honorary Flemish credentials were further boosted by his years as a rookie pro on the Belgian Flandria and Splendor teams. While at Splendor he often shared a room with genuinely Flemish Michel Pollentier. Although Kelly's Flemish language skills were reported to have improved during this period, this came at the cost of Pollentier's English becoming inflected with traces of Irish brogue.

'In a profession of iron wills, there is no one harder.'[119] This was Macgowan's appraisal of what helped to make Kelly one of the finest classics riders of all time – and notch up a total of 193 professional wins over a 17-year career:

> Kelly had all this in him from his Irish small-farm background: the outside loo; the dogs that have to be chained before you can step from your car; the one career possible, as a bricklayer on a construction site, stretching away and away into the grey mists. On the positive side, along with the self-reliance, came a physical strength that even by peasant standards is impressive.[120]

It's worth noting too that Ireland and northern Belgium share similarly unfavourable climates – unfavourable for cyclists at any rate – and both regions have produced more than their share of riders who excel in testing conditions, in wind, rain, mud and general nastiness. And Macgowan's unified theory of Flemish riders is one generally accepted by the cycling cognoscenti. The Velominati define 'Flemish tan lines' as 'artificial tan lines caused by mud, grit and cow shit'.[121] In their opinion, come the post-ride shower, the degree of contrast between areas of unsullied skin and those covered in Flemish road-gunk can be used as a reasonably accurate proxy of how epic the ride was and how much suffering it entailed. Sports retailer Adidas meanwhile has jumped on the bandwagon with its

'Flemish Weather Cap,' available from all good online cycle stores and promising 'climawarm technology' and 'moisture-wicking mesh' to keep the worst of the Flemish elements at bay. With its plain, workmanlike styling, you're unlikely to see many Spanish riders wearing one, but then no Spaniard has ever won Paris–Roubaix, that gloriously miserable race alternatively known as 'The Hell of the North'.

Sean Kelly remains a firm proponent of actions speaking louder than words, a detail that makes his current position in the Eurosport commentary box a somewhat curious one. When an admiring fan enquired which gear he'd selected for the finale of his last pro win, the 1992 Milan–San Remo, a deadpan Kelly replied 'the right one'.[122] For my part, any apparent deficit of Kelly-like grit and determination, any lack of hunger, is something I think I can reasonably blame on my parents; on my comfortable North London upbringing many miles from the nearest shite-strewn farm and with a choice of inside toilets. Had my parents chosen not to renovate the Edwardian semi-detached house they purchased as newly weds – and left the original outside loo *in situ* – it might have turned out quite different. I could have been more Flemish, or at least more Irish.

On the subject of farms, Epictetus also had important words to say. In the pages of the *Enchiridion* we also learn that it is considered unhelpful and decidedly unstoic to dwell upon any kind of loss. Never say of anything 'I have lost it,' advises Epictetus. 'I have given it back' is the preferred Stoic response. 'Is your child dead? It is given back. Is your wife dead? She is given back,' Epictetus goes on to explain. 'Is your farm taken away? Well, that also is given back.' Handy tips indeed for fielding those potentially awkward questions from inquisitive neighbours, whether down at the forum municipium or at its modern equivalent, the local Asda superstore.

On 23 July 1989, Laurent Fignon gave back the Tour de France. The blonde-mopped, bespectacled Frenchman wore yellow for a total of nine days in the race, but after a nail-biting final stage, a 24.5km (15.2 miles) time trial from Versailles to the Champs-Élysées, the race's heir apparent turned out to be American Greg LeMond, with his winning margin remaining the narrowest in Tour history. Fignon, Tour winner in 1983 and 1984, nevertheless displayed a certain stoicism in the aftermath of the race. In answer to a jibe that he was the guy who'd just lost the Tour by eight seconds, he responded, 'Non, monsieur, I'm the guy who won the Tour twice.'[123]

Fignon was no stranger to final-day disaster. With one stage remaining in the 1984 Giro d'Italia, Fignon led Italian Francesco Moser by almost ninety seconds. The race organizers, citing poor weather conditions, earlier had cancelled the toughest climb of the race, the Stelvio, a climb where Fignon had a good chance to extend his lead. Yet television footage had shown the road to be passable. During the final stage, a 42km

(26-mile) time trial from Soave to Verona, television camera helicopters flew slightly ahead of Fignon, creating a buffeting headwind, and behind their compatriot Moser, effectively giving him a helpful push. Moser beat Fignon by two and a half minues on the stage and secured overall victory. Fignon, filmed during the time trial shaking his fist skywards in a symbolic and uniquely Gallic gesture of defiance, later said the experience made him tougher and prepared him for hardships to come.

In the 1989 Tour, Fignon, once again clad in yellow with two stages to go, was almost home and dry. 'There was just one thing,' he later wrote in his autobiography, *We Were Young and Carefree*.[124] 'I'd felt a fairly sharp pain between my legs. That evening, it was clear. I had a sore spot in a very inconvenient place: just below the buttock, right where the saddle rubs on the shorts.' Fignon told himself not to worry; it was bearable, manageable. But before the final road race stage, Fignon was in so much discomfort that he found himself unable to urinate at the doping control. 'Just moving was a penance. Sitting down was horrendous.' He somehow survived the penultimate stage, still in yellow, still in great pain, but a tense Fignon was later involved in an altercation with a television camera crew, who this time chose to ambush him outside the Gare de Lyon train station rather than from a helicopter. He slept poorly the night before the time trial. The following morning, Fignon got on his bike and immediately dismounted. 'I just couldn't turn the pedals. It was completely impossible,' he wrote. But the Frenchman – perhaps familiar with Stockdale's Paradox – resolved to finish the race. 'Look, it's not as bad as all that,' he told himself. 'All that's left is a time trial … I'll hurt like hell but afterwards I'll forget it.'[125]

He never forgot it. LeMond clawed back fifty-eight seconds over the 24.5km (15 miles), overcoming an earlier fifty-second deficit. After more than 3,000km (1,864 miles) and eighty-eight hours of racing, the difference between first and second place was eight seconds, or about 100m (328ft) of tarmac. LeMond at that time was riding a revolutionary aerodynamic bike equipped with handlebar extensions, which in Fignon's opinion were against the rules. But the Frenchman never satisfactorily explained why his team had failed to lodge a complaint. 'You never stop grieving over an event like that; the best you can manage is to contain the effect it has on your mind,' he wrote. 'Even so, I was well aware that there were more serious things going on in life – and I had dreamed so much of coming back to the highest level to play a major role: I'd done that at least.'[126]

An hour before the 1989 Tour's decisive, *contre-la-montre* denouement, Fignon had warmed up alongside LeMond at the time-trial start area, grimly intent on hiding any discomfort from his rival. 'He had no idea that I was under the weather,' Fignon later wrote.[127] However, Fignon, who in 2010 died of cancer at the age of fifty, mostly came across as just a little too passionate, a little too *French*, to pass muster as a fully paid-up Stoic. It even strikes me as unfortunate that none of history's most celebrated Stoics have been French, since the Gallic name Loïc appears to be one of the few words that properly rhyme:

A Frenchman by the name of Loïc
Lived his entire life as a Stoic
When all turned to shit
It mattered not one bit
His resolve was really quite heroic.

Fignon, whose studious look earned him the nickname of '*le professeur*' (he'd passed his baccalaureate, but in fact had dropped out of university after only a year), brought a thoughtful, intelligent approach to bike racing. But he could be prickly too, with a quick temper. He was outspoken at times. Asked about LeMond's tactics during the 1989 Tour, he called the American 'the great follower'.[128] He also tended to downplay his achievements on the bike. 'I don't understand people who are nostalgic. I don't get nostalgia,' he said in a 2005 interview. He went on:

> I pushed myself to extremes. I did the maximum that I was capable of doing, and I will never again be able to do it. But in life I'm not happy. In fact, I am never happy. I am eternally unsatisfied with things. For example, when I won my first Milan–San Remo in 1988, I won it in a sprint ahead of Maurizio Fondriest. Great. But I said to myself, it would have been better if I had been on my own.[129]

The 1989 Tour is probably best remembered not as a race lost (or given back) by only eight seconds, but as a race decided by a saddle and a set of handlebars. The saddle, a Selle Italia Turbo, a sturdy, popular number in the 1980s peloton, was found guilty of inflicting a nasty boil on Fignon's *derrière*. (Had he been once again stymied by the crafty Italians, albeit more subtly this time?) The avant-garde handlebars, manufactured by Scott Sports, presented LeMond with an undeniable advantage, possibly as much as a trailing helicopter. Nowadays sanctioned by the UCI for use in most events against the clock, aero-handlebars broke no rules back in 1989 simply because the UCI had not got around to imposing rules for a piece of equipment that had only just been invented.

Half a century earlier, at the 1936 Tour de France, in a foreshadowing of Fignon's later travails, Henri Desgrange, now seventy-one, ordered the passenger seat of his race *commissaire* vehicle to be packed with soft cushions and that a doctor should accompany him for the duration of the event. Desgrange was overdue for a prostate operation and had been warned explicitly by his surgeons not to follow the race that year. Jacques Goddet, Desgrange's deputy, reveals in his autobiography how he was under strict instructions not to reveal to anyone else the extent of Desgrange's nether-regional suffering. On the first stage of the 1936 Tour, the car's jolty accelerations and repeated braking reduced a tight-lipped Desgrange to evident distress. The second day proved too much for him altogether and he reluctantly departed from his beloved race. According to writer and historian Pierre Chany, Desgrange ran the world's most celebrated bike race as a virtual dictatorship for several decades, accepting no interference, let alone helpful advice, and imposing arbitrary penalties on the field – penalties often so erratic that one year the entire Belgian team went home in disgust. But the pain, tenacity and stoicism that Desgrange demanded of his riders and of himself was not, in the final bumpy reckoning, without its limits.

CHAPTER 9

Mountain Men

'*When you are in the peloton and you come near the Ventoux, nobody's speaking anymore. You can hear a fly, because it's always very quiet, because everybody's afraid about the Ventoux.*'

Eddy Merckx[130]

'*I was f****d in the head a little bit.*'

Andy Schleck

Robert Millar was the first rider from an English-speaking nation to win the Tour de France climber's jersey. Britain's most successful cyclist of the 1980s also finished fourth overall in the 1984 Tour and second in the 1987 Giro. The taciturn Scot had a frosty relationship with the press, often seeming awkward and uncooperative in interviews. After he married in 1985, reportedly with none of his family in attendance, his Panasonic teammate Phil Anderson expressed astonishment that Millar was even in a relationship, commenting that he 'didn't seem to have the skills for getting on with men, let alone women'.[131]

To race is to suffer. As the other Scottish Millar, David, says, 'It's crazy what we do. We push ourselves beyond what we would do in any other sport and you do see a side of yourself and other people that you wouldn't see otherwise. You dig deeper and deeper, digging in for suffering beyond what you thought possible.'[132] Many of cycling's most iconic images over the years have shown this in stark detail, for example Tyler Hamilton riding an entire Tour de France with a broken collarbone, or Stephen Roche's incredible comeback – and subsequent collapse – at La Plagne. But a closer examination of cycling's image archive shows that the distribution of pain and suffering throughout the peloton is somewhat uneven.

Consider the sprinters, the peloton's version of Formula 1 drivers: dashing daredevils with supercharged engines. Think of Mario Cipollini, the fastest fast man of the nineties and early noughties. His fifty-seven Grand Tour stage wins must have registered somewhere on the pain scale, but the fact is that sprinters rarely need to go all out until the last few kilometres of a race. Until then, they're kept away from the hurt zone by a loyal cluster of *domestiques,* the galley slaves who shield them from the wind and fetch cold drinks on demand. Mountain stages might be a major nuisance for the big guys, but they can at least be tackled at a more manageable tempo, since the only strict requirement is to make the day's time cut. Indeed, a 'Cipo' career trademark was to grab as many flat stage wins as possible in the first week of a Grand Tour and then, before any tiresome hills beckoned, decamp straight to the nearest Mediterranean beach. Cipollini's aversion to steep gradients frequently irritated race organizers, leading to his team's exclusion from several Tours de France, most notably in 2003 when he was the reigning world champion.

Cipollini, the golden-haired 'Lion King', always enjoyed creating a bit of a stir, showing up at time trials in outrageous, rule-bending skin suits and leading a fairly flamboyant lifestyle off the bike. For a world-class bike racer, he never appeared to be hurting too much during competition. Of course, a sprinter can't always avoid collateral damage: the carnage-in-waiting of a tightly packed peloton veering erratically into a tight corner a few hundred metres from the line, when upended riders suddenly find themselves sans bike and surfing the tarmac on their backsides at speed. But the hard-man sprinters, the fast men of Cipollini's calibre, are simply patched up and put back on their bikes to fight the next day. After all, it's only a few layers of skin.

Ditto Mark Cavendish, the British rider and 2011 world champion, who in recent years has dominated countless bunch sprints. Cavendish is almost always outspoken and tends to let raw emotion get the better of him. While sprinting is to some extent a contact sport, his single-minded determination to be first across the line too often leads him into risky, high-speed tangles with other sprinters. In the 2013 Tour, both he and Dutchman Tom Veelers ended up on the floor after Cavendish tried to shoulder Veelers aside during the final dash. A year later, on stage one of the 2014 Tour, Cavendish, boxed in with 200m (650ft) to go, this time employed a headbutt – or, if we're being charitable, a head nudge – to remove an unwanted obstruction in the form of Australian Simon Gerrans. Both men clattered to the deck. A few minutes later a visibly distraught Cavendish rolled limply over the line: he'd separated his right shoulder and, in doing so, he'd separated himself from the year's showpiece event, on the first day of the race and in front of thousands of expectant home fans to boot. Gerrans meanwhile suffered the usual bruises and scratches, appearing to channel impressive restraint when later asked for his thoughts on Cavendish's sprinting tactics.

So Mark Cavendish does suffer, but rarely for very long. Under less traumatic circumstances – in other words when Cav simply fails to win a race, but avoids instigating the cycling equivalent of a motorway pile-up – his preferred therapy is to retire to the team bus where he can yell obscenities and hurl objects in relative safety. Fifteen minutes later he'll emerge with a cheeky grin and some quotable quips for waiting journalists. Cavendish, who took his cue from 'Super Mario' and married a former topless model, similarly doesn't seem much interested in proper, extended bouts of suffering.

Then we have the climbers. Alas, the poor climbers. If sprinters are the peloton's equivalent of racing drivers, then *les grimpeurs* are typically a strange hybrid of jockeys and chess players; lightweight loners cursed with fragile temperaments. Topless models don't gravitate towards them in quite the same manner, the plain truth being that it's not so easy to come across as desirable in a masculine way when your body fat percentage is less than your shoe size. It basically comes down to a simple choice: you can win the mountains jersey, or you can look fit and healthy. You really can't do both.

Michael Rasmussen, the emaciated Danish climber known to his teammates as 'Chicken', was also well known for carefully weighing all of his food, right down to the nearest gram. Instead of pouring milk over his breakfast cereal, he'd add a dash of plain water instead. He was fired by his Rabobank team while leading the 2007 Tour after it was revealed he'd lied about his whereabouts before the race, in what was a fairly unsophisticated attempt to evade the drug testers. Chances are that if the wafer-thin Rasmussen ever found himself in the company of supermodels, it was probably because they wanted to share weight loss advice with him. It seems highly unlikely they'd have wanted to share much else.

The late Marco Pantani remains the embodiment of the tortured climber. The last specialist climber to win the Tour, Pantani was afflicted with a crippling shyness as a teenager, in part caused by his protruding ears and prematurely receding hairline – and this in *La Bella Italia*, where good looks and style have been always paramount. His immense natural talent will be forever foreshadowed by the years of systematic doping, the failed drug tests and his isolated, untimely demise in a Rimini hotel room. A long-term cocaine habit compounded Pantani's health problems, after he'd first experimented with the drug following the shock of his expulsion from the 1999 Giro. Pantani's already fragile mental state then gradually unravelled, eventually leading him into the deep abyss of depression and substance abuse that claimed his life in 2004.

The career of the Spanish climber, Luis Ocaña, similarly plays out like a Greek tragedy. By the midpoint of the 1971 Tour de France, Ocaña had built up an improbable eight-minute lead over the dominant Eddy Merckx, whose combined winning margin in the previous two Tours had been an astounding thirty-one minutes. But on stage 12, Merckx crashed hard on the descent of the Col du Menté in the Pyrenees. Ocaña, following close behind, was unable to avoid Merckx and slammed into him. While Merckx was able to remount quickly, the Dutch rider Joop Zootemelk then ploughed into the stricken Spaniard. Too gravely injured to get back on his bike, Ocaña had to be airlifted to hospital, his dreams of winning the Tour shattered. Although he later won the 1973 Tour in convincing style, the tormented Ocaña always felt that it was an incomplete victory due to the absence of Merckx that year. Following his retirement in 1977, Ocaña suffered from depression and a series of health problems – reports vary of their exact nature – before taking his own life at the age of forty-eight.

The catalogue of climber woe continues. In 1999, José María Jiménez, another Spanish mountain specialist, won the first ever Vuelta a España finish on the feared slopes of the Angliru, one of Europe's steepest climbs. He was an explosive rider, often winning stages with brilliant, aggressive attacks, only to fade into anonymity the next day. As former teammate Miguel Indurain said of Jiménez, 'When things went well, they went very well. When things didn't go well, they didn't go at all.'[133] But his professional career was cut short by bouts of severe, drug-fuelled depression and he retired in 2002. Only a year later, Jiménez was dead at the age of thirty-two, after apparently suffering a heart attack in a Madrid psychiatric hospital.

Charly Gaul became the first out and out climber to win the Tour de France back in 1958, earning himself the nickname 'Angel of the Mountains'. The slightly built Luxembourger worked in an abattoir before turning professional, habitually wearing an expression of 'unfathomable melancholy'.[134] In 1956, Gaul achieved the first of his two Giro wins, effectively sealing victory on the long climb of Monte Bondone in atrocious weather, which, according to former Tour organizer, Jacques Goddet, 'surpassed anything seen before in terms of pain, suffering and difficulty'.[135] Behind Gaul, the rest of the field was spread out over several hours, with some riders having stopped at *pensiones* en route for a hot bath.

Gaul was popular with the fans, but not among other riders. British rider Brian Robinson, who rode as his teammate in the 1956 tour, claimed Gaul was always reluctant to share prize money with those who had helped him in a race. After his retirement, Gaul completely dropped out of the public eye, living for many years in self-imposed exile in a small hut in the Ardennes Forest. Some claimed to have spotted him at the roadside during later Tours de France, by all accounts paunchy, bearded and wild-haired. Gaul ended his hermit-like isolation in 1988 and subsequently offered an explanation for his post-career disappearance. 'Well, it's difficult to go back into normal society,' he said. 'Today, of course, I laugh about it, but that period was essential. Without it, I wouldn't have been able to tackle the final slope, that of old age.'[136]

The existential struggles of so many top climbers have even led some cycling commentators to ponder the possibility of a 'Curse of the Polka Dot Jersey'. Thierry Claveyrolat, who won the mountains classification in the 1990 Tour de France, was responsible for a 1999 road accident in which a father and son were badly injured, the fourteen-year old son losing an eye. Following the accident, Claveyrolat was arrested for drunk driving. According to friend and former teammate Paul Kimmage: 'His name was worth nothing any more. He had destroyed a family's life. The police were coming in the morning to take him to jail.'[137] A few weeks after the accident, Claveyrolat went down to his cellar and fatally shot himself with a rifle.

Tyler Hamilton, one of Lance Armstrong's cohorts turned arch-enemy, retired from pro cycling in 2009 after failing a routine drugs test. Hamilton had been taking a popular over-the-counter herbal antidepressant that included trace amounts of DHEA, an endogenous steroid. In 2004, Hamilton had tested positive for homologous blood transfusions, for which he received a two-year ban, and would likely have faced a suspension of at least eight years for this latest offence. Hamilton, who was diagnosed with clinical depression in 2003 (while still a teammate of Armstrong), explained he had switched to the supplement in a 'desperate' emotional state after quitting his prescription antidepressants cold turkey.

It's hard to dismiss the notion that cycling's mountain men are somehow more vulnerable and more prone to suffering – both on and off the bike – than their more gravity-bound peers; the sprinters and the *rouleurs*, those less angular, more flat-earth members of the peloton. Anecdotal evidence certainly seems to bear this out. It then becomes a question of cause and effect: if climbers typically share several key physical characteristics, might they also be predisposed to have certain mental and emotional traits in common?

American psychologist William Herbert Sheldon suggested exactly this in his theory of constitutional psychology. He proposed that there were three basic human body types, or somatotypes, each associated with distinct personality traits. According to Sheldon, endomorphs are typically heavy set and tend towards increased body fat, while mesomorphs possess a more muscular, medium build with lower body fat. The third somatotype, the ectomorph, is characterized by long, thin muscles and limbs, low levels of body fat, a narrow chest and abdomen and a large nervous system – in other words, a typical climber. After conducting a number of studies, Sheldon hypothesized that ectomorphs tended to be 'inhibited, introverted, hypersensitive to pain, and secretive'.[138] Although Sheldon's methodology was criticized at the time, several more rigorous experiments subsequently offered support for his theories.

Of course, the other possibility is that the wholly unreasonable, barely sane demands of repeatedly hammering up mountains on a bike, possibly the craziest part of what David Millar calls 'the sheer bonkers nature' of the sport, is what ultimately causes so many climbers to come apart at the seams. If some young riders start their careers as only marginally unstable, only slightly unhinged, then a handful of seasons on the pro circuit can be enough to complete the unravelling.

The seams of climber Andy Schleck started coming apart in mid-2012 when a moderate gust of wind blew the featherweight Luxembourger off his bike during a time trial at the Critérium du Dauphiné. Schleck fractured his sacrum and aggravated an existing knee injury in the accident. A runner-up in the Tour de France on three previous occasions (and the retroactive winner of the 2010 title following Alberto Contador's disqualification for a positive blood sample), Schleck's injuries meant that he was unable to start the 2012 Tour and on his return to competition later that season he failed to finish a number of races.

Although Schleck's raw climbing ability was never in doubt, his mental fortitude had been under scrutiny for some time, even during his Tour de France purple patch. Notoriously poor descending and time-trial skills, plus an apparent over-reliance on support from brother and teammate Frank (who himself received a twelve-month ban after failing a dope test during the 2012 Tour) had left many wondering if Andy Schleck was in fact the complete package. The 2014 Tour de France proved to be Schleck's final race as a professional. He crashed on stage three, en route from Cambridge to London, re-injuring his suspect knee. A few months later he announced his retirement, aged twenty-nine, to the press:

> In 2015 I will not be a professional cyclist any more, which hurts me a lot but I had no real decision. It was taken from me by my crash in the Tour. I could ride for three to four hours but when I went hard on a climb, my knee swelled up. I went back to the doctors and they said there was not much they could do.[139]

Yet some were not entirely convinced that the Luxembourger's latest mishap had been of truly career-ending magnitude. Persistent rumours of irregularities with his biological passport and even of a serious drink problem had continued to plague Schleck as he struggled to put the failures of 2012 and 2013 behind him. 'At night you sit there in your room and you know that you have to go through it all over again the day after,' Schleck told *Cycling News*, only days before the start of the 2014 Tour. 'Then it's onto the next race and it's the same scenario again and again and at night when it's just you and your thoughts and no one to talk with you lie there and you ask yourself "what's wrong with you?"'[140]

When quizzed about his feelings over his brother's earlier suspension, Andy Schleck all but guaranteed that his departure from the pro peloton would remain clouded by intrigue. As he explained: 'That wasn't the lowest point, there were harder moments but that was tough. There were a lot of knocks, one after the other and they all leave their scars. The biggest scar? I want to keep that to myself.'[141]

Mysterious, classified scars notwithstanding, Schleck was a natural climber of undoubted talent. He had shown huge early promise, finishing second in the 2007 Giro d'Italia at the age of twenty-two. 'We really thought he was going to do something special,' commented Tour de France director, Christian Prudhomme.[142] If his 2010 Tour win must remain forever asterisked, then his 2011 victory on the Col du Galibier, to crown a 60km (37-mile) solo break – and at 2,645m (8,678ft), the highest Tour stage finish in history – surely qualifies as the most impressive win of his career. Yet one still suspects that if the cherub-faced Andy were to turn up outside the well-sentinelled gates of The Great Pantheon, he would be respectfully but firmly turned away.

The enigmatic Robert Millar would have no doubt scored top marks in William Sheldon's somatype test. Classically ectomorph Millar (*inhibited, introverted, secretive*) was, according to former Scottish national champion Willie Gibb 'a loner and he put off a lot of people in Scotland with his attitude'.

Many years ago, on a morning training ride, I found myself pedalling along the same stretch of tarmac as Millar, who had finished a close second in the Vuelta a España just a few weeks earlier. When Team Peugeot's star rider completely ignored my casual greeting of 'Hey Robbie', he was in fact being relatively courteous: others received much shorter shrift.[143]

'Millar, he's been really awkward with us in the past,' said commentator Phil Liggett. 'Personally, I think it's a disgrace. He has a duty to his sponsor to represent the team.'[144] In the words of cycling journalist Steve Thomas, while 'that same basic mental strength lies within most climbers, there is also a great fragility embedded in many of them too, and it's ultimately this fragility that seems to destroy so many of them when they find themselves off their game, or even more so when the game is over.'[145]

In retirement, Millar appeared to take his cue from another climber, Charly Gaul, withdrawing entirely from public life. In 2007, Richard Moore, author of the biography *In Search of Robert Millar*, noted that the Scotsman was 'in very occasional email contact with one or two former acquaintances but his whereabouts are a mystery'. Moore also exchanged a series of emails with Millar, often receiving cryptic answers to his questions. After several days of this, a terse, three-word reply popped into Moore's inbox: 'No more questions'.[146]

CHAPTER 10

'If Your Thing is Gone ...'

'If your thing is gone and you wanna ride on'

J.J. Cale, 'Cocaine'[147]

Pot Belge is the derogatory French term employed to describe a mixture of illegal drugs used by cyclists. A potpourri of cocaine, heroin, caffeine, amphetamines and assorted analgesics might have found their way into a traditional pot, administered either before a race, or towards its latter stages if a rider looked to be in contention. And Belgium it was, appropriately enough, where I had my first glimpse of the seedy, performance-enhanced underbelly of bike racing. I'd arrived in the picturesque cathedral city of Ghent with a carload of other young London-based riders for a few weeks of midsummer racing. We were looking to test our mettle in the hotbed of cycle sport that is Flanders and also, to be fair, to sample some of that other world-class Flemish export – liquid, golden hued and handcrafted from the very best hops.

One morning after polishing off the ample breakfast provided by our friendly *kosthuis*, I returned to our dorm-style accommodation to find Max, our classiest rider, standing stark naked in the middle of the room. This in itself was not unusual. Max, all perma-tan and eighties-era blonde highlights, evidently felt rather good about his body and was keen for others to feel good about it too. What did strike me as not so usual, though, was the obvious presence of a hypodermic syringe, the contents of which Max was methodically injecting into his right buttock. Having registered the scene, I averted my gaze in the way that men are prone to do when confronted with male buttocks not their own. I honestly can't remember if I said anything, but Max seemed to think an explanation was required. 'Vitamins,' he explained. He may have winked as he said this – again, I'm unable to recall precisely. I exited the room and went back downstairs for another cup of coffee. Max had been riding most impressively in Belgium, forging his way into the lead group in races where the rest of us found ourselves drifting off the back of the peloton after only a few laps. And he was making good money: a top-ten finish could draw a cash prize of a few hundred Belgian francs, an amount that seemed to me quite obscene at the time. I was now at least a little more enlightened as to exactly how Max was doing it.

Later that week, on a scheduled rest day, our group crammed into the team car, a decidedly non-sporty, drab-brown Ford Escort estate, and set off for an afternoon of sightseeing around Ghent. At one point we stopped outside a small pharmacy on the outskirts of town. Nothing too remarkable about that: in a typical week of racing and training we could get through industrial amounts of energy drinks, muscle rubs and all sorts of emollients for chafed nether regions. But later that evening, after a tasty dinner in a local restaurant, Max handed me a surprise gift, a small packet of pills. 'Ah. More vitamins?' I enquired. Max, strolling alongside me, nodded, and once again he might or might not have shot me an impish wink. Back at the hostel, I studied the pills in their neat, silvery packaging. Despite my very limited Flemish language skills, I was in no doubt that Max had just handed me a supply of amphetamine, a drug classified as a class B controlled substance in the UK. Before I could lodge any kind of protest, Max explained that such things were legally available over the counter in Belgium. While it was probably the case that walking into a Ghent drugstore clad in full cycling race kit would have presented even a Flemish pharmacist with something of a moral dilemma, the local cyclists were not generally that transparent. Instead, they would turn up cunningly disguised as civilians – wearily overworked students to be exact – and request something that might help with their intensive exam revision. Less than two minutes later, they strolled out of the shop with a few grams of speed safely stashed in their 'student' pockets.

I will state categorically that I never once attempted to race while on Max's mega-vitamins. I'm not sure if my objection was strictly ethical; I think I was just scared of the unknown. To be honest, I've never been much good at drugs of any kind. In any case, I was merely trying to survive in the Belgian races, racing while under the effects of a nasty virus. Besides, as mentioned earlier, I eventually managed to race myself into unconscious oblivion without ingesting any drugs at all. It's alarming to imagine what might have happened had I been tempted by Dr Max's super pep pills. I could well have ended up as an anonymous redux of Tommy Simpson: the same tragic and pointless early expiration, yet without any of the fame and glory, and almost certainly with no commemorative roadside monument later built in my name.

My sole experiment with the amphetamines came a few months later. I'd started my second year at Manchester University and for the time being had lost all interest in the bike. The little package of speed pills, however, had made the trip up the M6 with me, lately loitering with questionable intent in my bedside drawer. One grey November Saturday, my friend Mark and I took the solemn decision to sample one Belgian vitamin apiece before heading out for a beery night on the town. Many years later, memories of the night in question are hazy at best. I vaguely recall Mark and I cornering a local female in a town-centre nightclub, where we subjected her to a barrage of rapid-fire, performance-enhanced drivel, each of us in an apparent bid for the title of Manchester's Most Boring Man. The unfortunate girl most likely judged our contest to be a nil–nil draw and without waiting for extra time suddenly made a desperate bid for freedom. Only momentarily nonplussed, Mark and I then bored each other senseless for a while longer before heading back to our student rooms as the sun, or at least the shamefully pale, watery orb that passes for Manchester's winter sun, came peeping over the horizon. I then spent the next few hours staring wide-eyed at the ceiling. So much for the wonder of amphetamines.

The intimate partnership between cycling and doping is of course no recent, twenty-first century phenomenon. The word 'bicycle' first appeared in English print in 1868 and yet as early as 1896 a competitor in the Paris–Bordeaux race, Arthur Linton, was reported to have died after ingesting a combination of caffeine, cocaine and strychnine, thereby becoming cycling's first recorded drugs casualty. Linton's coach was one Choppy Warburton, who found himself summarily banned from the sport, being later described as 'the instigator of drug-taking in cycling in the 19th century'. In the early years of the Tour de France, bull's blood and powdered wild boar's testicles were among the delicacies favoured by riders in search of go-faster snacks; delicacies often washed down with wine, cognac or champagne to dull the ache of overworked muscles. As Jacques Anquetil infamously retorted: 'Do you expect us to get around the Tour de France on Perrier water?'

In addition to the panoply of speedy cocktails abused by cyclists over the past century or so, there's the not inconsequential issue of recreational drug use in the peloton. Because once a rider has accepted that he's going to use a banned, performance-enhancing substance in order to get through a race, it's then easy enough to understand the temptation of supplementing it with a little something to take the edge off, a quick mood-lifter to relieve the pressure. For as glamorous as modern pro cycling may appear to be for its champions and podium-grandees – at least from an outsider's perspective – it's traditionally been a pretty tough way to make a living for the vast majority of riders. Consider this fact: Brazilian Aryton Senna was killed in the 1994 San Marino Grand Prix, but there have been no fatalities in Formula 1 races since then. Over the same period, professional bike racing has claimed lives at an average of about one a year and this is only taking into account fatalities during competition, a small fraction of the total. In addition to the sport's enormous physical and mental demands, it's also rather dangerous. And there's no question that it's much easier to get through the days with some chemical assistance, even if it's the kind that doesn't make you directly any faster.

Jan Ullrich was world amateur champion at nineteen and became Germany's first ever Tour de France winner at the age of twenty-three. Hailed by many as the biggest natural talent of his generation, the sport's new *wunderkind* then failed fully to capitalize on his early potential. As we're now aware, this was in large part due to the fact that Ullrich's Deutsche Telecom team was simply less proficient at doping than Lance Armstrong and his US Postal squad. Ullrich often seemed to struggle with the weighty expectations placed upon his shoulders, perhaps combined with the unbearable pressure of battling away, summer after summer, against a rival who appeared to be superhuman.

Many of Ullrich's toughest off-season battles were fought – and usually lost – in the pastry shops situated conveniently along his favourite training routes. 'I was totally fed up,' Ullrich said in early 1999, apparently unaware of his neat double entendre. 'Yet again I had not come through the winter well. I was even heavier than a year ago: a new record, which left me sad and hopeless. I had lost all interest in cycling. Everything that had to do with cycling seemed to me to be dark and depressing.'[148]

He recovered later that season to win both the Spanish Vuelta and the world time-trial championship. But he lost out to Armstrong in the 2000 Tour de France and again in 2001, a defeat that, according to Ullrich, nudged him into a full-blown depression. In May 2002, Ullrich crashed his Porsche sports car – straight into a bicycle rack, ironically enough – and was found to have a blood-alcohol level three times the legal limit. Two months later, Ullrich tested positive for amphetamine in an out-of-competition control and also confessed to having used Ecstasy, or MDMA. He was given a six-month suspension and lost his contract with Team Telekom. The massive fallout from the *Operación Puerto* doping investigation then ended his career prematurely in 2006. Ullrich appeared in recent years to have conquered most of his demons: 'After years of doubt, depression and physical problems, I have made peace with my personal case,' he announced.[149] But, in early 2014, Ullrich was responsible for another high-speed drink-driving incident, this time in Switzerland, injuring two people.

Former world champion Tom Boonen, another hugely popular rider, seems to gain the admiration of fans as much for his all too human fallibility off the bike as for his outstanding talents on it. And the same distractions of drugs, alcohol and fast cars have at times threatened to derail the Belgian's stellar career. Boonen tested positive for cocaine, first in 2008, then again the following year, a few weeks after winning Paris–Roubaix for the third time. 'The night before the drug test, I went out,' he said. 'I stayed for a while and I drank. At some stage I must have taken something. Then I had a blackout. I think I have a problem. After spending three to four months working, when I go out I probably overstep the mark and I become someone else.'[150]

In the omnishambles of a sporting spectacle that was the 1998 Tour de France, a succession of raids by the French police led to several team expulsions and eventual arrests, finally exposing the widespread extent of systematic doping within the peloton. After this unabashed airing of pro cycling's soiled laundry, the sport appeared to face an ultimatum. If its soul were to be saved, salvation would come only with a completely fresh start and a break from tradition. But, as we know, this never happened. The doping programmes of professional cycling teams simply became more organized, more professional and more secretive. After all, this was the same year in which an untouchable Marco Pantani sailed to victory in both the Tour and the Giro, while cancer-survivor Lance Armstrong had just re-emerged on the comeback trail, before going on to 'win' the first of his seven Tour pseudo-victories the following year.

Belgian Frank Vandenbroucke and Frenchman Philippe Gaumont were already regular training partners before becoming teammates at French team Cofidis in 1999. Initially hailed as the new poster boys for European cycling, the pair somehow morphed over the next few seasons into the sport's latest *enfants terribles*, the tales of their enthusiastic recreational drug use raising more eyebrows than the inevitable in-competition doping mishaps. As Vandenbroucke later explained in his autobiography: 'To Stilnoct [a hypnotic sedative] and amphetamines, I added Valium. Sometimes I didn't sleep a second in five days. I started seeing things, people who didn't exist.'[151] A 2006 French judicial enquiry into organized doping at Cofidis concluded that the team had spent up to 37,000 euros a year on controlled substances.

Vandenbroucke's career spiralled down into a succession of half-hearted comebacks amid worsening drug and alcohol problems. He made a failed suicide attempt in 2005, then while under suspension the following year hit the headlines after using a fake licence to enter an amateur race in Italy. He was hospitalized in 2007, reportedly in 'grave condition' after separating from his wife. Vandenbroucke died in Senegal in 2009 from a pulmonary embolism – or 'natural causes' as per the local pathologist's report, a verdict that apparently failed to take account of the various controlled pharmaceuticals found by Vandenbroucke's bedside. His teammate Philippe Gaumount retired from professional racing in 2004, after explaining to the official Cofidis enquiry that he'd used doping products throughout his career – and that he didn't believe it was possible to win a major tour without drugs. His 2005 book, *Prisonier du Dopage*, went on to explain his doping techniques – both competitive and recreational – in considerable detail.[152] Gaumont, like Vandenbroucke, had been an immense natural talent, an Olympic bronze medallist at the age of nineteen. But a few months after his fortieth birthday, Gaumont was also dead, having suffered a massive heart attack at his home in Arras.

David Millar joined Cofidis as a neo-pro in 1999. Although he later managed successfully to rebuild his professional career from the wreckage of his 2004 doping conviction and subsequent two-year ban, Millar was clearly on familiar terms with his alter-chimp ego during his formative Cofidis years. The Scotsman, who had spent his teenage years in Hong Kong and was no stranger to high-spirited nightlife, was at first taken aback by his continental teammates' fondness for recreational drugs and alcohol. But he soon adjusted to the life of an elite cyclist. Bored and miserable one evening at a high-altitude training camp, Millar decided to spice things up with a cocktail of vodka and sleeping pills. At some point during the party he jumped off a hotel roof, fracturing his heel and ruling himself out for the rest of the season.

The following year, a few months after a superb win in the Tour de France prologue, where he relegated Lance Armstrong into second place, Millar felt himself 'melting down' in the final countdown to the Sydney Olympics. By then alternating between a serious sleeping-pill habit and chronic insomnia, Millar went out partying in the athletes' village just three days before his principal event, the individual time trial. As Millar admits in his autobiography *Racing Through the Dark*: 'Looking back, I think it was quite obvious that I was a little unhinged.'[153] He finished an uninspired fourteenth in the time trial, then embarked immediately on a drinking spree that lasted forty-eight hours. Although Millar now identifies his younger self as a manic-depressive, he was never officially diagnosed. 'I didn't recognize it at the time,' he said. 'I spent so much time on my own nobody really noticed.'[154] Millar believes the bipolar traits that almost destroyed his career 'are not uncommon in the pro peloton'.

If so many pro cyclists feel the need to lie their way through their careers – to the sport's governing bodies, to the media, to friends and family, and even to teammates – then a hodgepodge of personality disorders can hardly be considered an unexpected consequence. And as numerous professionals, from Millar to Hamilton, from Ullrich to Armstrong, have attempted to explain (and, admittedly self-justify), in such instances both our minds and our morals must become rather flexible and usefully adept at reshaping awkward facts into a more palatable reality. 'Everybody's doing it,' said Hamilton in his autobiography. 'And beneath all that, the fear that if you don't find some way to ride faster, then your career is over.'[155] In the words of confessed doper Alex Zülle, a top Tour contender in the 1990s: 'I had two alternatives. Either fit in and go along with the others, or go back to being a house painter.'[156]

Although many psychologists dispute the existence of what's known as 'false memory syndrome', there have been several high-profile doping cases in recent years where the protagonists seem to be trying their best to convince themselves of their own innocence, no matter how flimsy the evidence. Alberto Contador maintained that his clenbuterol positive in the 2010 Tour de France was the result of a contaminated steak. Continued protestations of cleanliness from Floyd Landis, the disqualified winner of the 2006 Tour de France, appeared largely motivated by the contention that at least he was not quite as dirty as his former mentor, Lance Armstrong. Lithuanian Raimondas Rumšas surprised everyone with a third place in the 2002 Tour, but as Rumšas was waiting to mount the podium in Paris, his wife had been delayed several hundred miles due south. French customs agents were much interested in the contents of Mrs Rumšas' car, which on that particular day included 'empty syringes with traces of the blood-booster erythropoietin and a centrifuge of the type used to measure blood thickness, as well as human albumin, which can be used to dilute the blood to circumvent random tests.'[157] But just hang on a minute. This wasn't, so we were told, what it seemed. This massive carload of drugs, claimed Rumšas, with an impressively impassive face, was to be delivered to his ailing mother-in-law.

Tyler Hamilton's bestselling exposé, *The Secret Race*, offers a chilling insight into the life of a modern pro cyclist and in particular how to cheat most effectively in a sport where almost everyone is cheating. Yet as testament to modern scientific methods, the simple truth is that a correctly administered programme of recombinant erythropoietin, synthetic testosterone and human growth hormone – the drugs *du jour* of Armstrong, Hamilton *et al.* – can refashion almost any cyclist or mother-in-law into something stronger, faster and significantly better. In his confessional book, *The Doper Next Door*, amateur racer Andrew Tilin details his experiences with synthetic testosterone, which he took almost every day for a whole year, always under medical supervision.[158] Tilin had initially hoped to write a magazine article on what he calls 'citizen doping' – the ordinary weekend athletes who take performance-enhancing drugs – but after struggling to find enough willing interviewees, he decided instead to become his own guinea pig.

'Around the house, the T's presence had been palpable. The kids wondered why Daddy wanted to hug Mommy all the time,' wrote Tilin, after taking testosterone for four months. 'Meanwhile, on the bike, I recovered from hard workouts amazingly fast. I felt fresh the day after a training session that included multiple, intense ten-minute intervals.' Most often applied as a topical cream to the legs, synthetic 'T' is classed as an anabolic steroid that builds muscle mass and boosts recovery after intense efforts. Tilin received a two-year racing ban, after belatedly notifying USADA of his morally questionable experiment. 'Hard as it is to admit, I could see the benefits I was feeling on the bike outweighing the guilt I felt about cheating,' he noted. He goes on to reveal how a 'fabulously sinister' feeling washed over him as he felt a fresh surge of energy kick in towards the end of a race. 'I felt that same buzz and boost that I felt almost every time I competed as a doper. It was naughty and fun.'[159]

Tilin confesses to wondering how many weekend amateurs, largely free from the regular drug testing required of pro riders, are quietly going about their own home-built doping programmes. While the extra testosterone did not transform Tilin, who was aged forty-five at the time, into the next Eddy Merckx, he did see his results improve markedly. 'If you threw out the rules and put a doctor in front of me holding syringes? The temptation would be hard to resist.'

Another amateur racer, Stuart Stevens, went to the next level, adding EPO and growth hormone to his regular doses of testosterone – essentially the house specials from the old US Postal menu – in preparation for a double-century ride. 'The last time I'd ridden 200 miles, I felt awful the next day, like I'd been hit by a truck,' he wrote in *Outside* magazine. 'After the Solvang race I woke up and felt hardly a touch of soreness. I also felt like I could easily ride another 200, and I realized that I'd entered another world, the realm of instant recovery ... I could see why people might want to stay there.'[160]

In 2004, Spanish pro Jesús Manzano made detailed allegations of systemic drug use at his former team, Kelme, which in turn led to the watershed known as *Operación Puerto*. This major investigation into rampant blood-doping in Europe across several sports – and which focused on Dr Eufemiano Fuentes' extensive and illustrious client list – was what prompted Jan Ullrich's early retirement from the sport and led to lengthy suspensions for many of its top riders, including Ivan Basso and Alejandro Valverde. In a 2007 interview with *L'Équipe*, Manzano was asked about ill-fated Spanish climber José Maria Jiminéz and if he believed that drug use had been the real cause of death, rather than the official story of a heart attack. 'Of course, like it killed Pantani,' Manzano replied. He continued:

> The drugs lead you to other addictions. The anti-depressants almost automatically accompany other doping treatments. I took up to eight pills of Prozac a day when I was racing. Prozac cuts the appetite, keeps you in another world, a world where you're not afraid of what you're doing. You're no longer afraid to inject yourself with all the crap. It takes you to a world where you don't ask any more questions; especially you don't ask your doctor questions either or your sporting director. Then there are periods where you must stop doping: you feel like Superman. Then one day all of a sudden it stops and you become dramatically depressed.[161]

Manzano also claimed that as a pro rider he received daily injections of cortisone, which eventually destroyed his knees and left him unable even to pedal a bike. Cortisone is an effective anti-inflammatory when used short term. Longer-term use, however, not only debilitates the muscles and joints, but can also increase the chances of a depressive episode, according to a number of studies. Rapid withdrawal from testosterone supplements poses similar risks, as does any prolonged use of amphetamines, beta-blockers or cannabinoids. Evidently, any rider willing to submit to systematic doping on and off the bike is also subjecting himself to a physical and mental-health lottery.

A 2013 study of over 1,000 young German athletes by the University of Cologne found that more than 50 per cent admitted having experienced at least one of the following: depression; burnout; eating disorders or alcohol issues; and use of illegal drugs or other deliberate rule violations.[162] But if the study had been restricted to professional cyclists, it would not be a huge surprise to see significantly higher percentages. The likes of Hamilton and Manzano – to say nothing of the late Pantani and Jiminéz – would have ticked almost all of the boxes at certain points in their careers. There's now even a mutated strain of highly contagious depression doing the rounds in world cycling. In *The Secret Race*, Tyler Hamilton stated that Dane Bjarne Riis had actively assisted with Hamilton's doping while *directeur sportif* at the CSC team. This was then the spark for Riis himself to descend into a very public depression. Hamilton later apologized for any distress he'd caused his former boss; a little ironic this, considering Riis previously had gone by the soubriquet of 'Mr 60%', a reference to his admitted use of enormous amounts of blood-boosting EPO to win the 1996 Tour de France.[163]

Pro cycling is so outrageously tough that to ride clean is effectively an act of madness and professional suicide, or so goes the common argument. This, of course, might sound less than intuitive to the non-cyclist. But amateur racers at least can get some idea of the huge demands of a three-week race by thinking in terms of a large multiple of their own shorter and slower efforts. I've competed in events that lasted for a week or so, events that usually reduce me to a saddle-bound zombie by the fourth or fifth day. But in a regular Tour de France, the overall contenders are yet even to start racing in earnest by the end of the first week. Even were I blessed with more pro-like levels of speed and fitness, I suspect I would not be averse to a little picker-upper to get me through the second week of racing, let alone the third.

Not surprisingly, the ranks of not so tough sports are less burdened by doping controversy. The genteel game of lawn bowls, for example, has remained over the years almost entirely free of drug scandals. Almost. In 1991, Jean Wilson, aged fifty-five, was banned from national competition after failing a random drugs test at the Scottish women's championships. Traces of co-proxamol, a pain reliever – and which may also reduce heart rate – were found in her urine sample. But in endurance sports such as cycling and athletics, where engine power is usually the best predictor of success, a temptation to boost available power by any means possible has always existed. And as rewards for success head ever higher, so will temptation.

If there's no inherent reason why a mountain-top stage finish of a bike race should be more painful, any more suffer-worthy, than the bell lap of an Olympic 1,500m, or even the final length of the 200m freestyle, then cycling's fraught relationship with doping may have much to do with the sheer number of hours spent in the saddle. Even today's comparatively truncated Tour de France is the equivalent in duration of forty or so elite-level marathons. Completing two Grand Tours over the course of a summer, a common enough practice for team leaders and *domestiques* alike, similarly equates in time to roughly 100 games of football. Cristiano Ronaldo, 2013 FIFA player of the year – and a man who evidently hates to be out of the spotlight – made a total of forty-nine appearances over the entire 2013–14 season, a season that for him included a trip to the World Cup.

In May 1965, Jacques Anquetil won the eight-day Critérium du Dauphiné Libéré; a mere forty hours of racing at an average speed of just over 37km/h (23mph). After showing his face at the early evening prize ceremony, he was ferried to Nimes airport, where he boarded a charter flight to Bordeaux. Anquetil then reappeared several hours later at the 2am start of the Bordeaux–Paris classic. Although fatigue caught up with him not long into the 567km (352-mile) event, the Frenchman persevered through the night, and through the suffering. He later dropped his two breakaway companions as the race approached Paris and entered the Parc des Princes velodrome alone to a thunderous standing ovation. If no telltale vials of EPO were to be found secreted in professionals' fridges back in those relatively innocent days, then we also can state with some confidence that neither was *le frigidaire de Jacques* stocked exclusively with bottles of sparkling Perrier water.

CHAPTER 11

Peloton Mindfulness and the Zen of Jens

'Shut up legs'

Jens Voigt

Dope, drugs and pharmaceuticals. Therapeutic use exemptions. Drugs to suffer harder on the bike, drugs to soothe the suffering off it. Uppers, downers, twisters, benders. A magnificent sport seriously compromised, its aura tarnished. Far too many riders reduced to unholy, quivering wrecks, or worse. Plainly the drugs either don't work – or they work too well. Our cabinets full of prescription medicines might be a comparatively new-fangled method of holding suffering at bay, but in the quest for a brief interlude of bliss and pain relief we've always been willing to sip, smoke or swallow whatever gets the job done. The ancient Egyptians consumed blue lotus flowers to induce ecstatic states; psilocybin or 'magic' mushrooms have been identified in Algerian murals dating from over 7,000BC, while plain old nutmeg has long been used as a popular sedative over in India and other parts of Asia. More recently, Malcolm X reportedly drank nutmeg-infused tea as a cannabis substitute while in prison.

But some powerful, non-narcotic remedies with fairly limited side effects also have been with us for thousands of years. For example, the Buddhist prescription, via the delivery mechanism of the Eightfold Path, that promises a longer lasting, drug-free salve for our suffering. This does seem a bold claim, when a cursory glance around at the current state of world affairs, a daily click-through of the non-stop TV newscasts, would suggest that most of us have not been paying much heed to this whole cessation of suffering thing. But some have. Anyone even remotely familiar with the life of the Dalai Lama would have to concede that those Buddhists might be on to something. After all, the cuddly guru has surely known real suffering in his time. But we simply can't ever imagine seeing him in a bit of a sulk, or having an off day, or without that serene smile permanently spread across his features. To most of us, it seems nigh on impossible to be that peaceful and contented, all of the time – at least not without some kind of chemical assistance. But we rightly refuse to countenance the idea that the fourteenth High Lama of Tibet might be on something. His Holiness is emphatically not a doper. So when he tells us that peace and contentment must come from within, we want to believe him – and then maybe wonder how exactly to get started on that journey.

In recent years, the originally Buddhist concept of mindfulness has gained a higher profile in many traditionally non-Buddhist parts of the world. The UK's National Health Service, as one example, now promotes mindfulness as a first-line treatment for various mood disorders, such as anxiety, depression and obsessive-compulsive disorder, none of which are entirely foreign to the ranks of the pro peloton. As French ex-pro, Erwann Menthéour, discussing what might be loosely termed 'The Armstrong Decade', states frankly: 'I don't think there are many people who got through a career in cycling in those years with their mental health intact.'[164]

Mindfulness, in the Buddhist tradition, is all about stilling the 'monkey mind', a precursor to – and for most purposes synonymous with – the mischievous inner chimp as conceived by Steve Peters. Buddhists tend to liken the unfocused mind's churning maelstrom of chaotic thoughts to so many chattering monkeys, leaping excitedly from tree to tree. But modern theories of mindfulness have been recently branching out from their Buddhist roots. Jon Kabat-Zinn, Professor of Medicine at the University of Massachusetts, who studied under renowned Buddhist masters such as Thich Nhat Hanh, is the creator of the university's Mindfulness-Based Stress Reduction programme (MSBR). While the MSBR approach grounds itself firmly within a modern, scientific context, it still includes elements of more traditional methods such as meditation and Hatha yoga. These days it's practised worldwide, notably in hospitals and clinics, and has helped countless patients manage pain, anxiety and depression, and also to improve immune function. According to Kabat-Zinn, 'Mindfulness is the act of increasing present-moment awareness of physiological, mental and environmental events without imposing judgment on the quality or meaning of them.'[165]

The high anxiety crucibles of elite sport make obvious candidates for any stress-reduction or mindfulness programme. While much of athletic performance unfolds at a reflex, instinctive level, when athletes have too much time to ponder their next play or move, stress can easily build to a crescendo. Consider the World Cup football game still tied after extra time, with a penalty shoot-out to follow, or the pro golfer suffering from an attack of the putting green 'yips', or what's been defined as 'nervous tension affecting an athlete in the performance of a crucial action'. A 2004 study from LaSalle University suggested that more traditional remedies for such high-stakes situations – that negative thoughts and emotions 'must be controlled, eliminated, or replaced'[166] – often proved unhelpful and even counterproductive in practice. Instead, they proposed 'the development of mindful (nonjudgmental) present-moment acceptance of internal experiences such as thoughts, feelings, and physical sensations'[167] as a more reliable strategy for optimal performance. In other words, the centre forward who's booted his last three penalties into the top tier of the stands is not doing himself any favours by avoiding such unpleasant memories; likewise, the golfer who keeps fluffing his putts.

The concept of flow is a key element of mindfulness. Hungarian-born psychologist Mihaly Csikszentmihalyi, who emigrated to the USA in the 1950s to further his studies, is considered the grandfather of flow. Csik-szentmihalyi, who much enjoyed painting in his spare time, began to study artists and other creative types who became completely absorbed and immersed in their work, noting that the creative process itself seemed at times more important than the finished product. 'The best moments in our lives are not the passive, receptive, relaxing times,' he observed. 'The best moments usually occur if a person's body or mind is stretched to its limits in a voluntary effort to accomplish something difficult and worthwhile.'[168] Csikszentmihalyi became fascinated by what he called the 'flow' state, which he later defined as 'the state in which people are so involved in an activity that nothing else seems to matter'.[169] He set about identifying the different elements involved in achieving such a state.

The flow concept is so named because during Csikszentmihalyi's early research, a number of his interviewees described their experiences by using a metaphor of being carried along by a current of water. Flow and mindfulness are clearly two separate qualities, but they have a certain amount of overlap. Mindfulness is characterized by the redirecting of attention inwards, most commonly through some form of meditation, whereas flow focuses one's attention on a specific external process. In Csikszentmihalyi's model, flow is achieved when degree of challenge and level of ability to complete a task are able to strike a balance, a perfect harmony. Simple tasks that require only minimal skill might lead to apathy and boredom, while tackling more difficult activities with only limited ability may cause undue stress and anxiety. But during an optimal flow state:

> one's skills are adequate to cope with the challenges at hand in a goal-directed, rule-bound action system that provides clear clues as to how one is performing. Concentration is so intense that there is no attention left over to think about anything irrelevant or to worry about problems. Self-consciousness disappears, and the sense of time becomes distorted. An activity that produces such experiences is so gratifying that people are willing to do it for its own sake, with little concern for what they will get out of it, even when it is difficult or dangerous.[170]

The principal common ground between flow and mindfulness is that both will anchor us securely to the present moment: athletes who in the midst of competition have a tendency to dwell on past mistakes or on future fears are being neither mindful nor in a state of flow.

And so to a sun-dappled, mountain descent: difficult, yes, dangerous, almost definitely, but paired with a well-tuned, two-wheeled machine and the appropriate handling skills, we get to experience pure exhilaration, not stress and anxiety. Well, okay: some stress and anxiety, but to be fair this is only natural. Or, if it happens to start teeming down with rain and the road is narrow and potholed, with an off-camber turn here and there, then a slug of fear and dread might worm its way into the pit of our stomach, but this serves only to deepen our immersion, to focus our complete concentration on the task at hand. In a proper state of flow, as Csikszentmihalyi observed, action and awareness are merged, while distractions and self-consciousness both disappear and this is what should define our finest moments on the bike. Nervy, buttock-clenching descents aside, we find our own states of flow on twisty country lanes, on forested single track and even on the daily commute to work, on those clear-skied mornings of auspicious traffic-light phasing. Perhaps, too, we discover a semblance of flow on the steady, repetitive tempo of a long climb, although Csikszentmihalyi appears not to have elaborated on whether flow – which he also called 'optimal experience' – can be properly achieved while also experiencing crushing amounts of pain.

At any rate, bombing through the hairpins of an extended stretch of downhill – for most cyclists this is the epitome of bike flow. When Nic (he of the war-torn legs) and myself took ORICA GreenEDGE professional Christian Meier up into the mountains around Chiang Mai one time, we made sure to warn him before we started the twistiest descent of the ride. Flow states are all well and good, but it was a testing downhill where two of my teammates had recently crashed at high speed. Christian nodded his acknowledgement, perhaps made a quick mental comparison between the task currently at hand and the downhill horrors he'd confronted in that year's Giro d'Italia, and then sprinted towards the first corner, flying around it with all the panache and crazed leaning of a MotoGP rider. Nic and I set off in pursuit, but a couple of corners later Christian had vanished completely from sight. It was galling to realize that even if I had a small electric motor concealed in my bike frame to help me *climb* at pro-like speed, I stood no chance at all of ever remaining in contact on the descents. Our warning did, though, prove prescient when later in the ride Christian was sideswiped by a stray minibus, luckily escaping with only cuts and grazes. If Christian's descending skills were beyond reproach, he still had a thing or two to learn about Thai driving habits.

Buddhists, of course, understand the idea of flow just as well as any psychologist. Recall that *sukha*, the mercurial counterpoint to the more pervasive *dukkha*, signifies a sense of flow as much as it does a feeling of happiness or bliss – it's the smooth-spinning wagon axle, free from obstructions and hindrances. The trickier concept of 'oneness' as emphasized by the Taoist approach, or *jhana*, the Theravada Buddhist cornerstone of right concentration in which the mind becomes fully immersed and absorbed in the chosen object of attention; these are also essentially states of flow. And so it is with the state of velo *Dharma*, with bike *sukha*. Joyful memories of high-speed descents, when I'd yell ecstatically at the onrushing trees, at the sky, at my handlebars, for no reason other than feeling very much alive.

Although Team GB psychologist Steve Peters might accept that yelling at trees is not always a cause for concern – indeed, if practised with discretion it can be seen as a healthy response to feeling joyful – it could be also a warning that the inner chimp is trying to assume ascendency. And in order to exercise effective control over our 'jungle centre' – Peters' colourful phrase for the base instincts that make us act in irrational and emotional ways – we need to remain mindful and focused on the task at hand. Besides which, a chimp descending a mountain on a bicycle is most unlikely to be in a state of flow. Professor Mark Williams, whose work has been instrumental in introducing mindfulness to the masses in the UK, talks of bringing 'intentions and actions back into alignment'.[171] Indeed, a number of ancient Buddhist texts state that one key characteristic of mindfulness is 'not wobbling', which in itself has obvious benefits for cyclists everywhere.

Right mindfulness, along with the other Buddhist Eightfold Path qualities of right effort and right concentration, offers a promising start for any bike racing manifesto worth its salt, any esteemed collection of cycling *sutras*. To win a race without having those three attributes firmly dialled in is a big ask indeed. After all, Lance Armstrong had them in spades, albeit in addition to the special-order contents of his fridge. To better appreciate how mindfulness can be useful in a race, we should first take a look at what might happen in its absence, when mindfulness finds itself tossed to the roadside like an empty *bidon*, supplanted instead by the mistruths of delusion and impulsivity. As it happens, I'm on fairly good terms with a man who knows about racing bikes the mindless way, along the bumpy path of wrong effort and poor concentration.

A five-day masters stage race, a peloton coasting along in dazzling morning sunshine, approximately halfway through a hilly third stage, and I was feeling good. Extremely good, in fact, and this, in hindsight, was not so good. Because the problem with feeling good is that it can stop you from worrying about all the things you ought to be worrying about. And I wasn't worrying at all. One known reason why I was feeling good was that I'd arrived at the race in excellent condition, coming off several months of focused training and the best string of results I'd put together in many years of disjointed attempts at being a bike racer. This was not only a known; it was, to borrow from the Rumsfeldian combat phrasebook, a '*known* known'. But something else was boosting my sense of well-being that day, affording me 'good sensations' on the bike, as those funny Continentals like to say. Something that in theory belonged in the general category of knowns, but in the terrible fog of racing had slipped into an adjacent, less accessible area of my awareness.

Nutmeg and blue lotus flower may have had a limited impact on the world of cycling, but countless studies have shown that caffeine boosts performance in endurance sports. The exact mechanism is still not fully understood, but it's thought to alter the way in which the brain regulates fatigue – maybe as a helpful spanner in the works of the Noakesian regulator. Caffeine is also an effective painkiller, as anyone familiar with over the counter headache remedies should be aware. In 2004, the World Anti-Doping Authority (WADA) removed all restrictions on caffeine use in competition, no longer appearing on its prohibited list. These days, caffeine and bicycles are culturally intertwined to the extent that a 'coffee shop ride' – usually meaning a sociable, easy-paced spin – has become part of everyday cycling parlance.

That said, it's not so easy to drink a double espresso or a skinny latte while actually on the bike, which explains why many sports drinks and power gels now come preloaded with caffeine. But at some point during the race my prior knowledge that the half-dozen gels stuffed into my jersey pockets contained zesty amounts of caffeine had drifted across a mental divide and into the poorly demarcated border territory of previously known. This is simply another way of saying completely forgotten. The sachets of sugary goo tasted rather nasty, that much was still known, but what with it being a longish stage, I was knocking back gels on a regular basis, each one washed down with swigs of a lemony drink. Of course, feeling less fatigue and pain during a race might be considered a good thing. And it could be, if it were not for the caffeinated foolishness that, in my case, almost always ensues – the foolishness that tricks you into believing your effortlessly spinning cranks are a testament to physical superiority, rather than a short-lived, stimulant-induced high.

I drifted off to the side of the peloton and popped another gel – now even stickier and less palatable after several hours under the tropical sun – and came to the conclusion that the race needed some pepping up. No one seemed interested in doing much. Was this a race or a club ride? I launched a sneak attack at the base of a small hill and glanced back to see a handful of riders bridging across. We soon regrouped and formed a steady, efficient rotation. I surveyed the other escapees: all overall contenders; all willing to do their share. No passengers on board. Yet the pace soon slackened. What on earth was wrong with these people? Surely the only thing worse than missing a break was making a break, only to be quickly reabsorbed by the bunch. And this decisive break was now looking decidedly indecisive. I attacked a second time, stomping on the pedals, soon putting some daylight between the chasers and myself. I had hoped to be in contention for the overall win, but had not expected the competition to capitulate like this. With 10km (6 miles) to go, I was already savouring the prospect of victory.

With the road now beginning to undulate more noticeably, and in the best tradition of Thai races, I passed a sign signalling 25km (15.5 miles) to go. This was unfortunate, if not entirely unexpected. Unfortunate, too, was the soaring temperature; it was now past midday. A headwind had sprung up from nowhere. I felt twinges of cramp in my thighs. Caffeine haze notwithstanding, it was beginning to hurt and I was no longer feeling quite so superb. If I was not yet suffering *per se*, then I was rattling, express-like, through all intermediate stations between the termini of superb and suffering. I eased off and waited for the others, who offered me puzzled glances as they drew level. We ground out the last 12km (7.5 miles), all feeling the effects of riding for four hours in the tropics. The uphill finish was contested with a comically cramp-affected sprint. Teeth gritted, I willed myself over the line a few bike lengths ahead of the others.

The comedy continued back at the hotel. In my hyper-caffeinated state, I couldn't settle into my usual post-race routine, namely a nap. In a brief window of clarity, of something close to mindfulness, it dawned on me that my state of extreme alertness might be due to that day's race nutrition. Mid-evening, and the comedy took a more tragic turn. I badly needed rest, but my body was unwilling to negotiate. By midnight, desperation had taken hold: I had a vivid premonition of what the next day's hilly stage held in store for an exhausted insomniac. As the caffeine ebbed out of my system, it was then my failure to stop *thinking* about caffeine that kept my head spinning into the small hours. The premonition proved accurate. I struggled throughout the stage, losing time to my rivals and ceding any chance of the overall win.

Defeated by chocolate-flavoured energy gels: this is bike racing, or at least bike racing the not so mindful way. Mistakes are made, chances are taken or missed; the best man does not always win. And in amateur races at least, unforced errors often outnumber the good decisions. We're only amateurs, after all. We drop chains, jam gears and overcook corners. There's the nameless friend who a few hours before his debut Iron Man triathlon raised his saddle by 2.5cm (1in) – to make space for a water bottle and spare tube to fit underneath. His swim went very well, but the sudden onset of crippling backache ended his race less than halfway into the bike section. Another triathlete friend suffered a shock defeat by projectile vomiting after leading a race to within metres of the finish line, the messy result of a last-minute change to his regular pre-race meal. Race nutrition is a tricky and often sticky science; trickier and stickier still when the weather is hot. My main regret over the Gelgate incident is not that I massively overdosed on caffeine, but the equally amateurish error of not having anything handy to bring me down afterwards. In deference to the sport's all-time greats, any rider remotely serious about his 'preparation' would have at least a few Valium pills stashed in his kitbag. Me? I had some multivitamins and a jar of peanut butter.

Pro riders evidently crash with alarming regularity and are also prone to tactical errors at key moments, but you might imagine they would be largely exempt from the kind of mindless lapses in concentration that punctuate lesser races. But perhaps not. Jan Mathieu, team doctor at Lotto-Belisol, believes that the pro peloton's ongoing affinity for Tramadol, a powerful painkiller, might have contributed to a spate of bad crashes in the 2014 spring classics.[172] Tramadol, a powerful opioid, is known to cause drowsiness and can affect concentration. It is not currently prohibited by WADA, although it was recently added to their watch list. That a substance administered to relieve suffering might end up causing greater suffering might elicit a wry smile from some, not least from the Buddhists.

But if the key quality of mindfulness does have a rightful place in the peloton, where exactly might it be found? Probably not so much with the sprinters, whose races typically condense down to two minutes of pure madness, the raw instinct needed to manoeuvre into position for a highly explosive finish. More possibly the climbers, or at least the less tortured variety of climbers, up there on their windswept mountain passes, tapping out a metronomic rhythm on the pedals and coaxing themselves into a trance-like state. But for the most authentically mindful approach to bike racing, we must look instead to the *rouleurs*, the peloton's solid and dependable all-rounders. Because, for that largely unsung majority of riders who do not possess a lethal finishing sprint, or the ability to defy gravity for extended periods of time, much of road-racing success is indeed about mindfulness, about focus and concentration, and about choosing the right moment to make the *right effort*. This, of course, is not always so much in evidence at amateur races, where impulsive, inexperienced riders tend to chase down each and every move off the front of the peloton, fearful that they will miss the one that eventually gets away. This kind of grasping, possessive behaviour – an ego-driven desire to be part of the break, or indeed a craven attachment to it – is unfortunately a strict no-no in all teachings of mindfulness.

Many Buddhist texts on mindfulness emphasize the importance of non-attachment, of 'freedom from craving and desires'. If this type of detached, considered approach to racing requires more than a modicum of experience, it is then no great surprise that the most convincing displays of racing the mindful way come from cycling's *bona fide* champions, the true masters at the pinnacle of their sport. Masters of the stature of Fabien Cancellera, who has claimed three victories in Paris–

Roubaix and another three in the Tour of Flanders. It's in these cobbled spring classics that M. Cancellera, or 'Spartacus' as he's known to his legions of fans, has most often wreaked chaos and destruction on his rivals by finding exactly the right time to attack – almost invariably a devastating, unanswerable attack – and thereby freezing in time a race's 'perfect moment' as effectively as any Henri Cartier-Bresson photograph. For Fabien Cancellera, right concentration plus right effort normally yields right result.

As an important caveat, it should be noted that, as a nation, the French generally do not adapt too well to all this mindfulness stuff. Cancellera, for the record, is from Switzerland, the German-speaking part, and comes across in his interviews as a profoundly measured and even-tempered individual – exactly what you'd expect from that part of the world. But as for the typical Gallic temperament, well, what can we say? *C'est un problème.* It's a temperament that's a little too combustible, too volatile. It does afford the French a level of passion – one often deemed lacking in their Anglo-Saxon neighbours – that can pay off handsomely in the sporting arena. But these cupfuls of Gallic sporting passion do have a frequent tendency to runneth over. Take football, for instance: Eric Cantona, launching his infamous kung fu kick at a spectator whose verbal taunts had upset him, or compatriot Zinedine Zidane's well-executed headbutt in the 2006 World Cup final, witnessed live by billions around the world.

No Frenchman has won the Tour de France since Bernard Hinault in 1985, a shameful blot on their history book and one fast approaching a national crisis now that two Englishmen in succession have won the race. To be fair, French cycling has enjoyed something of a renaissance in recent years, a rebirth that's led some to the obvious conclusion that, as a nation, they may have been doping marginally less than others during the Dark Ages of Cycling. During those ignominious years, it was Laurent Jalabert's fondness for the doomed solo escape that seemed to personify the Gallic preference for passion over mindfulness. Among the current crop of French riders, it's Tommy Voeckler who appears to have inherited Jalabert's predilection for the showy but futile attack. But M. Voeckler, for reasons unknown to the public, rarely, if ever, looks comfortable on his bike and also has the distinction of owning what is surely the most enjoyably expressive face in the peloton. Cycling writer Eben Weiss describes Voeckler as 'sort of the anti-Jens Voigt, in that while both undertake long and ultimately fruitless breakaways, Voigt seems to be enjoying himself whereas Voeckler rides with his shoulders hunched up and a look of disgust on his face – he always looks like he's plunging a particularly foul toilet'.[173]

So what then of this fabled Voigt character, the laid-back German who apparently derives pleasure from suicidal breakaways? On stage sixteen of the 2009 Tour de France, Voigt crashed on a fast descent. Sliding across the tarmac at high speed, he appeared to be using his face as a front brake. He suffered a fractured cheekbone and concussion. During stage sixteen of the following year's Tour, Voigt's front tyre exploded and he crashed again. Still somehow able to ride, but with his bike destroyed, the 1.9m (6ft 3in) Voigt borrowed a miniature yellow bike from a youth group who were following the race. He rode it for a good 15km (9 miles) ('it made me look like a bear riding a circus bike') until he could get a replacement from his team. Voigt, as always looking on the brighter side of life, later told reporters 'my ribs are hurting, but hey, broken ribs are overrated anyway. Fortunately, I didn't land on my face this time, and I'm still alive.'[174]

In 2014, Voigt rode in his seventeenth and final Tour de France. A couple of months later, he celebrated his forty-third birthday, hopped on to his track bike to break the world hour record, then announced his retirement from professional cycling. He's always been one of the peloton's most popular figures, this in large part stemming from his reluctance to point a finger at anyone else when his race didn't go to plan, combined with his obvious enthusiasm and passion for the sport when it did. A committed family man, Voigt has six children; his Twitter feed is crammed with photos of the kids, their pet rabbits and other minutiae of domestic bliss. If you were to conjure up a scenario of an engaging and fruitful conversation between the Dalai Lama and a pro cyclist, then German Jensie would be your man.

Despite no shortage of success in his eighteen years as a pro, Jens Voigt's enduring legacy is his signature phrase: 'Shut up legs!' Initially offered as a throwaway explanation to a television journalist of how he was able to suffer so much during a race, his words seemed neatly to encapsulate the Tao of Jens. Voigt's minimalist mantra has since spawned T-shirts, posters, smartphone apps and also featured in a custom paint job for his Trek road bike. Voigt wrote a longstanding blog for *Bicycling* magazine called 'Hardly Serious' (no longer online), where he got to ask himself important philosophical questions on a regular basis. 'Geez, what are you doing, Jensie? What are you thinking? Are you crazy, man? Why do you still want to suffer like a pig?' And most of the time he seemed to have the answers. 'When you go hard, your body says, "stop!" and your mind says, "body shut up!" And, sometimes it works! And then you go!'

Calm detachment in the face of injury or other misfortune may be a highly worthy trait of the mindful mindset, but it's in the placid incantation of 'shut up legs' where Jens duly reveals himself as a classically mindful bike racer. Jensie, far from surrendering to the unwholesome delusions of attachment and aversion to the pain in his legs, was merely observing what was going on with them – and asking politely if they could just turn the volume down a little.

In Zen philosophy, a follower practises detachment from personal thoughts and opinions, so as not to be harmed mentally and emotionally by them. This might help to explain why countless cyclists, possibly inspired by the Tao of Jens, find it convenient to develop a stand-offish, third-person relationship with their legs. Earnest confessions along the lines of 'the legs didn't have it today', or 'the legs just suddenly went on that last climb' are tossed around liberally post-race amongst those who had frankly hoped to do better. The legs themselves almost certainly haven't *gone* anywhere, of course. But when they've let you down and caused you to suffer, you might choose simply not to associate with them for a while. A cooling-off period after things get fraught is what helps to keep a relationship healthy.

The key difference here is that Jens and his impressive legs were able to remain in the present moment at all times. To put this another way, Jens always remained mindful that his legs had a mind of their own; that they had their volume tweaked up and down more times than he could remember, but never knowingly went missing in action. They hurt, they ached. They cramped, screamed and burned, but they always kept going. And this is the essence of Jens. The Lord Buddha's final words were reportedly 'strive on diligently, don't give up'. Jensie was saying much the same thing. It's the remarkable Zen of Jens.

CHAPTER 12

Race Hardness

Rennhärte (n), German: 'Racing Hardness'

'It was by far the farthest my mind has ever pushed my body.'
Andy Hampsten, winner of the 1988 Giro d'Italia[175]

The Tour of Thailand, the country's only pro-am international stage race, has been a fixture on the UCI Asia Tour since 2006. Each year it attracts a number of the region's pro teams, a smattering of Asian national squads and occasionally a team or two from further afield, perhaps looking to escape the early spring gloom in Europe or North America. The 2009 edition, also known colloquially as the Princess Mamackakri Sirindhon's Cup, was to cover a *parcours* of 929.81km (577.8 miles), a number that struck me as curiously precise, since Thai bike races had a general habit of ending up with substantially different distances – and even entirely different routes – to those listed in the race programme.

Thailand's emerging bike racing scene now features a host of expat riders, with growing numbers of road-racers, mountain bikers and tri-athletes choosing either to base themselves in the country year-round, or for the winter months only, as an escape from grey and chilly northern climes. While some head straight for the palm-fringed beaches of Phuket or other well-touristed resort areas, others favour the northern cities of Chiang Mai and Chiang Rai, both of which are surrounded by lush, forested mountain ranges and enjoy cooler temperatures than the south.

In late 2012, Canadian Christian Meier, a trusty *domestique* on the ORICA GreenEDGE Pro-Tour team, selected Chiang Mai as his base camp for several weeks of low-key, pre-preseason training. A confirmed coffee fanatic, he soon pronounced the local lattes and cappuccinos superior to anything he'd found in Girona, his Spanish home during the European racing season. Thailand's other attractions include the ability to train outdoors throughout the year, an affordable cost of living, excellent and plentiful fresh produce and a decent highway infrastructure populated by mostly Buddhist drivers whose fundamental creed is to do you no harm, at least not intentionally.

The Thai bike-racing calendar continues to expand each year, albeit from a narrow base. In an unexpected development – as if to mark the true coming of age of cycle sport in the Kingdom – The Tourist

Authority of Thailand (TAT) announced in late 2014 that it was planning to host the Tour de France. According to Reuters, senior officials from the TAT had recently returned from Paris, where they'd been in fruitful and encouraging discussions with the Amaury Sport Organisation (ASO), the organizers of the Tour de France. The likes of England, Germany, Luxembourg and the Netherlands have hosted multiple stages in recent editions of *La Grande Boucle* – a likely source of inspiration for the TAT. And yet it may have overlooked the minor detail that all these nations are France's close neighbours. To pre-empt any logistical quibbling, TAT governor Thawatchai Arunyik told Reuters 'We're not sure yet how many stages we will hold, whether it is one or two stages or the whole competition. This is something that still needs to be discussed.'[176]

Informed expats in Thailand viewed this as an entirely understandable misunderstanding. 'The words "France" and *farang* (foreigner) sound almost identical in the Thai language,' noted one. 'The TAT evidently believes the 110 year-old race is actually the Tour de *Farang*. Thailand already plays host to millions of *farang* visitors each year, so no problem at all to accommodate another two hundred or so on bicycles.' Whether a race held entirely within Thailand would still be named the Tour de France remains for the moment a moot point. The ASO soon set the record straight, confirming that something had been lost in translation, a hardly uncommon occurrence in any dialogue between Thais and westerners. 'There are talks indeed, but not to bring the Tour to Thailand,' the ASO clarified.[177] He suggested instead that a one-day professional criterium was a possibility sometime in the future.

As somebody once said, it's the taking part that counts. A freak surge of this *esprit de corps* may account for how I came to find my name on the 2009 Tour of Thailand start list, if only because more rational explanations are sorely lacking. American Chris Horner raised a few eyebrows when he won the Spanish Vuelta at a near-superannuated forty-one, but he's been a professional rider for half of his life. At roughly the same age as Horner and an amateur part-timer, I was starting my international stage-race career about twenty years too late. Decent preparation would certainly have helped, but it had not worked out that way. I would be lining up against top-flight competition with only a few months of proper training in my legs. I was going to suffer.

A place on a local semi-pro team became available after a couple of their riders were unable to make the journey from Europe and had to cancel at short notice. As Lex Nederlof, the team captain and former Dutch national squad rider explained, the team jerseys were already on order, so I might as well try one on for size. It was, after all, only a bicycle race. Still, the CCN team's three core members, two Dutch and one German, had oodles of experience and were all more than capable of challenging for honours at this level. Making up the numbers were my friend Marco, another Dutchman and a recently converted triathlete, and myself; a pair of international stage-race rookies consigned as mere cannon fodder for the big guns of the peloton. Until recently, Marco and I had been leisurely connoisseurs of coffee shop rides around Chiang Mai. Now we found ourselves thrust directly and uneasily into the line of fire.

Yet it seemed the unease was mine alone. Marco, one of life's incorrigible optimists during his more contemplative moments and a raving maniac at all other times, was raring to go. 'We're going to kill them,' he announced. As I scanned the names on the start sheet, I had serious doubts. A US pro team, Kelly Benefit Strategies, were a late addition to the race roster. They'd initially applied to race the Tour of California – to compete alongside the likes of Armstrong 2.0 and his Astana team – but after missing out on a slot, opted instead for an early-season jaunt to South-east Asia. If killers were indeed lurking in the peloton, then I had a rough idea where to find them.

For the uppermost two-thirds of Thailand's landmass, the months of December and January comprise what is euphemistically known as the 'cool' season, which in effect means slightly less scorching than the remaining ten months of the calendar. Towards the end of each year, the locals exhort you to make the most of the eagerly anticipated Thai 'winter' because in a startlingly quick turnaround, the hot season (maximal scorch) starts to simmer in early March and reaches boiling point by mid-April. A Thai race promoter with any humanitarian leanings might then look to the cool season as the ideal period in which to stage a week-long event. Not so, unfortunately. The Tour of Thailand takes place every year in early April, when shade temperatures can hit 40°C (104°F). The Thai Cycling Federation, by hosting its signature race in the hottest month of the year and only a few hours' drive from Bangkok – the world's hottest city, according to the World Meteorological Organization – may be under the impression that its perverse scheduling favours domestic riders. There is certainly some truth in this: any pasty, pale-skinned teams turning up for a race in the sun after a long winter of hibernation are destined to suffer horribly.

The first stage of the 2009 Tour of Thailand was listed as 187.7km (116.6 miles), give or take a few centimetres. While I'd hoped for a quasi-sensible start time, say, 8am or thereabouts – which if all went well would have us back in our air-conditioned hotel rooms not too long after midday – it was no great surprise to find the Thai Federation had decreed a 10am start. Flocks of local bigwigs are a standard fixture at major Thai races and they prefer not to get out of bed too early.

By 10am, the sun was already blazing down and the assembled VIPs had bagged all the available shade at the start area. As we lined up, I glanced around at some of the other teams. The general degree of seriousness was disconcerting. As far as I could recall, I was doing this for fun, but it did not look as if too many of the others were. The Chinese team especially, all square jaws and steely gaze, looked as if they had been assembled in a Guangzhou factory. By a quarter past ten, a series of speeches from various local dignitaries was under way, but there seemed little prospect of a bicycle race starting any time soon. With my head already pounding from the heat and the sun, I tried to align myself behind a lamp post, hoping to appropriate a tiny sliver of shade. A momentary pause in the speeches then gave way to a troupe of traditional Thai dancers: half a dozen pubescent girls, each one heavily made up, their winsome smiles barely concealing their desire to be elsewhere, preferably somewhere dark and air-conditioned.

After a couple, or possibly twenty more speeches, the shimmering orb of the sun had gained sufficient elevation in the sky for pedalling hostilities to begin. At the pop of the starting gun, Lex, our team captain and a veteran of the UCI Asia tour, turned around to offer me some sage words of advice. 'Just sit in and don't get caught at the back,' he cautioned. In other words, I was to remain at all times inside the protective cocoon of the peloton and under no circumstances attempt anything complicated or risky, such as actually racing. With no need to be present at the sharp end of the race, the stage should be a pleasant opportunity to sit back, follow a wheel and enjoy the scenery; in bike racing terms, this was almost a day off. At least that was the idea.

European races typically start at a comparative dawdle, then steadily pick up pace before finishing in a manic, teeth-bared frenzy. But my hopes that the peloton might want to take it relatively easy for the early part of this stage were blown away almost immediately. For the entire first hour of fast, flat highway, my bike computer display refused to show me anything below 50km/h (30mph). Trying to position myself out of harm's way proved an elusive goal. Whenever I managed to pull myself up to the safety of mid-pack, a stream of riders would then pass on either side, dragging me – as if on some kind of doomed conveyor belt – towards the forbidden rear end of the race.

I survived the first hour, physically and mentally intact for the most part, and somewhere around the two-hour mark my suffering seemed to reach a steady state; it wasn't going to get better, but it might not get too much worse. It was getting hotter though. It was getting very hot. As a team *domestique*, I was tasked with dropping back to the team car at regular intervals to fetch fresh bottles for the others. But the idea of loading up with several kilos of water and then trying to zigzag, at full race pace, through the crazed convoy of vehicles was totally unrealistic. I stood a better chance of surviving a solo mission to Mordor and back. Thankfully, our resident German pro, Timo, soon realized that my first trip back to the car would probably also be my last and graciously took command of the communal water duties. Timo, a powerful track rider, had introduced me to the German word *rennhärte*, which, roughly translated, means 'race-hardened'. Back in the days of steel frames and five-speed shifters, prevailing wisdom was that the best preparation for the rigours of long, tough races was to ride plenty of long, tough races. Training theory may have advanced since then, but the mantra still applies. At one point I glanced behind to see Timo on his return from a refill sortie, floating through the team cars towards the high-speed peloton, hands off the bars, jersey overstuffed with refilled bottles, and I'm fairly sure he was whistling. *Rennhärte* indeed.

A split occurred in the 140-man field shortly after the stage's halfway point, but with the stretched peloton now snaking its way along narrow, potholed country lanes, I only became aware of this well after the fact. So focused was I on doggedly following the wheel in front, kilometre after scorching kilometre, that a tactical nuclear device could have detonated at the front of the race and I would not have known. After the split, the pace finally relented, but our *grupetto* of sixty-odd riders still had to get to the finish and within the time limit. With almost all the team cars now following the lead group, water became a scarce commodity. I squeezed the last few drops out of my *bidons*, while trying to banish increasingly intrusive thoughts about swimming pools and ice-cold beer. Eventually someone handed me a nearly empty bottle of what tasted like warm dishwater. On my left, a New Zealander, patriotically if unwisely kitted out in Kiwi-standard all-black, gestured that he was also thirsty and could I please save him a sip. The salty tidemarks of dried sweat decorating his jersey and shorts gave him the sorry look of something washed up on a beach.

It is a truth universally acknowledged that any cyclist, upon finding himself being inexorably stir-fried under a tropical midday sun, is then quite likely to observe his mind trawling through wistful memories of cycle rides in cold and bleak conditions. The bracing chill of a Peak District winter club run perhaps: a lightly frosted nose and fingertips, but after half an hour on the bike, a warming inner glow developing as positive affirmation of that morning's selection of high-tech layering garments. Then, rosy-cheeked and redolent of damp dog, piling into the cosy confines of the village café for double beans on toast and steaming mugs of tea. Of course, it is equally axiomatic that on the long haul homewards, feeling overfed and sluggish, belching audibly on each climb, the multiplicative effects of the low flat cloud, the steady drizzle and the buffeting crosswind are what lull you into daydreaming of those bucolic midsummer rides, all warm breezes and cloudless blue skies.

Before the start of stage fourteen of the 1988 Giro d'Italia, technical race director and former Giro winner Francesco Moser had urged race director Vincenzo Torriani to cancel the stage. The mountainous *parcours* included a climb of the notorious Gavia pass, a 'glorified goat track' in the words of 7-Eleven team doctor, Max Testa.[178] But Torriani explained that while it was indeed snowing at the top of the pass, the road remained more or less clear. 'The show should go on and the riders should suffer through,' he told the assembled team managers, thereby setting the scene for what *Sports Illustrated* described as 'misery on a scale rarely seen even in this suffering-intensive sport'.[179] The Gavia had not been part of the Giro since 1960, when Charlie Gaul won the stage ahead of eventual winner Jacques Anquetil. That the Giro had for a number of years since avoided many of the country's more notorious climbs had led to accusations that the Italians were favouring their own contenders, the likes of Guiseppe Saronni and Moser himself, neither of whom were noted climbers. But by 1988, the Italians' protectionist policy was over. 'Those sons of bitches put every mountain they could find in the race that year,' said Bob Roll, an American rider on the 7-Eleven team. While not quite as glamourous as its Tour de France sister, the Giro showcases equally rugged and spectacular scenery and, as many believe, offers even larger doses of misery for its participants. 'I despise it in some ways,' Bradley Wiggins told reporters on the eve of the 2013 race. 'But there is an attraction.'[180] The usually implacable Jens Voigt called the 2008 edition of the race 'stupid' after encountering 24 per cent gradients during the individual time trial. David Millar went one better, describing the race as 'ridiculous' and 'insane'.[181]

As the peloton approached the lower slopes of the Gavia in the 1988 race, Andy Hampsten, 7-Eleven's specialist climber, glanced across at Bob Roll and noted: 'This will probably be the hardest day on the bike of our lives.'[182] 7-Eleven manager Mike Neel had prepared the team for the extreme conditions as best he could, slathering each rider in lanolin – as used by cross-Channel swimmers – and equipping them with neoprene ski gloves. During the stage, the 7-Eleven team car regularly refilled the riders' water bottles with hot tea. Once on to the climb itself, the lead riders had to follow in the tyre tracks of vehicles to find a path through the mud and snow. But the climb was not even the main concern – climbing at race pace should generate sufficient body heat to keep the muscles functioning, even at the summit where the temperature was a reported –4°C (25°F). The bigger problem would be the 25km (15.5-mile) descent, on twisty, wet dirt roads, into a howling headwind and a blizzard. But as the lead riders approached the top, television commentators noted that the weather was affecting not only physical strength but mental reasoning too. Hampsten was observed zigzagging across the road in an agonizing attempt to zip up his rain jacket.

Dutchman Johan Van Der Velde embarked on his descent of the Gavia, but soon turned around and rode back to the top. He then had to be helped into a team car, where he sat shivering, sipping cognac and hot tea.

Aussie rider Allan Peiper borrowed a motorbike jacket for the descent. He later recounted passing 'riders who were crying, and some who were walking in ones and twos, the snow blinding their vision'.[183] Hampsten continued downhill into the snowstorm, on his way to the leader's pink jersey and eventual race victory, but by now shaking uncontrollably and braking and pedalling at the same time in a desperate attempt to generate more body heat. Ice crystals formed on his bicycle frame, freezing his gears. 'It was by far the farthest my mind has ever pushed my body,' he later noted. 'I looked down at my legs and they were bright red with a sheet of ice on my shins.'[184]

In the seemingly interminable first stage of the Tour of Thailand, my legs were also looking rather reddish. Mind was still pushing body, but body was showing increasing signs of dissent, this time from over five hours exposed to Thailand's brutal midsummer. The redness on the tops of my thighs was incipient sunburn. A sheet or two of ice would not have gone amiss: one for the legs; another down the back of my jersey. We passed a sign indicating another 15km (9 miles) to go moments after my bike computer clocked up 200km (124 miles) for the day. I ground out the last dozen or so clicks in an almost hallucinatory state and as we rolled over the finish line, a wave of exhaustion, utter depletion, crowded out any sense of triumph I might otherwise have felt. I had the dissociated urge to call my mother, to ask if she could please come and take me home, take me far away from this madness. Powerful water jets from a local fire truck soared skywards, then fell as a cooling shower on the stunned racers, transforming the roadside finish area into a large paddling pool. Had a German physician (neatly trimmed beard, small round spectacles) been present at the stage finish to give me a quick once-over, he might have diagnosed a straightforward case of *Frühjahrsmüdigkeit*, otherwise known as 'spring fatigue', and possibly the co-morbid presence of moderate *Ichschmerz*, the all-pervasive condition of 'dissatisfaction with the self'. Certainly there was dissatisfaction with my lack of *rennhärte*, my evident deficit of Hampstenesque race hardness.

The key to stage-racing survival is recovery, but back in the hotel that afternoon it was obvious that my body was in no mood to cooperate. And from a non-partisan point of view, why the hell should it, if only to be horribly abused again the next day? The standard post-stage recovery protocol was simple enough: replenish fuel supplies immediately; then remain as horizontal and comatose as possible until summoned for the next refuelling. But any hopes for a speedy recovery seemed like wishful thinking. My body was still trying to figure out what it might have done wrong to deserve such cruel and unusual punishment.

The following morning, as I checked in with my legs at the start of stage two, a message came through loud and clear that the previous day's injustices were neither forgotten, nor forgiven. The first hour or so of the undulating stage sent the race eastwards, head on into a stiff breeze. To harness my remaining energy reserves, depleted as they were, I anchored myself this time securely inside the phalanx of the peloton. Thus concealed from the wind, head down and crouched low over the bars like Count Dracula caught outdoors on a sunny day, I began to feel almost comfortable.

Without the day's first intermediate sprint, I might have stayed almost comfortable. But as the sprint loomed, the pace quickened, elongating the peloton as it wound through a town centre and a series of 90-degree corners. Riders were starting to overtake me as I clunked into top gear, intent only on staying glued to the wheel in front. But the glue was coming unstuck, as the gap gradually stretched to a bike's length. I looked around in mild panic, hoping for some sort of joint offensive to tackle this invidious gap, but there was now only one man behind me, a young rider from the Malaysian national team, who duly responded by sprinting past me at full speed, closing the gap on his own. I clung on to his wheel for a few seconds, but then began to slip backwards. I was absolutely at full throttle, but it was the whiny rattle of full throttle on a clapped out 4-cylinder engine, an engine sorely mismatched against a collection of thoroughbred V8s.

At some point, a gap is no longer a gap; it grows into a handsome divide, a gulf, a chasm. The convoy of team vehicles – primarily Toyota pickup trucks in this part of the world – were now careering past me, with several drivers signalling that I should try to follow in their slipstream and thread my way back into the peloton. But I'd blown a gasket; my crankshaft had seized and my big end was possibly a write-off. More to the point, my heart was no longer in it.

The rearmost vehicle in a bike race is known as the broom wagon, usually a medium-sized bus or truck tasked to sweep up discarded riders and other detritus. The Tour of Thailand's broom wagon announced its presence behind me with a polite toot of its horn. But as I rolled along in the morning sunshine, it suddenly felt like a pleasant day for a bike ride – admittedly one at 25km/h (15.5mph) rather than race speed. I'd only been on the bike for an hour and a half. My engine might have been frazzled, but I wasn't feeling too terrible at this more sedate speed. I signalled for the truck to overtake, but the driver tooted again and pointed to my back. Ah. My race number – I was still technically part of the race; the broom wagon was obliged to follow behind. I stopped and removed the safety-pinned number, stowing it in my jersey pocket. The driver gave a wave and drove off, leaving me numberless and alone on a deserted back road somewhere in the north-east of Thailand.

I cycled down the lane at a tourist's pace, past rice fields and banana plantations, enjoying the rural scenery for the first time. After twenty minutes I came to a village. A group of roadside spectators cheered and waved red, white and blue Thai flags as I freewheeled along a gentle stretch of downhill. The loudest cheers came from several latecomers who'd missed the peloton hurtling through earlier and believed they might be witnessing the current race leader, the yellow-jersey elect. I continued on my countryside tour, reconnecting with the simple, calming sensations of just sitting on a bike, casually turning the pedals with no particular place to go. Actually, where was I going? I hadn't the faintest idea. I'd continued in much the same direction since parting company with the race, but now I remembered that the stage map had featured many loops and turns. There were no signposts and even if there were, I wouldn't be able to read them. Asking directions would be a pointless exercise – Thais invariably gave you the answer they thought you most wanted to hear.

Eventually I came to a T-junction where I spotted the brown and white livery of a Royal Thai police truck parked under some leafy shade. Two officers were leaning against the cab, taking a mid-morning cigarette break from the rigours of police duties. I explained in rudimentary Thai that I'd been separated from the race and needed to get to the stage finish. How far was it, I asked them. Forty kilometres? Fifty? 'Oh, it's at least 100 kilometres from here,' said the senior officer. In that case, I was definitely lost. 'No problem, no problem,' said the other policeman, smiling. 'We must to take you there.'

I slung my bike in the back of the truck and climbed into the cab. We sped off with a wheel spin and a cloud of dust, the piercing siren and flashing roof light not strictly necessary, but clearly a source of pleasure for the officers. Before too long we'd joined the rear of the race convoy. Team vehicles pulled over frantically to the side of the road, making way for what was obviously a grave emergency. More highly reckless driving then brought us within sight of the peloton. My police driver was keen to place me back in the race, perhaps even at the front. 'No, no. Never mind,' I said. 'It's better if I get out here, behind the race.' The driver, looking exasperated at my apparent lack of fighting spirit, mumbled something to his colleague about ungrateful foreigners. He pulled over and stopped abruptly, causing momentary chaos and several near collisions amongst the team cars behind. I retrieved my bike and thanked the officers for their kind assistance.

This time it was a flat 30km (19 miles) back along the main highway to the finish and the nearby race hotel: an easy hour or so to spin the legs and to reflect upon my all too brief career in the UCI Asia Tour. I hopped back on the bike. Two minutes later my front tyre blew out with a loud hiss. I had no spare. After a brief roadside hiatus, I managed to hitch a ride in another pickup truck, this time driven at implausibly low speeds by a local farmer, who was at pains to lecture me on why this really was not the right kind of weather for a bike ride.

Back at the hotel that evening, I received a visit from our team manager, former Thai national champion Wisut Kasiyaphat. As an up and coming young rider, he had signed with the Mapei Asia team, appearing destined to become the first Thai cyclist to race professionally in Europe. But when Mapei, the Italian building materials company – which had bankrolled the most iconic and successful pro team of the 1990s – withdrew the sponsorship coffers in 2002, Wisut's European ambitions also stalled. Known to most simply as 'The Wizard' and nowadays occupying an unofficial position as the godfather of Thai cycling, Wisut coaches the women's national track squad, promotes a raft of bike races and events, while still managing to spend enough hours in the saddle to maintain his killer sprint.

'I have good news for you. And I have bad news,' beamed The Wizard, loitering for a second or two in the teak-panelled hallway and then shuffling into the room. Supine on the pleasant horizontality of my bed – where I'd spent the entire afternoon – I slowly manoeuvred myself into a seated position.

'The good news,' said The Wiz, 'is the race commissaire let you start tomorrow. I explain him that you had serious mechanical problem.'

'And the bad news?' I asked, sensing that this sketch required a straight man.

'The bad news is the race commissaire let you start tomorrow,' punchlined The Wizard, displaying a knack for pithy, Wildean wit fairly uncommon around these parts.

By breakfast time the next morning, the race officials had overturned their decision, decreeing that in all matters of non-finishing and police-escort hitching riders, the UCI rulebook trumps any gestures of Buddhist compassion or community spirit. I would follow the remainder of the race from the passenger seat of our team Toyota. Still hanging in, however, was my fellow canon-fodder conscript, Marco, if now looking a little frayed around the edges and sounding less ebullient than a few days earlier. Battling mightily on the fourth day's lumpier *parcours*, he was finally jettisoned from the bunch with an hour left to race and spluttered over the finish line more than ten minutes in arrears. Several hours later, Marco decisively settled any debate over his continued participation in the Tour of Thailand by strolling into the hotel bar, seating himself comfortably and requesting from the bartender one bottle of wine (red), lightly chilled as per local custom, and one wine glass (large).

CHAPTER 13

Race Face and the God of Safety Pins

'Bluffing is a massive part of the Tour de France.'

Bradley Wiggins[185]

Liar's Poker, a game popularized by Wall Street traders, calls upon statistical reasoning, some knowledge of behavioural psychology and, as the name implies, an ability to lie convincingly. Bluffing and dissembling are useful skills in any form of poker, but they're critical in this version, since each player is dealt only one card. This 'card' is in fact typically a dollar bill, although any banknote with a serial number will suffice. To start the game, each player first checks his card's serial number. The *Investopedia* explains the rules as follows:

> If one player bids three 4s, he predicts that within all of the dollar serial numbers held by all players, there are at least three 4s. If the player's bluff is not called, the next player must either bid a higher frequency of any other digit (five 2s) or can bid a higher number at the same frequency level (three 6s).[186]

In *Liar's Poker*, Michael Lewis' revelatory tale of 1980s Wall Street excess, Salomon Brothers' CEO John Gutfreund challenges head bond trader John Meriwether to a game with a one million dollar stake. Meriwether, after pausing for a moment of reflection, replies: 'No, I'd rather play for real money. Ten million dollars.'[187]

The total prize pot for the 2001 Tour de France was a more modest 2.4 million euros. The overall win was worth 400,000 euros, a decent mark-up from the 20,000 francs awarded to Frenchman Maurice Garin, the winner of the inaugural 1903 Tour, if not quite in rarified bond-trader territory. But as the 2001 edition of the race headed up into the mountains for the first time, something odd was afoot. Midway through stage ten, Lance Armstrong, winner of the two previous tours, was hanging off the back of the thirty-man lead group of riders. 'Armstrong *en difficulté*,' chattered the French commentators. Big Tex certainly was not looking his usual indomitable self; instead, he was grimacing, rolling his head and pedalling a bike length or two adrift. Teammates Roberto Heras and José Luis Rubiera hovered attentively, chaperoning their dear leader.

Several riders on competing teams offered a supportive pat on the back, a small push even, as they rolled past the flagging Armstrong on their return from team-car sorties.

Rudy Pevenage, manager of the Deutsche Telekom team, following events from the team car, detected a whiff of subterfuge, not to mention a mighty bluff. As did Jan Ullrich, Telekom's star rider and Armstrong's perennial rival. But the Texan's histrionic gurning soon forced Telekom's hand: there was simply no way of knowing for sure what kind of legs Armstrong had up his sleeve that day. Pevenage ordered two of his Telekom riders to step up the pace at the front, to probe the slim possibility that Armstrong was not play-acting after all. US Postal's two Spaniards, Heras and Rubiera – neither of them apparently poker fans – started to fret. 'We wanted to go to the front,' said Rubiera. 'But he told us to keep calm, that everything was fine. I was amazed by how cold and detached he could be.'[188]

As the race approaches the 10 per cent lower ramps of L'Alpe d'Huez, the day's third and final climb, bluffer Armstrong finally reveals his cards. The two little Spaniards scuttle to the front, setting a fearsome uphill tempo that soon dispatches most of the lead group, including Ullrich's now exhausted teammates. Only Armstrong, Ullrich and the Kazakh cyclist, Andrei Kivilev, are able to hold the pace. In the defining moment of the race – if not the bike-racing decade – Armstrong, features once again locked in grim determination, then launches his own unanswerable attack. A short way up the road he turns his head and appears directly to eyeball Ullrich before returning to the task at hand, that of conquering the mountain, alone. Armstrong, whose two-minute winning margin at the summit of L'Alpe d'Huez paved the way for his third Tour win, later claimed to be merely searching for his two teammates, not staring down his German rival. Might there be a shred of truth to this? Since Lance's entire career in hindsight bears striking resemblance to a game of high-stakes poker played out over two decades, such claims are probably better taken with a hefty pinch of salt. 'We couldn't believe what we saw,' said Ullrich's teammate, Udo Bölts, after the L'Alpe d'Huez stage.[189] An understandable comment at the time, but one now wonders if the intended emphasis was more one of suspicion than admiration.

Miguel Indurain – the last man to dominate multiple Tours before Lance Armstrong – was another rider often accused of a cold and detached demeanour. But the big Spaniard – who always came across as extremely affable away from the bike – was perhaps just one more highly skilled exponent of the race face. 'Everybody tells me that I never look as if I'm suffering,' he said. 'But, when I watch videotapes of a race, I always remember the pain I had to endure.'

Of course, neither Indurain nor Armstrong was among the first to resort to such games of facial one-upmanship, but, according to Bradley

Wiggins, the Texan was one of the best. 'He was always talking to me on these climbs,' said Wiggins of their intimate, head-to-head contests in the mountain stages of the 2009 Tour.[190] 'His tactic was to talk to you as if you were his best friend. Then he'd slip the knife in your back. He was the master of that.' Not that Wiggo himself can claim complete innocence in this regard. In a recent BBC interview, he confessed to pulling a race face on his own teammate, Dave Zabriskie, in the same 2009 Tour: 'I was suffering but I pretended for one second that I wasn't. I looked at him as if I was just looking for a pint of milk on the top shelf in the supermarket.'[191]

While it's not often possible to win on duplicity and guile alone, if the legs aren't quite up to it, it's always good to have a 'Plan B'. In the 1904 Tour, the second edition of the race, Maurice Garin looked to have scored a second consecutive victory but was later stripped of his title, thus setting the precedent for many future strippings. The *Union Vélocipédique de France* that year disqualified a total of twelve riders for a variety of rule infractions, which included making use of the local train service during stages. 'The Tour de France is finished,' wrote a dejected Henri Desgrange afterwards. 'I'm afraid its second edition has been the last. We have reached the end of the Tour and we are disgusted, frustrated and discouraged.'[192] The Tour was even provisionally cancelled, but the show was back on the road by the following summer. 'We must continue the great moral crusade to clean up cycling and it is something only the Tour de France can achieve,' said a revitalized Desgrange, unfortunately overlooking the actual nature of so many of history's moral crusades.

Suffering of the racing kind is inevitable. It lays patiently in wait at the foot of every high mountain pass. It's submerged in the muddy puddles of a cobbled spring classic. But hiding the suffering to the best of your ability, maintaining the appropriate race face for as long as possible: this is the price of admission into The Great Pantheon. Mild to moderate pain must be stoically dismissed. Yes, the legs are going to hurt, but when did Epictetus ever complain? Only after attaining the suffersphere proper are any cracks allowed to show – and then only sparingly. And as we'd expect, a leaf through cycling's image archive confirms that The Great Pantheon of a generation or two ago – Coppi, Anquetil, Poulidor, Merckx – were most definitely on intimate boudoir terms with Lady Pain. But it's almost as if there's a degree of rawness, of explicitness in their suffering, that's somehow less evident today – *viz* the more controlled, more programmed, high-octane exertions of a Nibali or a Contador or a Froome. How can this be? Races were certainly longer a few decades ago. Pharmaceutical assistance has come on leaps and bounds since the days of *Pot Belge*, and the modern team buses are exponentially more comfortable. Perhaps it's nothing but an illusion: the romanticized, visceral appeal of grainy black and white footage versus our super pixelated plasma displays. Some will no doubt blame the presence of the ubiquitous power meters and race radios: Grand Tour contenders now climbing mountains on a pre-determined schedule; racing by computer algorithm, toeing the red line, and minimizing the chances of a spectacular blow-up, or, equally, a superhuman, Pantheonic feat.

Or maybe, despite our wall-sized, high-density televisions, we just can't see as clearly as before. If it's true, as Shakespeare observed, that the eyes are the windows to the soul, then ever since 1985, when Greg LeMond contested that year's Tour de France sporting what appeared to be a pair of blacked-out lab safety goggles, the soulful windows on the pro peloton have been mostly shuttered. LeMond's Oakley Eyeshades, which came in a variety of colours, covered at least half of his face. This outsize eyewear, especially when used in combination with another 1980s bikewear innovation, the brick-like Giro helmet, made LeMond look noticeably less like LeMond and more like a saddle-bound astronaut. In sports where full-face helmets are the norm – in motor racing, for example, or in many of the Winter Olympic events – spectators sometimes can feel a sense of disconnect between player and audience. When helmets were introduced for test cricketers in the early 1980s, similar objections were raised. That international test matches and cycling's Grand Tours were played out without a helmet in sight until fairly recently is a sobering thought indeed. Although high-fashion eyewear had become omnipresent in the pro peloton by the early 1990s, the UCI only mandated compulsory use of helmets as recently as 2004. LeMond's giant Oakleys did reduce in size over the years to more sensible proportions, but then along came Mario Cipollini and his preposterous collection of dayglo Briko eyewear.

With beards enjoying a recent resurgence in the pro peloton – and amongst the male population in general – some riders' faces are now disappearing from view altogether. In the 1990s, Italians Marco Pantani and Fabio Baldato tested the waters with their neatly trimmed goatees, but within the current peloton we have lumberjack lookalike Luca Paolini (reddish bristles to boot) and Laurens ten Dam, whose facial hair serves as a type of mucus magnet during more intense efforts. Sir Wiggins himself sports a more hirsute look these days, possibly in an effort to distance himself further from baby-cheeked Chris Froome. Ursine Aussie track sprinter Sean Eadie even went for a full Fidel Castro number during his career; an odd choice, aerodynamically speaking, in an event where milliseconds matter. A decade or so ago, when a shaved head and a tidy goatee were still a novel look, Brian Sieger, the inaugural beige-jersey winner, opted for one of each. Three different razors were thus required: scalp, beard and legs, with a colour-coding system to prevent mix-ups. Although Brian always made sure to allocate reasonable bathroom time for his girlfriend, she was encouraged not to linger unnecessarily – and not to touch his razors.

Facial disappearance is now all but complete in elite time-trial events. To reduce wind drag, today's alienesque helmets encase as much of the rider's head as possible; a mirrored or tinted visor then prevents us from taking any kind of peek inside his soul. The rider's mouth is still mostly visible, though, so the degree of suffering often has to be gauged by the precise angle of an out-hanging tongue. Of course, in a world championship time trial, unlike a road race, your rivals aren't usually close enough to observe any of your facial ticks or tells – the dead giveaways that you're on the verge of cracking. But your rivals' team managers are watching; watching closely, on the small TV screens in their team cars and will eagerly relay news of your impending implosion to your competitors via race radio. Henri Desgrange most probably would not approve.

Although some claim that recent innovations such as race radios have made pro-level events more predictable and less spontaneous, many others point out their utility as a vital safety feature, with the ability instantly to relay information about road and weather conditions – and accidents. Spaniard Pedro Horrillo, languishing off the back of the peloton during the eighth stage of the 2009 Giro, then fell 60m (197ft) into a ravine and suffered multiple injuries, including fractures to his legs and spine, as well as puncturing both lungs. Teammate and fellow laggard Jos Van Emden then spotted Horrilo's bike laying by the roadside: 'There was nobody else around and there was nothing behind the guard rail. In a reflex I called out over the radio that Pedro had probably fallen into the ravine.' A rescue operation was mounted and the Spaniard was quickly located. As Van Emden concluded: 'Pedro almost certainly owes his life to the race radio. So if you save the life of a man, the debate of abandoning it seems pretty absurd.'[193]

While the UCI recently moved to restrict the use of race radios in second and third tier events, it would seem that, in general terms, the technological genie is out of the bottle – and there's no going back. 'The advances in technology and human applications are just exploding,' an excitable Dave Brailsford told the *Guardian* in January 2015. 'I'm off to San Francisco in a couple of weeks and I've got my fingers in quite a few pies over there to get abreast of all the latest technologies and see how we can apply those to our sport.'[194] The Sky boss also waxed lyrical over how Chris Froome has been growing into the role of team leader:

The way, for example, in the Vuelta when he's suffering and he's riding back up and he's getting dropped again and he rides back up. He refused to give in and he refused to quit and he suffered and suffered and suffered. The riders see that, they see the suffering that he does, as it were. They respect him.[195]

Yet it's not only other team members who are able to scrutinize their leader's efforts. With so much useful data outpouring from his bike-mounted computer, Froome himself is able to keep close tabs at all times on his real-time suffer score. Indeed, Froome's evident fascination with his own handlebars accounts for much of his ungainly, face-down comportment on the bike, where he's all bobbing head and jutting elbows, placing him somewhere between giant grasshopper and Lycra-clad turkey. And if we don't know yet in which particular pies Mr Brailsford is getting his fingers sticky, then the real game-changer may come when the top contenders are able to hack into *other* riders' data during an *hors catégorie* climb, to see precisely how much hurt they're putting on their rivals.

The Three Noble Truths of Competition: suffering exists; suffering shall be minimized; suffering shall be concealed. A relatively straightforward *troika* this, at least on the face of it. Yet, as Buddhists will remind you, a proper understanding of complex canonical truths may require years, if not decades, of dedicated study. Of course, that physical suffering exists should be readily apparent by the time you're a lap or two into your first bicycle race, if not well before. A better appreciation of the need to minimize suffering logically should follow, but the hands-on skills necessary to achieve this can be only acquired through years of painstaking experience: how to ride in a crosswind; how to fake fatigue in a breakaway (*see* Armstrong, L. above); and the dark arts of slipstreaming, both sanctioned and non-sanctioned (other riders, motorbikes, team cars, articulated lorries and very occasionally helicopters), to cite a few examples. The novice rider likewise will not initially excel at the hiding of suffering. But through much dedication and practice, he will cultivate for himself a more neutral race face, progressing in due course towards a more exalted, stoical in-the-saddle status.

This second truth, the minimization of suffering, turns out to be much like an underground car park – many levels deeper and less navigable than meets the untrained eye. It claims jurisdiction over a far wider spectrum of events than those that simply unfold on the bike. The all-knowing deities of cycling, so we're led to believe, also monitor everything that goes down off the bike; all thoughts, words and actions before a race. The slightest deviation, the tiniest slip from an established, approved routine, is to usher in bad luck, misfortune and all-out calamity. Just as actors will go out of their way not to mention 'The Scottish Play', bike racers remain mindful to steer clear of certain topics before a race; indeed, some topics are best never spoken of at all.

Racing cyclists are a superstitious bunch. If so much of what we witness in pro cycling is best digested with a pinch of salt, then there are also many pros that remain wary not to spill any of the stuff, or to tempt misfortune in other ways. In *The Secret Race*, Tyler Hamilton relates how teammate Michael Sandstød did exactly that during a dinner at the Giro d'Italia. 'He purposely knocked over the salt shaker, then poured out the salt in his hand and tossed it all around, laughing, saying, 'It's just salt!'[196] The next day, Sandstød crashed on a descent, breaking eight ribs, one shoulder and puncturing a lung. Hamilton elected to start subsequent stages with a small vial of salt in his jersey pocket. 'Since there's so much we can't control, we do our best to make our own luck,' he later noted. 'Some riders cross themselves constantly, some whisper prayers on climbs, some tape holy medals to their handlebars. I tend to knock on wood a lot, or if there's no wood around, I use my head.'[197]

Drawing number '13' in a race is clearly not an ideal way to begin. In theory, this number could be skipped altogether, as with the thirteenth floor of buildings in many countries, but the sensible folk over at the UCI clearly have no time for such primitive twaddle. But at pro races, the unlucky rider will usually wear his race number upside-down. Number 113 may do likewise. Many riders will refrain from shaving on the morning of a race and crashes – both past and prospective – remain for the most part a taboo subject. A fairly rigid race-day routine is standard practice for many riders and this sense of familiarity can help to keep nerves under control. While some aspects – for example, adhering to the same pre-race meal – seem to make perfect sense, others, such as having to clip into the left pedal before the right, or wearing a lucky pair of socks, veer closer to psychological disorders. Multiple Tour champion Jacques Anquetil was famously superstitious. On a rest day at the 1964 Tour, he refused to leave his hotel room after the *France-Soir* newspaper reported that a fortune-teller had predicted Anquetil would die on or around the thirteenth day of the race. That evening, perhaps in an attempt to overcome his fears, he consumed several glasses of wine – and was promptly dropped on the first climb of the next day.

There is no 'one size fits all' with superstitions. We all get to choose our own form of madness. Steffen Rasch, a German masters racer, pays regular homage to The God of Small Safety Pins, one of the lesser-known sporting deities. I first met Steffen in a corner of a near-empty car park, where he was busy prepping bike and body for his weekly dose of suffering – a race, in other words. Our conversation was a little stilted: Steffen was not only a German, but also a former East German, where as a schoolboy he'd learnt Russian rather than English as a second language. The East German coaches, who would scour the nation's schools in search of potential Olympic talent, had directed a younger Steffen towards the cycling pool, where he later made the fringes of the national squad.

In the car park, Steffen was presently preoccupied with pinning his race number on to his jersey. Eight safety pins were required, he half-explained, half-demonstrated. Not seven, not nine. Eight. One at each corner, one at the mid-point of each side, with the head of each safety pin precisely aligned in a clockwise direction. To stray from this ritual was to invite certain disaster. To omit or misplace even one tiny pin would be no less irresponsible than using orange marmalade to glue a new set of tyres to your rims. I peered inside the opened boot of Steffen's estate car. Not for him the usual assortment of oily rags and decaying inner tubes. Assorted spare wheels were arranged tidily in alphabetical order, or some similar system. A selection of towels, sized and sorted according to specific function and perhaps also thread count, was close to hand. There was even some sort of hi-tech mobile bike bath for restoring any race machine back to pristine condition within minutes of crossing the finish line. Meanwhile, I needed somewhere to lean my own bike. Steffen, safety pins in hand, his race jersey laid out flat on the driver's seat, glanced up to gaze levelly at me. I decided that rubber on rubber was the only viable option here: a precarious equilibrium achieved by lightly grazing the rear tyre of my bike against one of the rear wheels of his car. No other point of contact permitted. Steffen grunted his acceptance and returned to his pinning duties. A curious combination this: quintessentially German applications of technik and methodik, and yet moderated with an appeal to a benevolent higher power.

An hour later, we were both sitting mid-peloton, working our way up the first climb of the race. Steffen was tight on my wheel, as the peloton's elastic began predictably to lengthen. I glanced around. Steffen's race face was duly impassive; impressively so, I thought, and not far off Wiggins' in-supermarket nonchalance. I naturally hoped mine was of a similar calibre, although I wasn't at all sure I'd survive any further stepping up of the pace. But as we neared the top of the climb, Steffen, now pedalling alongside me, began to chunter like a broken steam train. The loudest sound in the entire race was Steffen's laboured breathing. This sort of thing, while of course understandable, is frankly best avoided, just as your average poker player, as the stakes start to mount, is best served by not dropping his cards face up on the table, or acquiring an unexpectedly twitchy eyebrow. Not easy at all, this bluffing game. For the two-wheeled version of the game, not only will you require whispery quiet legs and a set of sphinx-like features. The ability to inhale in total silence while close to maximum heart rate will also come in handy.

CHAPTER 14

Veterans' Day

'Aging and ultimate death seem characteristic of all living organisms.'
Encyclopedia of Sports Medicine and Science[198]

'It isn't pretty.'
Joe Friel, 'The Aging Athlete'[199]

As those wily Buddhists are always keen to remind us, suffering – also known as *la souffranc*e, *la sofferenz*a, *el sufrimiento*, or, more simply, *dukkha* – is alas universal and inevitable. However, it nonetheless seems to thud on to our doorsteps parcelled and packaged in a surprising variety of ways. The basic starter package, that of plain vanilla *dukkha-dukkha*, is the suffering or pain inherent in birth, in growing old, and in falling sick and in death. It's the intrinsic *suffering of suffering* and few would have any real beef with that.

Team Sky's grand unified theory of marginal gains may help to explain much of its recent success, but for lesser bike racers suffering primarily from the inescapable truth of aging, for the herds of Sunday morning MAMILs, this particular aspect of the gospel according to Sir Dave is not the main preoccupation. Of course, one of the most enjoyable aspects of taking up a new sport – or returning to an old one – is that almost anyone can improve for a few years, can eke out their own marginal, and often super-marginal, gains. But for racers of advancing years, over yonder on the horizon lies a plateau – a monolithic, Ayers Rock-sized plateau – and after bumping along the top for a while, they will one day discover that they're all out of marginal gains and may soon find themselves sliding down the greasy slope of marginal declines.

The average age of all Tour de France winners is twenty-eight. Belgian Firmin Lambot, who won his second Tour in 1922 at the age of thirty-six, remains the oldest champion in the history of the race. Lambot claimed his first victory in 1919, the first Tour since the outbreak of World War I five years earlier forced the race to be suspended. The 1919 event was by all accounts a downbeat affair, with blown-up roads, sketchy logistics and a number of former contenders unable to compete on account of being deceased. Only ten riders managed to finish the 5,560km (3,455-mile) race. Similarly, the average age of recent world champion middle-

and long-distance runners is thirty. In 1988, Albert Hill of Kenya at thirty-one became the all-time oldest Olympic 1,500m winner. American Patrick McDonald won the 1920 hammer competition at the undignified age of forty-two and remains the oldest gold medallist in Olympic track and field history.

After the age of forty, our maximal aerobic capacity, or VO_2 max, begins a steady and inexorable decline. For untrained individuals, this drop can be as much as 10 per cent per decade, although a trained athlete, in conjunction with a balanced training programme, can limit the decline to around half this amount. Since VO_2 max is a direct measure of both the oxygen-pumping ability of the heart and the efficiency of the muscular system to utilize this oxygen, an experienced masters bike racer who can maintain a consistent level of performance over a period of years is therefore ahead of the game. Marginal gains for older riders are not entirely out of the question, of course, but they will most likely stem from a source other than increased aerobic capacity, such as improved muscular strength, or reduced bodyweight. And these days anyone who knows how to use a web browser has access to an array of options not strictly within the rules of the sport. If we have citizen dopers in our midst, then the existence of senior-citizen dopers also cannot be ruled out. A cursory skim of any amateur bike-racing forum reveals that it is not only the pros that resort to performance-enhancing pills and vials.

Age-related declines in aerobic capacity are still not fully understood, but the simple and well-known formula of how an athlete's maximum heart rate will decrease over time best illustrates how male-pattern hair loss and expanding love handles are by no means the gravest concerns facing the masters peloton. The accepted formula for estimating maximum heart rate (in beats per minute) is 220 minus age. A twenty-year-old might hit a heart rate of 200bpm during a finishing sprint, but the forty-year-old trying to keep pace alongside will top out somewhere around 180. Unless the older racer has a higher stroke volume (quantity of blood pumped per beat), he's unlikely to win the sprint on pure physical ability. He will instead try to win it either by employing superior tactics, or if that fails, his elbows.

It gets worse. Muscle mass also declines with age. But muscle does not just disappear. Recall that energy cannot be created or destroyed; it can only be changed from one form to another. And so all muscle inevitably comes around to the realization that it wants to become fat instead. Oh, those perfidious midlife transitions: an oft-discussed topic this, and hereby be forewarned that your own muscles will insist on being part of the debate. Our middle-aged muscle fibres, especially the so-called 'fast twitch' type II fibres that we recruit for short, explosive efforts, will callously retire themselves from active duty, and in increasing numbers each year, until by the age of eighty or so, we will have lost a full 50 per cent of our initial allotment. And since the overall decline will encompass loss of aerobic capacity *and* reduced muscle mass, the total age-related drop-off in endurance sport performance can be as much as 2 per cent per year. Perhaps a cleverer idea then is to abandon all attempts at physical excellence and refocus one's efforts instead on more cerebral pursuits. But bear in mind that the current world chess champion, Swede Magnus Carlsen, is only twenty-five and became a full grandmaster at the age of thirteen. In fact, none of the world's current top 100 players is over the age of 50. But finally, some better news: the average age of all Nobel Laureates is fifty-nine, a fifth of whom were aged seventy or over at the time of their award. There's still hope.

In the words of Joe Friel, revered author of the *Cyclist's Training Bible* and who remains a determined competitor despite recently embarking on his eighth decade:

> Let's say that one is 'old' over age 50. By this age it is usually apparent that an athlete is experiencing several life and performance altering physical changes: lower levels of testosterone, lost muscle mass, increased risk of osteopenia and osteoporosis (especially in cyclists and swimmers), an increased tendency for acid-base imbalance further contributing to bone and muscle loss, a greater propensity for weight gain, lost soft tissue elasticity with an increased likelihood of injury, reduced enzyme activity, less tolerance for heat, and more.[200]

It's not at all pretty, as Mr Friel concedes. His advice to long-in-the-tooth racers is to reduce their weekly training mileage, but to *increase* the overall intensity, with a minimum of a couple of high-power efforts per week. This goes against the observed norm, where greying members of the peloton – often with plenty of time on their hands – seem willing to go out and ride all day, every day, but at a gentler pace.

One notable drawback of cycling – or at least a drawback of cycling to the exclusion of all other physical exercise – is that the former utilizes only a few major muscle groups, all of which are located south of the waist. But lean muscle mass and bone density are best preserved through heavy resistance training and impact exercise. Riding a bike actually offers neither of the above. A 2011 study in *The Journal of Strength and Conditioning Research*[201] tracked changes in bone mineral density (BMD) of competitive masters cyclists over a seven-year period. Adjusted for age differences and other variables, the study found a consistent pattern of lower BMD in cyclists compared not only to other sporty types, but also relative to non-athletes. A sizeable majority of the tested cyclists also met the accepted criteria for osteopenia, the precursor of osteoporosis. The study concluded:

The high percentage of male master cyclists with low BMD, combined with a high risk for fracture from falls associated with competitive cycling, warrant attention among this population. Coaches and health professionals interacting with cyclists need to promote alternative exercise such as weight training, plyometrics, or other high-impact activity as a complement to cycle training.[202]

This is certainly something I've witnessed myself: older guys bumped off their bikes at relatively low speeds in run of the mill training spills, but then shattering hips and splintering elbows, where a more youthful cyclist would have simply bounced back up again.

At my most recent annual health check, the doc duly ticked off the relevant boxes, then inserted a brief comment to the effect that one of my heart valves had sprung a small leak. Fairly common at my age, he explained, no intervention required. And here came the dawning realization that I'd reached an age where 'at my age' was suddenly meaningful in a medical context. In any event, my mitral valve, one of a complement of four valves, was allowing a fraction of pumped blood volume to leak backwards into the main chamber, in a process known as valve regurgitation. No cause for concern, I was told, with the caveat that it might worsen over the longer term. (Leaks rarely improve over time: just ask the Dutch.) And this really should not have come as a surprise. If you can somehow locate a forty-something-year-old bicycle pump, you will find that it won't inflate your tyres anywhere near as effectively as a new one. And still no need for alarm, at least for anyone *not* preoccupied with transporting gallons of blood muscle-wards as fast as possible; not too alarming for most chess players, perhaps. But for we leaky, regurgitative MAMILs, the prospect of squaring up against riders half our age, with their showroom-condition tickers and their snugly airtight valves, is not an especially appealing one.

As author Terry Pratchett quipped: 'Inside every old person is a young person wondering what happened.'[203] It is indeed hard to fathom why anyone over the age of twelve would get excited about an upcoming birthday. No adults in their right mind look forward to taking the car in for its annual MOT test. Yet birthdays and MOTs represent essentially the same thing: an opportunity to take stock, certainly, but also confirmation of *temps perdu*, confirmation of further marginal declines in the state of chassis and bodywork. And the unwelcome but ever-present possibility of unexpectedly rapid wear and tear of critical parts, or even wholesale failure, and the attendant hefty repair bill. A solemn shaking of the head, a sharp intake of breath: 'Oof. It's gonna cost you, mate.'

Fortieth birthdays are meant to be a bit special, though. Life Begins At. Forty is the New. And so on. No matter that for most of human existence, forty-somethings have been considered pretty much past it, well over the hill. Upper Paleolithic man, despite the apparent excellence of his diet, had an average lifespan of only thirty-two years. Any sensible Paleo bloke thus would have opted for retirement sometime in his mid-twenties, perhaps looking forward to spending more time with his grandchildren and a few extra hours each week to potter contentedly in his allotment. But for the *homo modernicus*, forty marks the statistical halfway point and – even if it feels altogether too much effort to paint the town red – this milestone is at least worthy of commemoration. Of course, any Paleo man who had managed to evade woolly mammoths for long enough to clock up his fortieth year of hunter-gathering would have had good reason to celebrate. It's a great pity in this sense that the Paleolithic period lacked both a monarchy and telegrams, since the occasion of a fortieth Paleo birthday (no cake, of course) would merit a citation at least on a par to that bestowed on modern-day centenarians. And Paleo man evidently did his entire hunter-gathering on foot. There were of course no Paleo bicycles, as even later Paleo man predated the invention of the wheel by several thousand years. Again, this a shame: it seems that Paleo man, largely on account of his diet, had the potential to be pretty damn quick on a bike.

Joe Friel is also the co-author of *The Paleo Diet for Athletes* (Dr Loren Cordain, the modern high priest of Paleo, is the other co-author).[204] The book's central premise – and indeed the basis of the Paleo Diet – is that there has been no significant change in the human genome since the end of the Paleolithic Period, over 10,000 years ago. But our eating habits have changed dramatically, first with the advent of wide-scale agriculture and the domestication of farm animals, then through more recent breakthroughs such as Pot Noodles and TV dinners. Modern diets heavy in dairy, grains, processed oils and refined sugar, so the authors claim, will compromise our health and limit our athletic performance.

There's also much evidence to suggest that a decent diet is of increased importance for aging athletes. As the book's authors observe, 'an acidic diet due to a high consumption of cheese, grains and legumes escalates the loss of bone minerals and muscle mass'.[205] As we become ever more wizened and wrinkled, our bodies are unable to recover as quickly from exertion and also become less tolerant of sudden fluctuations in blood sugar levels. In the so-called 'recovery window' – the immediate aftermath of a high-intensity workout – creaky-kneed cyclists are therefore urged to make a habit of timely refuelling with the appropriate micro- and macronutrients. Much easier said than done, of course. It's during this critical recovery period that the urge for beer and pizza is typically at its strongest.

For much of his twenty-year pro career, American Chris Horner seemed hell-bent on rewriting the rulebook. Winner of the 2013 Vuelta a Espana just a few weeks shy of his forty-second birthday – the oldest Grand Tour winner in history – the Oregonian was also a self-professed junk-food addict. 'I could eat whatever I wanted,' said Horner. 'The junk food didn't affect my weight any if I wanted to stay 145 to 147 pounds.'[206] At the 2004 World Championships in Verona, Italy, Horner, after finding the team hotel seriously lacking in his customary cuisine, then 'hijacked' his team director's car for a trip to the local McDonald's. 'I was a little disappointed to see that the large Coke looked like a US medium, so I had to make up for the missing calories with a hot fudge sundae,' he recounted. But with his fortieth year looming, Horner decided to ditch the junk food – most of it – and focus on a healthier, faster diet. 'I added a lot of fruits and a few vegetables. I mean, seriously, let's not get carried away here.'

But Horner concedes that he probably would not have achieved his belated Grand Tour victory on his old daily staples of Cokes and chips, Snickers bars and Swiss Rolls. 'Changing my diet has been huge. There also comes a time in someone's career when you just want to do everything you can. You want to do the maximum sleep, the maximum recovery, the maximum diet,' he said in 2010. 'While training the diet is very manageable, but is more uncomfortable when there is no training. With several long periods off the bike last season because of injury, I spent a lot of time being uncomfortable, but it paid off, as I am a few pounds lighter and climbing better than ever.'[207]

To commemorate my own fortieth birthday, I booked a weekend getaway at the swanky Anantara Golden Triangle hotel. This upmarket hotel occupies a prized perch at the northernmost tip of Thailand, where the confluence of the Ruak and Mekong Rivers demarcates the national border with Myanmar to one side and sleepy Laos on the other. Picturesque? Why, yes indeed. It also presented the ideal surroundings for a spot of midlife contemplation. Not the place at all for raucous crowds or parties. It would be a quiet affair and just for the three of us: myself, my girlfriend Dee and my bike.

For the morning of my birthday, I set the alarm clock for 6am. By 6:15am, I was out of the door and on the bike. This ride, this groundbreaking first expedition of my fifth decade, would be necessarily something of a test run. My primary goal was to gather sufficient data, to ascertain which parts of me still functioned and which no longer did. The pedals were soon spinning free and easy in the slight chill of the postdawn, with the occasional motorbike or pickup truck burbling past me. I stole intermittent glances at the heart-rate read-out on my handlebars: all systems normal, as far as I could tell, even if my theoretical maximum was exactly one heartbeat lower than it had been a day earlier. Mindful of the fact that I was no longer nineteen years old – or even thirty-nine – I felt for once no need to push the system to its limits, which in itself was a source of relief. A steady tempo ride would suffice. The road hugged close to the placid waters of the Mekong. Lightly misted mountains rose abruptly from the Laos side, on the opposite river bank. On my first trip to the area, several years earlier, I'd experienced a lost-in-translation moment with my Thai guide, who had decried the local Burmese habit of tossing cabbages into the river. 'So dirty,' he'd complained. 'Very dirty peoples.' I didn't understand. Why dispose of perfectly good vegetables in this way? If what I'd read about the state of Myanmar's basket-case economy was correct, how could they afford to be so profligate? I finally worked out what he meant a few days later. *Garbage*. Of course.

A couple of hours and forty or so miles later, I coasted to a satisfied halt in the gravelled hotel forecourt. Forty miles for my fortieth: this felt about right – although therein lay a dangerous imperative. Sixty on my sixtieth? Eighty on my … No. Absolutely not. Far better not to establish this ride as some sort of precedent. Back in the hotel room, Dee was in the process of getting up, a nano-sized woman emerging sleepily from under thick folds of king-sized duvet, very much in the manner of someone enjoying a restful weekend break. I dived into the shower, hungry after my test ride and ready to wreak some damage on the hotel breakfast buffet.

After a quick rinse, I ceded the bathroom to my now wideawake girl-friend. A full-length hallway mirror offered me an opportunity for a routine leg inspection. The thighs were lesser in girth by an inch or so since their glorious heyday, I had to admit, while scrutinizing my half-naked reflection. Perhaps not exactly Chris Hoy-like in shape or form, yet there was still definite definition here. There was rippling. Even *ripped* might not be too much of a stretch. The thighs still had it. I experimented with various positions, twisting here and tensing there in order to extract maximum ripple effect.

'Back to front,' said a scrubbed, fluffy towel-clad Dee, emerging from the steamy interior of the bathroom.

'What's that?'

'Your underwear,' she said. 'You're wearing it back to front.'

And so I was. Here was chilling confirmation. The incontrovertible evidence. The thighs, the legs, the entire corporeal self might still have had it, but the mind – the mind was clearly on its way out. I registered straightaway that in all likelihood, a few decades from now, I would find it wholly impossible to dress myself, not as the result of any physical infirmity, but because I no longer even understood the concept of dress-ing, or indeed understood much of anything at all. This was the first ominous forewarning. The writing was on the mirror. I quickly corrected my wardrobe malfunction and we headed off for my birthday breakfast – a hearty, Paleolithic breakfast and yet one overshadowed by a sense of almost Proustian regret, the chastened realization that one's own under-pants could be so cruelly complicit in marking the passage of time.

A couple of years later, with my mental faculties still mostly intact, I travelled to Cape Town to compete in the Absa Cape Epic, a two-person team mountain-bike race held over eight gruelling days. Billed as one of the toughest events of its kind, it receives the top *hors catégorie* rating from the UCI. The world's best mountain bikers descend upon the Cape to contest the professional event, while another 2,000 assorted riders compete for the amateur categories – or in many cases simply aim to reach the finish line. My friend Hamish and I signed up for the masters race as Team Thailand, albeit a fairer-skinned Thai-based team than most were expecting.

A week before the Epic, I took part in the Cape Argus, the world's largest timed cycle sportive, with up to 35,000 riders participating each year in the single-day event. South Africans don't much care for half measures when it comes to bike races. The Argus, a 100km (62 miles) undulating and twisty route around the Cape peninsula, distinguished itself by being both the most sumptuously scenic and – with a gale blowing in off the southern Atlantic – the outright windiest morning I have ever spent on two wheels. The big buzz beforehand was that a mid-comeback Lance Armstrong was due to race in the Argus's pro event. A few days earlier, however, an inbound Lance had run into difficulties at Cape Town's international airport. What was he *on*? It turned out he was on the last page of his passport. South African immigration, in common with most nations, requires several blank passport pages, the absence of which will have you summarily returned to your country of origin. But what with Lance being *Lance*, calls were made and the former ex-retired now ex-champion made it to the Argus's start line on time.

The Cape Epic was established in 2004, when South African mountain biking was very much in its infancy. The Epic quickly grew to become one of the premier events on the worldwide race calendar, often being referred to as the Tour de France of mountain-bike racing. The Cape area boasts some of the best mountain biking terrain to be found anywhere and South Africa, after seeing a huge surge in the sport's popularity, now also has a number of world-class riders. The Epic course itself, which changes from year to year, winds its way around the Western Cape and showcases the wine-growing region's fantastic off-road trails and scenery. Leon Evans, who otherwise goes by the pseudonym of Dr Evil, is the man tasked with putting together the race route. So named for his predilection for toying with riders' fragile minds in addition to turning their legs to quivering jelly, a favoured Dr Evil tactic is to lead a weary pack of racers, after many hard hours in the saddle, to within sight of a finish line, only to send them back out again on a dastardly detour. Such detours might involve another half an hour of flailing through deep sand traps, or bouncing along the wooden sleepers of a disused railway track.

Considering that this edition of the Epic was my teammate Hamish's first major competitive event, our two-man Team Thailand performed creditably enough, finishing inside the top half of the masters field. A higher placing seemed on the cards earlier in the race, but that was before Hamish's aging knees suffered their crisis of loyalty. Knees that on certain days did play a useful role in Team Thailand's progress, helping their owner to negotiate rock-strewn trails and slippery sections of single-track. But on other days, the mutinous knees appeared to be on a different team, or at least demonstrably not on ours; precisely 50 per cent of Team Thailand's allotment of four knees was on a defiant work to rule, a go-slow and threatening a walkout. And indeed creaking and rattling much like a 1970s' British Leyland automobile.

Former world champion Christoph Sauser, a Swiss native and one half of the winning pro team in that year's Epic, made the valid point that the Epic is often markedly less epic for elite riders than it is for the amateurs. The pros typically storm through each day's stage in four to five hours. After a shower, a massage and lunch, they then have the entire afternoon to recover. In contrast, Hamish and I would roll across the finish line sometime around mid-afternoon, where – still caked with mud and dust – we would make a beeline for the nearest platefuls of calories on offer. But the Cape Epic becomes truly epic for the slowest riders in the race, those struggling each day to make the 5pm time cut – after which they have twelve hours or so off the bike before rousing their aching bodies to do it all over again. Burry Stander, Sauser's young South African teammate in their 2010 Epic victory, was tragically killed in early 2013 after being hit by a minibus taxi during a training ride.

Halfway through the Epic's final stage, Hamish and I were joined by a small group of competitors that included Joel Stransky. A former rugby international, Stransky had scored all of South Africa's fifteen points in their historic 1995 World Cup final win over New Zealand, the first World Cup in which a post-apartheid South Africa had been allowed to take part. Stransky was clearly enjoying every minute of his mountain-bike race and would offer real-time commentaries on how he was feeling on each climb. As the race finish approached, my adrenalin levels vetoed my common sense and I attacked off the front of the group, taking Hamish and both his knees with me and dropping the others. While your average bike racer would not much care for this kind of showboating – coming as it did at the end of a week-long race with absolutely nothing at stake – Stransky, a genuine sportsman, came up to me after the finish to offer a bone-crushing handshake. 'Great ride, mate,' he said. Yet this act of dropping the gracious Mr Stransky, who was a good 23kg (50lb) heavier than me and while halfway up a hill, amounted in the end to a singularly meaningless accomplishment. A no less ridiculous scenario might be the powerfully built Stransky punching the air in triumph after felling me in a flying rugby tackle.

CHAPTER 15

Young at Heart

'One night men go to bed and all is well with the world. Then they wake up and everything has gone to shit.'
Mike Carter, *Uneasy Rider: Travels Through a Mid-Life Crisis*[208]

'Deep down, I knew it was gone.'
Eddy Merckx (aged thirty-two)[209]

To paraphrase Benjamin Franklin, nothing is certain in life except the passing of time and the paying of taxes. Early Buddhists, who were not much bothered with filing their annual returns, might well have chosen to insert *dukkha* in lieu of taxes. But since filing one's tax return is in any case an experience largely indistinguishable from pure, unadulterated *dukkha*, the distinction is somewhat blurred.

Suffering, so we're told, will punctuate our lives as metronomically as the passing of time. But Buddhists are quick to point out that we humans are prone to heap suffering upon suffering. Not content to merely wallow in regular *dukkha dukkha*, we then seek out opportunities to suffer in more esoteric ways. The suffering of impermanence, or *viparinama-dukkha*, refers to the pain caused by trying to hold on to things in a world that is constantly changing. It gnaws steadily away at our inner selves, at the elementary human design flaw of being mostly clueless about what we really want out of life. It's the suffering of not getting what we want and of getting what we didn't want. And if we happen to get what we think we might have wanted, we find out we actually wanted something else instead. And so on. It's the suffering of repeatedly grabbing the wrong goody bag from life's lucky dip.

The photogenic Alpine town of St Johann in Tirol plays host every August to the World Masters Cycling Week: a proud testament to the passage of time, or a colourful deluge of 3,000 bike racers from over 50 countries, depending on your point of view. A sleepy market town for much of the year, St Johann occupies a narrow valley between the peaks of the Wilder Kaiser to the north and to the south, the famous Kitzbüheler Horn. The event's previous and slightly overblown title, the World Masters Championships, was discarded a few years ago. The UCI, organizers of the competing World Cycling Tour – the sport's *de facto* age group world championships – intervened to suggest a more appropriate billing for the popular Austrian event, for which anyone with a decent bicycle and sufficient birthdays behind them may be considered eligible.

The standard of racing at St Johann may not be strictly world class, but it's still classy enough. The men's thirty to thirty-nine field – the youngsters, the neo-masters of St Johann – are typically the speediest competitors on display throughout the week. The race categories then graduate upwards in five-year increments towards the lofty heights of the seventy to seventy-fours, the even loftier seventy-five to seventy-nines, and the casually open-ended eighty-plus. Strolling through the sun-dappled town centre, past patisserie and biergarten and dodging *grupettos* of freewheeling octogenarians astride their thoroughbred race machines, it was hard to know whether to be impressed or horrified by these superannuated *roulers*. Both, probably. But the key question on my mind: when was enough enough? Justifying to myself yet another week of suffering in the saddle was proving no simple matter. It had felt like a good idea at the time – several months earlier – and completing the online registration form had taken only a few suffer-free minutes. But now I was actually here and a creeping sense of impermanence was starting to run rings around my earlier steady resolve.

I was in my mid-forties. But these silvery-domed seventy-plus contenders, sipping their cappuccinos and shooting the breeze in the town's outdoor cafés: what in the name of Merckx were they thinking? These were not MAMILSs, not in any realistic sense. Their MAMIL sell-by date had long expired. These were more like BONIGUYs: Brazenly Old, Not Interested in Giving Up Yet. Or YAHWEHs: Young at Heart Wrinklies, Ever Hopeful. But either way, millions of their contemporaries across the globe were choosing, quite sensibly, to spend their weekends out on the golf course. Golf: the sporting solution for those who'd rather have fun. (The fresh air, the camaraderie, a light aerobic workout if desired, an electric buggy on standby if not.) A near perfect pastime for the oldies, dreamt up centuries ago in the heart of the Scottish lowlands and now played throughout the world, from the Amazon basin to the Himalayan highlands. Not entirely suffer-free, of course: there's always the angst of the sliced drive, the agony of mistimed putts. But this was merely suffering-lite and a far cry from what this grandfatherly peloton was going to endure over the next couple of hours. No shortage either of spectacular golf courses on offer right here in the North Tirol. Select from one of the following: a leisurely nine holes contested against a most pleasant Alpine backdrop, or an entire morning spent trying to haul your backside up that same backdrop. You takes your pick. Not that I'd ever attempted golf, but the time could well come when slinging a bag of clubs in the back of the car instead of a bike would make more sense. This much I could foresee – and yet I'd be heading defiantly against the current trend.

Recent data from the UK and the USA shows that middle-aged men, in ever-increasing numbers, are discarding their expensive golf clubs in favour of lightweight racing bikes. How to explain such acts of collective madness? Well, for a start, further data suggests that male competitiveness reaches a peak around the age of fifty and the singular pastime in which such testosterone-driven urges appear to reign most freely requires skin-tight Lycra, not a pair of silly trousers. And for those who have never had much aptitude or affinity for ball games, riding a bicycle requires only basic levels of motor coordination. The evident physical dangers of biking, however, clearly outweigh those of golf – where collisions between golf buggies are highly infrequent – and the data also suggests these physical risks increase with age. Fifty-four-year-old singer Bono required three metal plates and several rounds of surgery to repair fractures to his face and shoulder when he crashed his bike in New York's Central Park. A recent study of cycling accidents in Melbourne found that MAMILs 'were the road's most endangered species on a bicycle. Three-quarters of crash victims surveyed were men and about two-thirds of those men were aged 35 to 54'.[210]

In 2010, *The Economist* ran an article entitled 'The U-Bend of Life'.[211] It explains how our sense of happiness and well-being tends to follow a U-shaped curve as we journey through our lives: 'When people start out on adult life, they are, on average, pretty cheerful. Things go downhill from youth to middle age until they reach a nadir commonly known as the mid-life crisis.' Academics first suspected the existence of the existential U-bend in the early 1990s and numerous surveys have been conducted since. The Swiss, for example, sink to the bottom of their spotlessly clean U-bend at a comparatively early thirty-five, while Ukrainians become most miserable at sixty-two. But a global average of available data puts the nadir squarely at forty-six. The surprising claim made by *The Economist* was that as men (and women) progress into old age and start to lose all manner of things they once held dear – their looks, their car keys, their memories, their *minds* – they actually become happier.

The mid-life crisis, and in particular the male mid-life crisis, has been extensively documented, most often by contemplative males of a certain age. Journalist Peter Aspden, then aged forty-nine, noted in the *Financial Times* that the male mid-life demographic seemed to attract more than its share of 'ridicule, contempt or sarcastic admonishment'. Aspden also lamented how the aspirations of his peer group were so often the target of derision, 'whether it is planning barbecues in the comfort zone of his back garden or plotting to climb Everest. He is a bore or a charlatan ... .'[212] Perhaps it's precisely this latter attribute that helps to account for the recent emergence in society of the middle-aged bike racer: these startling metamorphoses whereby previously drab and lacklustre MAMs re-emerge into the sunlight as gloriously technicolour MAMILs.

On the unseasonably wet weekend of my forty-sixth birthday, I travelled to a Thai bike race with a friend. We agreed to share the driving. He'd volunteered for the outward route; I then grabbed the keys for the three-hour return leg. Approaching a moderate incline, I gave the pickup truck some right foot. The rear-wheel drive Toyota responded by spinning on the rain-slicked surface, a neat demi-pirouette that left us facing from whence we came: a stylish manoeuvre, a staple of movie stuntmen. But the truck, like a puppy on ice, was in no mind to stop. It began a slow-mo slide towards the road's edge, a move that despite my having zero say in the matter, felt briefly manageable – and might have been, were it not for the ditch that lay beyond the tarmac border. The truck lurched over to starboard and with our rudely shifted perpendicular, we came to rest with a thud. A quick exchange established that neither of us was hurt and we clambered out through the driver-side window as if from a submarine's top hatch – the passenger-side door was now effectively the lower deck. The truck was in rather poorer health: glass shattered; metal dented and deformed. As for the bikes, wrenched from their mountings behind the cab, it was not a fair contest. A pair of carbon race machines versus a truck. I had to avert my eyes.

On the venerable theme of non-bicycle specific suffering, it's those Germans who again more than prove their worth. Could there be a more definitive symptom of our times – of the *Zeitgeist* – than the German *Weltschmerz*? Translated literally as 'world pain', it's a corollary of the similarly commonplace condition of *Ichschmerz*, or self-dissatisfaction. In the words of linguist Arika Okrent, *Weltschmerz* is the sadness brought on by the realization that the world is not how you wish it to be: 'It's more emotional than pessimism, and more painful than ennui.'[213] But the Germans don't stop there – not by a long shot. There's *Zeitkrankheit*, or 'illness of the times', a generic term for whatever's damaging the mindset or preoccupations of a particular era. *Lebensmüdigkeit* translates as simple despair or world-weariness, while *Zivilisationskrankheit*, or 'civilization sickness', is simply any malady caused by the modern world: stress, sleeplessness, eating disorders, and so on. The German people evidently possess an astonishingly broad vocabulary to convey the fundamental condition of feeling fed up. Germanic or not, as we tiptoe towards our half centuries, we may well find ourselves afflicted with one or two of the above. But fretting about the overall state of the world is usually not a productive way to pass the time, especially when the state of oneself, the general condition of *ich*, is not all it might be.

Age is a relative concept. At an impressionable eighteen years old, I'd entered into a complicated relationship with the owner of my local bike shop. Not in any romantic sense of course, because bike-obsessed teenagers position themselves by default well out of the running for anything of that ilk. In *The Meaning of Liff*, Douglas Adams and John Lloyd's glossary of redefined place names, Wormelow Tump is a small village in Herefordshire no longer, but instead describes 'any seventeen-year-old who doesn't know about anything at all other than bicycle gears'.[214] I'd been ruthlessly outed as a Tump by my two younger brothers; serious allegations that at first I denied, but as the damning evidence mounted, my denials took on a decidedly Nixonian tone. The bike shop owner, Alan, had ridden many years earlier for the Great Britain Olympic team and was now staging a comeback at the unlikely age of forty-one. With both of us maybe a decade or so off our primes – in opposite directions – we found ourselves closely matched in local time trials. I naturally hoped to beat Alan each week, maintaining all the while a healthy respect for his *palmares*. And since I had no *palmares* to speak of, Alan certainly did his utmost not to get beaten by the young upstart. In hindsight, I might have prevailed more often had he not sold me a bike frame several inches too large, on the pretext that I'd soon grow into it. In fairness he wasn't to know that I'd top out – indeed, had already topped out – at 1.68m (5ft 6in), about the average height of the average tricksy Colombian climber – and arguably too the average height of the Jewish climber, although for reasons detailed elsewhere, the data points are far fewer. But I had to wonder why Alan, at his advanced age, was even bothering to turn up each week. Surely the pipe and slippers were beckoning?

But the times they have a-changed: forty-year-olds now routinely win Grand Tour stages – and in the lean yet freshly nutrient-rich form of Chris Horner, they have even won Grand Tours outright. In September 2014, the inimitable Jens Voigt boosted the spirits of forty-somethings worldwide by breaking the world hour record at the age of forty-three. In his final ride as a professional before easing into a well-earned retirement, Jens commanded silence from his legs one last time. As he told reporters: 'The first ten minutes I could not feel the pedals and thought, "Oh, this is easy!"'[215] For the lanky German, who for years had demonstrated not only an immense capacity for suffering, but also an apparent ability to enjoy it, it was time to sign off with a declaration that he was, after all, not immortal: '33 years of cycling behind me. This was my last attempt. I'm in so much pain. But what a way to retire.'[216]

For my part, I'd arrived at my mid-forties with a clearer appreciation of why the pipe and slippers could wait. It was indeed all relative. In early 2014, several months before Jens Voigt took his last bow in the limelight, Robert Marchand, a 102-year old Frenchman, beat his own age-group world hour record, cycling 26.93km (16.7 miles) at the Saint-Quentin-en-Yvelines velodrome. This comfortably eclipsed the time of 24.25km (15 miles) he'd set two years earlier in Aigle, Switzerland. 'I'm not playing at being a champion,' said the diminutive, white-haired Marchand, after his first record ride. 'I just wanted to do something for my 100th birthday.' He continued: 'I haven't cycled on a track for 80 years. ... I prefer cycling outside but that is impossible at the moment. I don't want to catch the flu. So I am short on training.'[217] Doctors cautioned Marchand not to raise his heart rate above 110, a warning he claimed to have heeded for the most part, on regular training rides that he restricted to a maximum distance of 100km (62 miles). 'There is no point going overboard,' he explained. 'I want to keep cycling for some time yet.' And it turns out there's even a Nietzschean, *Wille zur Macht* element underpinning his late success. 'I've never abused anything. I don't smoke, I never drank much,' he said. 'The only thing I did in excess was work. I retired at 89 years old.'[218]

In October 2014, Matthias Brändle, an Austrian on the Swiss IAM pro team, and Marchand's junior by roughly seventy-eight years, powered to a new non-age restricted world hour record of 51.85km (32.22 miles), improving on Voigt's time set only a month earlier. Perhaps it was the case that the young hopefuls of the seventy-plus peloton saw the likes of Marchand as sufficient justification to keep the pedals turning – turning for another two, three or twenty-five more seasons.

Not too many centenarians get to attempt – let alone break – a world record, if only for the simple reason that not many of us get to be centenarians. My own grandfather had appeared to be sailing effortlessly towards his century when the Great Umpire in the Sky abruptly raised his index finger. Ninety-nine and a half – a decent innings and the basis for our family's assumption that subsequent generations would proceed to rack up even higher scores: no obvious reason why 125 or so would be out of range for me. Several years ago, my father, with a certain degree of trepidation, was on final approach for his seventieth birthday. An avid sports news junkie, he then made the discovery that the existing world centenarian 100m athletics record was a shade under thirty seconds. Following a satisfying Sunday lunch, Dad strolled out to the front gate one afternoon, levered it open (rusty hinge, minor squeak), checked his watch, then proceeded at a fairly brisk pace to the end of the street – roughly 100m (328ft) away. Inspired and only slightly breathless on his return, he announced that he'd stopped the clock several seconds inside the current world record. He lit a cigar in celebration. A thirty-year training plan then transpired, founded upon the well-established principle of not peaking too early. The sheer lack of any need to improve encompassed the plan's simplistic beauty. Not getting any slower would suffice.

On a more recent outing, the annual occasion of Dad's week-long winter tennis series against his closest friend, the two, now both aged seventy-seven, checked into the same Miami Beach hotel that had for a decade or more hosted this important event in the sporting calendar. But they managed to play zero tennis and instead spent much time comparing their various aches and ailments. It then transpired that neither of them had bothered to bring their tennis gear. They had settled for a no-tennis tennis week. The veteran competitors were feeling more sprightly after

a few days of extended beach time, of soothing their muscles in the sub-
tropical warmth, but the idea of having to rent equipment just to play a
set or two when they could be sunbathing or eating: it all felt like too
much effort. The times were still a-changing.

Turning up for a bike week without my bike: not something I'd previously considered, but the idea was not entirely lacking in merit. It was
early afternoon in St Johann and my bike and I were stationed kerbside.
From my vantage point behind the start line, elbows resting lightly on the
handlebars – a brazen attempt at insouciance – I watched as the men's
thirty to thirty-nine peloton animated itself into life. Shoe cleats snapping
into pedals, squeals of brake on rim, the smooth click (or mashing grind)
of shifting gears and, as usual, no shortage of oaths and expletives, in a
selection of dialects, as the fool alongside or in front of you does something you really hoped he wouldn't. The whirring mass of these thirty
to thirty-nines, this self-contained, homogenous unit, then swept along
the finishing straight and disappeared around a bend, which left a little
under twenty minutes until the start of the over-forties race.

St Johann attracts bikers from several dozen different countries, but
each year Germans and Italians turn up in sufficient numbers to form a
clear working majority – unremarkable, I suppose, given the event's location. And this particular year the Italian caucus was most in evidence.
The Italians were easy to spot. A perfectly turned-out rider atop a
perfectly set-up bike: an Italian, 99 per cent guaranteed. Someone with
perhaps the outer seams of his jersey and shorts not perfectly aligned,
or a few flecks of road grime defiling his frame's chain stays: any other
nationality. It simply must be the case that every male Italian of primary
school age receives several years of mandatory instruction on proper
bicycling deportment: *Essenziale per Biciclette: A– / B+ Young Gianni
shows promise but still lacks application at times.*

And now here were the forty-plus Italians, milling languidly around the
start area. None of them even looked middle-aged. (Note to self: read up
on Mediterranean diet.) Most of them looked as if they'd arrived directly
from the Giro d'Italia, perhaps riding in support of compatriot Michele
Scarponi, who earlier that summer had scored an impressive double; the
pink jersey for overall and red for the points classification. Everywhere
on display: lean Italian torsos; smooth, olive-skinned Italian limbs; and
regulation Fabien Cancellera haircuts – tousled, shoulder length, calcu-
latedly scruffy. This Cancellera-style haircut is in fact a secret weapon:
when just enough hair extends from the rear of the helmet, a swift hour
or so on the bike – in a cunning circumvention of UCI rules – wind-
sculpts the rider's *coiffure* into an altogether more aerodynamic arrange-
ment. The Swiss suits might be swarming all over helmet design, but they
have not yet thought to regulate hairstyles. Finally, the sheer amount of
gold jewellery on display from the Italian contingent looked sufficient to

count as a possible weight impediment once the serious climbing began, but for some reason none of them appeared overly concerned.

As our race got under way, the Italians' degree of collective concern – or lack of it – was soon confirmed as correctly calibrated for the circumstances. They had everything under control. Not too much of an exaggeration then, a quarter-way through the first lap, to suggest that they had it all sewn up. As with the world road-race championships, where riders on competing trade teams join forces under the colours of one national flag, so all Italians in this race were set on a common goal: an Italian win, ideally accompanied by a couple more Italians on the podium. Italians would decide when the key break would get away; Italians would decide who got into that break. (Hint: mostly Italians.) For us non-Italians, well, the scenery wasn't too shabby.

I was racing with a German teammate, Fidel. An ex-ski racer, Fidel hailed from the Bavarian spa town of Bad Wörishofen, where his family owned a hotel – a hotel in which I was currently a guest. The hotel's heyday had been way back in the 1970s, but more recently had suffered a slide in visitor numbers. To my surprise, many of that week's modest tally of guests were elderly Israelis. The comfortable rooms were large and airy, with extensive use made of pinewood: a sort of 1970s porn movie ambience, for those who were into that sort of thing. The Bavarian food, though, was outstanding. I now had a better appreciation of why Fidel, for a bike racer, was quite solidly built. A comprehensive jump start was also generally required to activate Fidel into racing mode. Coffee alone was not sufficient. A double espresso or two – merely a warm-up for the main event, which in Fidel's case was several cans of Red Bull. This sickly, semi-viscous substance, which for the uninitiated looks and tastes like jet fuel, is the most successful Thai–Austrian joint venture in history and an absolute godsend for those bored by the quotidian chore of sleeping. At a supermarket on the outskirts of St Johann, a Red Bull sales promotion took the form of several metre-high *faux* cans situated by the main entrance. Delight soon turned to disappointment when Fidel realized that the oversized cans were completely empty, but he posed for a photograph anyway.

Aside from the many Italians, the problem in the St Johann race was that they had installed the hills, two of them, in the wrong place. They featured too early in each lap, followed by a long flat run into the finish. This would be a sprinter's race. (An Italian sprinter's race.) We climbers dutifully attempted to eke out some sort of margin as we hit the climbs on each lap, but the climbs, in addition to being misplaced, were also not long enough. The gapped sprinters would invariably regain contact on the way down – gravity-friendly Fidel hurtling past me at 85km/h (53mph), giant-slaloming his way through the twists and turns of the forested Alpine descent.

The Italians, unquietly confident that all was well on track, began to strike up their own intra-peloton dialogues and commentaries. I had no idea what they were saying, but it sounded pretty good. Italian is, of course, the *lingua franca* of the peloton. Accompanied by just the right amount of gesticulation, medallion tugging and minor adjustment of sunglasses, it makes one ashamed to speak English in the presence of Italians. And as a means of remonstration (of which in a peloton there is always much), a phrase such as *'Ehi, cosa diavolo stai facendo?'* sounds vastly more impressive and carries far more authority than 'Oi mate, watch where you're going.' The Italians' other clear advantage, as if they needed one, was to do with surnames. Coppi, Bettini, Nibali; these names are undoubtedly *faster* than their Anglo-Saxon equivalents. Harris, Simpson, Wiggins – all worthy British world champions, true enough, but would they have gone even quicker had their names ended with a vowel? Probably. Not to labour the point, but 'Ferrari' is the third most popular surname in Italy. Imagine signing on at an important race as a Ferrari. What would that be worth? A greater confidence boost surely than scrawling your initials next to Austin, Morris or Hillman. The only part of the race not going to plan for the Italians was the weather. Afternoon temperatures were creeping into the low thirties Celsius and cries of *'agua, agua!'* filled the air on each climb, as clusters of roadside helpers frantically attempted to direct fresh water bottles to the intended recipients. Water? Oh, come off it, chaps. Hot? This was nothing. This barely made it over the minimum threshold of *la sofferenza*. Any Thai racers (of which there were none) would still be wearing their arm-warmers.

The race trophies were duly presented to a selection of beaming, well-coiffed Italians later that evening in St Johann's main square. Former Tour de France winner Jan Ullrich held centre stage, shaking hands and handing over silverware, looking fit and healthy after his years of absence from the sport. And on the subject of things silver (and shaky), a number of weathered-looking BONIGUYs and YAHWEHs – at least those who had not opted for an early night with a mug of hot cocoa – were also present to collect awards from their races earlier that day.

Eddy Merckx achieved his five Tour de France victories between the ages of twenty-four and twenty-nine. He finished sixth in his swan-song Tour in 1977, announcing his retirement early the following year. Merckx said of his final season in the peloton: 'I prepared well and actually won my first big race, the Tour of the Mediterranean. But as soon as more racing came along my body failed. I kept catching colds and other minor illnesses, where before I rarely did.'[219] There was to be no twilight masters racing for this former champion. And by his mid-fifties, the former Cannibal had ballooned to outsize proportions. Merckx, who turned seventy in 2015, has since shed some of his excess bulk and is these days even occasionally spotted out on his bike. In *The Cannibal*,

Daniel Friebe's biography of Merckx, he writes how Guillaume Michiels – who would later become Merckx's masseur – once told the cycling-obsessed eight-year-old that his backside was too fat.[220] A couple of years later, a ten-year-old Eddy then informed a local pro rider of his ambition to be a bike racer. 'In five years,' the pro responded, 'you won't get through that door, Eddy, given how fat you are.' So when a decade later, Merckx was selected to take part in the 1964 Tokyo Olympic Games, he made sure to issue Michiels a pointed reminder. 'You said my backside was too fat – and now I'm going to the Olympic Games.'[221] That Merckx was driven by a powerful fear of failure seems beyond dispute, but can we dismiss out of hand the terrible stigma of being labelled a fatty?

As Will Fotheringham notes, 'the greats of cycling rarely make exits that are truly worthy of their careers.'[222] Eddy Merckx was no exception. By the mid-1970s, he was clearly suffering from serious burnout: the only question was how much of it was physical and how much was mental. Mostly the latter kind, believed his compatriot Jean-Luc Vandenbroucke. When questioned about former rivals Raymond Poulidor and Joop Zootemelk, both of whom raced into their forties, Merckx responded that there 'wasn't the pressure on them to make their presence felt all the time. If you are number one, you end your career more quickly'.[223] It seemed entirely natural that Merckx would later strike up a friendship with Lance Armstrong. As Fotheringham explains, the American, like Merckx, 'was unmatched in the depth of his competitive obsession, or *rage de vaincre*, as the French term it'.[224]

In late 2014, Lance Armstrong, now forty-three years old, told French magazine *L'édition du soir* that he now rides his bike only about once a week. Following a charity bike ride in California – one of the few events in which he's permitted to take part – Armstrong admitted that he'd struggled with the 125km (75-mile) *parcours*. 'The route was very hard, much more than I expected. I'm not used to these kinds of climbs,' he confessed. 'I don't train that much anymore, not more than once a week. And when I do a bike ride, it's mostly on my mountain bike.'[225] Armstrong, who has climbed L'Alpe d'Huez in under thirty-eight minutes, a feat equalled only by Marco Pantani, continued his poker-faced explanation: 'In Austin, where I live, the routes are not as hilly.' If Mr Armstrong were not subject to a lifetime competition ban, one suspects he still might enjoy a weekend hobby of ripping apart masters races. But he also admitted that he no longer even follows pro cycling results. Following the suicide of his close friend Robin Williams, Armstrong spoke of his renewed determination to live life to the full – a life mostly off the bike.

'When you've devoted your life to a sport, you realize at the end of your career that you've missed a lot,' he said. 'I've been trying to make up for lost time, either with my children or by travelling.'[226] For Lance Armstrong, for the foreseeable future, it is definitely not all about the bike.

CHAPTER 16

Too Close to the Sun

I'm not the first or the last
to stand on a hillock,
watching the man she married
prove to the world
he's a total, utter, absolute, Grade A pillock.

'Mrs Icarus', Carol Ann Duffy, Poet Laureate[227]

A general rule of thumb for anyone wanting to bike up mountains as fast as possible is that your weight in pounds, divided by your height in inches, should come to a value below 2.0. Almost all the specialist climbers in the pro ranks score below this figure. Bradley Wiggins hit the magic 2.0 right on the nail to win the 2012 Tour de France. But to achieve this, he'd shed a tenth of his previous racing weight and in doing so dropped to a precarious 5 per cent body fat – a wholly unsustainable number and potentially dangerous for anyone not under close medical supervision. The black and white photographs of a shirtless Wiggo taken at the 2012 Tour by Team Sky photographer Scott Mitchell are of the genre typically used to launch famine relief appeals. But there was much method in Wiggins' leanness: while 1kg (2.2lb) weight loss might be worth only a handful of seconds over a fast sixty minutes on the flat, it can save you a minute or more on a one-hour climb. In the former instance, wind resistance is the major impediment to speed, but when the road starts to curl upwards, the force of gravity takes over as the principal foe. The classified climbs of a Tour de France typically amount to over 20,000m (65,620ft) of vertical elevation, which in turn translate to twenty hours or so of uphill pedalling. Shedding 7kg (15lb) of bodyweight, as Wiggins achieved before his 2012 Tour victory, might have saved him a full two hours over the duration of the three-week race, assuming of course that he achieved his weight loss without any concomitant loss of power. At the 2006 Tour, a heavier, track-specialist Bradley had finished down in 121st place, three and a half hours off the podium. Of course, slimming down (or stretching yourself on a rack) in order to sneak inside the critical 2.0 marker is no guarantee that you will then go out and climb like a mountain goat. Too many other factors are involved, with the key always being to drop weight without losing power. But this does help to explain why a flatland powerhouse like Fabian Cancellera, who registers around

2.5 before sitting down to his high-energy breakfast, tends not to worry too much about racing over the high Alpine passes.

Nicolas, one of our local powerhouses, was looking unhappy. The source of his unhappiness was a podium photograph from a recent stage race, where Nic – he of the refurbished, but once again superfast legs – had finished third, behind two pro riders. Nic felt no shame at all at finishing a few bike lengths behind a couple of younger guys who raced for a living, but he was mortified at the evident difference in size between the third-place finisher and the podium's two top spots. 'I'm huge,' complained Nic. 'I am enormous.' I stared at him across his kitchen table. This was a man in superb physical shape. His arms and legs were road maps of muscle, vein and sinew. If he was concealing a spare pound or two of body fat anywhere, I had no idea where it might be.

I studied the photograph again. And yet he did have a point. While Nic was clearly leaned out, well-conditioned and race-ready, in comparison to the pros he did look a bit, well, wider. He was taking up more three-dimensional space than the other two, for whom 'wraith-like mutants' would be an unkind, if not entirely inaccurate, description. The issue was that Nic had already shed a dozen or so pounds over the past year, a statistic that made his wife rather uncomfortable. If he lost any more weight, she cautioned, she'd have to reconsider sleeping in the same bed as him. This illustrates another very useful rule of thumb for bike racing. The very point at which your wife or girlfriend throws up her hands in revulsion at your emaciated figure is probably also the point where you're ready to go and cause major mayhem on the hills. And if you can live for a while without basking in the glow of female approval and affection, you can at least expect a few nods of appreciation from other gaunt, sunken-eyed climbers admiring your skeletal form.

Anyone who has wandered around the start or finish area of a pro bike race will know how surprisingly flimsy, how anatomically insubstantial, many of the top riders appear in the flesh. After Alberto Contador (1.985, give or take) crashed on the tenth stage of the 2014 Tour de France, TV coverage showed him receiving medical attention on his injured (later found to be fractured) right leg. When Contador's team boss, the now bulked-up Bjarne Riis, then puts a consoling arm around his Spanish rider, it looks as if he's sheltering a particularly delicate and rare species of exotic bird. Contador's body mass index (BMI) hovers around 19, a shade above the 18.5 cut-off that the World Health Organization officially defines as 'underweight'. But if you walked past Alberto on your local high street, you still may feel the urge to buy him a steak sandwich. Likewise Christian Meier, the ORICA GreenEDGE *domestique*, who isn't a specialist climber and nor is he especially skinny in pro terms. But when he spent a few weeks training with us in Chiang Mai – and was inevitably pestered each day for group photos – it was surprising how little space he took up in the resulting images. Drafting behind Christian during the rides also offered very little in the way of wind protection, but it was worth it just to marvel at the sublime smoothness of his pedal stroke.

Yet for the occasional exception, the issue of weight loss appears superfluous to requirements, no more critical for racing success than a bike-mounted kickstand or a shopping basket. Pavol Križan is one of these physics-defying mould-breakers; weighing in at roughly 110kg (243lb), he has a marked tendency to break other things too. No one meeting Pavol for the first time ever mistakes him for a pro. A pro bike rider that is, since many instead surmise, after a quick visual appraisal, that he might just be a champion bodybuilder – which he often times is, at least on those days when the Herculean Slovakian is not out riding his bike. But in addition to a prodigious talent for lifting heavy slabs of lead, Pavol has found time to win several national cycling championships on the road and the track. There's a photograph of an immense, skin-suited Pavol, stationary on a start ramp and you have to look at least twice to ascertain that there is actually a bicycle underneath him. Pavol himself – all bulging arms, legs and torso – fills the entire frame and from a frontal perspective his skinny time-trial bike is barely even visible. Pavol weighs over twice as much as our group's smallest rider, a diminutive Thai. Whenever they pedal side by side, I'm reminded of one of those kitsch father and son Hallmark cards.

The phenomenon of Pavol is possibly best explained as a corollary of Malcolm Gladwell's 10,000-hour maxim. While Pavol certainly puts in the requisite training hours, he's also what the same author would term an 'outlier', or someone who does not fit into our normal understanding of achievement. Gladwell's book *Outliers* deals with those who 'operate at the extreme outer edge of what is statistically plausible'.[228] This aptly sums up the impression Pavol generally leaves with those he competes against. Whether any one individual may in fact be 'larger than life' remains of course a metaphysical imponderable, one best left to a roomful of Zen monks and a pot of jasmine tea. But Pavol's philosophy of living large certainly gets him closer than most. He'll polish off a 200km (124-mile) solo training ride on a sudden whim. To honour such feats of endurance, one of South-east Asia's principal transnational highways has been unofficially renamed Route Pavol. But, as the sun goes down and with the day's training done and dusted, Pavol will dutifully shoulder his nocturnal responsibilities, those of ambassador at large for cultural affairs; responsibilities that require some seriously in-depth knowledge of local nightspots and which are often only completed to his satisfaction once the sun is coming up again.

It goes without saying that you wouldn't buy a used bike from Pavol. Another friend, another Jon, a sensible man for the most part, bought a used bike from Pavol. Not so long after, he found himself the not so proud owner of a handful of sundered carbon-frame tubes. It's not that Pavol abuses his bikes; it's just that he subjects them daily to a degree of torsional stress testing for which they were not designed. Pavol's flat-line power output is on a par with – or better than – many world-class pros, although admittedly not many of them weigh 110kg. The one thing you never wish to hear on a group ride is when a mildly bored Pavol intones 'now I make *looong peloton*', and from his helmsman's vantage point starts to pull harder, and then harder, slowly elongating the groaning line of sufferees until the elastic inevitably snaps. Pavol in full flight is nothing less than a bicycling B-52: battle-ready, road-blasting Rolling Thunder. First the ominous low rumble in the distance, then the deafening, earth-shaking fly-past, laying waste to all that lies in his path. It goes without saying that you would not want to get in a breakaway with Pavol.

The first time I raced against Pavol, I got in a breakaway with him. Like many breakaways, it was not planned that way, but at the halfway point of Thailand's annual Queen's Cup road race, I found myself in a lucky escape with the thunderous Slovak and a skinny climber from Colorado. Pavol, clearly in charitable mood, was doing most of the grunt work upfront, while the American and I fought for the prime real estate close to his back wheel. Thus positioned – using Pavol's body as a massive bulwark against the wind – the turbofan roar became a subdued whoosh, my peripheral vision blurred and time itself seemed to warp as if in the eye of a tornado, as if in the churn of Pavol's wake we'd discovered a black hole from which no light or sound could escape.

But as the day warmed and the road, at times, began to point skywards, even Pavol started to tire and the Coloradan and I had to assist more with pacing duties. On the steeper inclines, I heard Pavol behind me, swearing colourfully yet incomprehensibly in Slovakian. As the final kilometre approached, an insanely steep climb up to a hilltop temple, I let myself drift behind the others. The three of us were technically in separate races – the over-forties category for me, the thirty-plus for my companions – even if we had started as an ensemble. This therefore meant that I could take it nice and steady up the last hill, safe in the knowledge that a victory was in the bag. As it turned out, I was almost reduced to crawling the last 100m (328ft) over the line, dragging my bike behind me. After two hours of riding in the company of a B-52, my legs had gone missing in action. No point here in asking the legs to shut up, because in an act of gross irresponsibility, the legs had already left the building. Thirty seconds before I lurched across the finish line, Pavol had won his race. With the finish in sight – and still neck and neck with the slightly built American – Pavol briefly inverted the laws of gravity, engaged full thrust on each of his eight engines and, roaring something valedictory in Slovakian, blasted his bike over the line.

I spent the next half an hour laying close by the finish line in a virtual fugue state; not much interested in moving or speaking. This proved much to the annoyance of Captain Lex, who, in addition to having won the elite race, was eager to promote his new bike clothing business and was occupied presently with setting up a rack of assorted cycle gear right on top of my inert form.

'Can't you just move out the way a bit?' asked an exasperated Lex. I signalled in the negative by twitching an eyebrow. But I needed to recover, and quickly, because we still had the trophy ceremony to contend with. As I well knew by now, prize-giving awards at Thai races often last longer than the races themselves. For events held under Royal patronage, such as the Queen's Cup, this was especially true. The Thais do love a parade. And with such ceremonies generally held under the full glare of the midday sun, a well thought-out ceremony strategy is essential. Hydration and calorie intake, optimal position with respect to both the sun and the huge, over-amped PA systems: all have to be carefully worked out ahead of time. Depleting all of your energy during the race itself is never advisable: a decent reserve needs to be retained for the prize ceremony. In a cruel and unusual twist on standard ceremony protocol, the trophies this time were to be awarded before the speeches from the roster of local dignitaries. Myself, Lex, Pavol and a young Thai, winner of the junior event, climbed on to the beribboned stage. For ten minutes, we stood there blinking and sweating in the blinding sunshine. After sweating some more and after paying our respects to a life-size portrait of Her Majesty, we received our awards from a man in a sharply pressed white naval uniform who possibly wasn't a genuine sailor. The legs, unsteady and aquiver from the morning's exertions, almost crumpled under me as I took custody of my substantial trophy. Then the speeches began.

Pavol, alongside me, beaming for the local press photographers, appeared to be dangling his trophy from his little finger. Even the spindly Thai junior was bearing up well. But as the third or fourth speech got under way, I started to feel distinctly unwell, swaying dizzily from side to side. For a moment I thought I might be suffering an attack of *Kreislaufzusammenbruch*, which is German for 'circulatory collapse', but which can also denote feeling a bit woozy. My trophy, seemingly hewn from solid gold or plutonium, was threatening to rip my arms from their sockets. I'd trained well enough for the race itself, but I was clearly not in any sort of condition for the rigours of the prize ceremony. I could count upon sufficient endurance to tackle either one of these events on a given day, but not both together. I reckoned I would need to hit the gym well in advance of next year's race, establishing a regular routine of dead lifts and bench presses. Perhaps Pavol could coach me.

For the majority of cyclists – us non-outliers – shedding excess weight is a relatively suffer-free way to improve performance on the bike. Passing up a doughnut or an ice-cream sundae may cause a momentary pang of regret, but you will feel that much more virtuous on the next climb. While it's not necessary (or advisable) to remould your silhouette into one of Contadorian svelteness, paying attention to your daily calorie ledger will pay dividends over time. Cyclists at all levels typically will know their best time on a given climb – particularly since the advent of Strava and other apps – and improving a personal best is always a strong motivator, even for those who don't race. As Michael Hutchison, winner of fifty national titles has noted, 'all that bike riders want to do is compete. Deep down, there is an urge to measure, and the more accurately you can measure, the more people you can measure yourself against, and the greater the span of time over which you can do it, the better.'[229]

Those cyclists most inclined to record intricate details of their performance nowadays can go and buy themselves a power meter. A relatively new (and therefore prohibitively expensive) cycling gadget, it attaches to a bike's cranks or pedals and gives a real-time reading on the actual force applied through them. Unlike a heart-rate monitor, which offers a more approximate guide to how much effort you're expending, the power meter informs you in no uncertain terms of the exact wattage propelling the bike forward at any given time. All else being equal, wattage then translates directly into speed. It can be an invaluable training tool and in a race setting also functions as a kind of fuel-economy gauge, similar to that of a car. You start a race with only so much fuel in the tank and the power meter helps to raise your awareness of wasting precious watts, of making ill-judged efforts and attacks that will only lead you towards fuel starvation later in the race.

Of course, the general idea behind training with a power meter is to see your wattage improve over time. But, as the saying goes, an amateur cyclist buying a power meter is like hiring an accountant to tell you how poor you are. After training with a power meter for several months, my own numbers were resolutely staying put. Instead of amassing more muscular wealth, my legs were starting to feel a little impoverished. 'A power meter is like a tattoo,' says Michael Hutchison. 'You get one when you're young and naive, and when you think you'll be young forever. Then when you get older, you start to really, really regret it.'[230]

My relationship with the bike-specific strain gauge was clearly under some strain. A perfect inverse relationship if you like: the less physical strain felt by the power meter, the more mental strain felt by me. 'As you get wrinklier and wrinklier, your power output gets wrinklier and wrinklier as well,' says Hutchison. 'And you can't hide from it. You can't look at it in a steamed-up bathroom mirror and kid yourself that those downward plunging power traces are laughter lines. Nothing is that funny.'[231]

I was also discovering that power meters can be peerless masters of passive-aggressive behaviour – or rather they are mistresses, since mine was undoubtedly female. Although restricted to a basic digital read-out, they are able to manipulate the numbers to construct an ongoing sub-narrative with which to grind you down. And to top it off, my power mistress was German in origin. 'Oh. You have only 290 watts. This is the best you can do,' observed the power *mätresse* at the conclusion of some morning hill intervals. In truth, I'd been expecting more from myself too, but I refused to apologize to this autocratic bike-*Frau*. I asked former French champion Peter Pouly, nowadays living the celebrity lifestyle of Thailand's premier cycling expat, to cast an expert eye over my training data. 'No, no. It is too hard,' he told me. 'You are pushing too hard. You must train more easy if you want to race fast.' He was right of course and merely repeating advice I'd first heard decades ago. But training slower to race faster seemed an incredibly hard habit to acquire.

Another relatively pain-free method of boosting performance for the amateur racer is to upgrade equipment. With the exorbitant prices of bike gear these days, some suffering must be reckoned with in due course, but credit card damage feels less immediate than other varieties of pain. I already owned several bikes, but bike owners rarely, if ever, reach a steady-state equilibrium. A manic flurry of energy goes into acquiring the perfect bike, which gives the owner a brief respite until a better bike becomes available, usually within the next six to twelve months. According to the website of The Velominati, the self-professed 'Keepers of the Cog', the optimal number of bikes to own is *n+1*, where *n* is the number of bikes owned.[232] But there's also an important corollary, *s–1*, where *s* is the number of bikes that will cause your wife or partner to leave you. Nicolas, who had augmented his stock of bikes at the same time as dropping below his spouse-approved weight limit, was clearly skating on thin marital ice. And some are more adept than others at juggling these large numbers. Ian, another cycling expat in Thailand, has a collection of around twenty bikes at his home, for which he has built an extension – known to all as the Chiang Mai Bike Museum – in which to store them. As he only ever rides two or three of these bikes, he clearly derives most of his pleasure from being a collector. It is perhaps with precisely this collector's mindset that Ian recently acquired his fourth wife, although I should clarify that the previous three wives are no longer part of his collection. And as I'm no great mathematician, I have no idea where this leaves him in terms of *n+1* or *s–1*.

Numbers alone don't tell the whole story. Jeff, aka the Second Fastest Jew in Thailand, firmly believes that a daily outing on the bike is the secret to enduring marital bliss. As Jeff is now several decades into his first marriage at a time when many of his peers are hitched to third, fourth or *nth* wives, his theory is worth a listen. The *modus operandi* here is to argue, bicker and generally annoy the hell out of other riders in the group until all pent-up aggression dissolves and only a serene calmness remains. It seems to work. After each ride, Jeff goes home to spend pleasant afternoons and evenings in the company of his wife and his four dogs. That said, the sight of two men on bicycles, both into their fifties and if not quite coming to blows, then coming to *elbows* over where to stop for a coffee, is always faintly ridiculous.

When not upgrading complete bikes, there are faster wheels and faster components to consider. Or even faster clothing. Evaluating whether one particular jersey might be quicker than another might sound odd to the non-obsessive cyclist, but up at the sharp end of bike racing, Team Sky employs several people to do exactly that. It is the irresistible lure of free speed. Not that any of this technology is ever free in a monetary sense: far from it. But with a group of athletes already pushed to their limits in training, anything that offers incremental speed without adding more exertion and pain is welcome. It is the classic theory of marginal gains, as popularized by Dave Brailsford. I pointed out to Nicolas that the science of marginal gains might not be all that relevant when he was already winning his races so easily. He agreed with me wholeheartedly, then went back to researching a new helmet, one that claimed to save twenty seconds over an hour. Beating up the amateurs was no longer of much interest. Nic had his sights set on the pros. In preparation for a forthcoming time trial where he would face top competition, he joked that he might set up a tent near the start line and camp there for a few weeks in order to familiarize himself with the course. At least I hoped he was joking.

Nic then arrived at one race having left his shoes at home. A couple of weeks later, it was his helmet. In my experience at least, such forgetfulness can be an early warning of a mind not entirely at ease. I'd learnt more about Nic's diagnosis of post-traumatic stress disorder, the result of having been almost sliced in half by a Taliban bomb several years prior. But in racing terms at least, Nic was still on his way up, heading towards the sun, while I was on my return to earth. But on any voyage to the sun, you should always know when it's time to turn around. I told Nic I might have to rename him 'Nicarus', and resolved to keep an eye on his carbon-fibre wings.

For my part, I had been racing consistently for four years without taking any extended breaks. There is little concept of a race season in this part of the world; the climate allows for year-round racing. With events sprinkled at random across the calendar, it was easy to find yourself training more or less the whole year round. Pro riders might be on their bikes for eleven and a half months each year, but they have no real intention of being race-fit for the entire time. It's considered a major challenge for a rider to be in peak condition for both the Giro d'Italia and the Tour de France, held a couple of months apart. The so-called Triple Crown of Cycling – winning all three Grand Tours in the same calendar year – has never been achieved. Eddy Merckx got closer than anyone, winning four consecutive Grand Tours in 1972–3. But to date, only thirty-nine riders in total have managed even to finish all three Grand Tours in one season, and of those only Raphaël Géminiani and Gastone Nencini achieved top-ten positions each time. Lance Armstrong's career was notably built around only one race each year, which for many commentators, even before his fall from grace, rendered any comparison with Merckx wholly untenable.

Modern coaching manuals emphasize the need for 'periodization' in any rider's racing and training programme, where peak fitness might be targeted no more than two or three times per year. Veteran coach Joe Friel describes periodization as the gradual increase of physical workload and stress over a defined period. While there are many ways to skin this particular cat, Friel believes that the key element is to adopt 'a methodical system for gradual physical adaptation that avoids exhaustion'.[233] Friel notes that another critical aspect of periodization is that 'the closer in time you get to the race, the more like the race your workouts must become'.

In places such as Europe or North America, with their well-defined racing seasons, incorporating periodization into a training regimen is straightforward. Riders take post-season breaks, then build up stamina on the bike through the winter and spring. High-intensity conditioning is used selectively before big races. But in Asia, in lieu of a race season, I had aimed instead for a decent level of fitness throughout the year. Not only does this increase the risk of eventual burnout, but it also prevents an athlete from properly peaking. While this strategy won't leave you in last position in a race, you're also unlikely to win too many. Even for elite riders, the lengthening pro season is a cause for concern. In the past, European pros rarely needed to venture too far from their heartland. But with new events from as far afield as Australia, the Middle East and the Far East now on the race calendar, a critical task for any team boss is to determine exactly where and when he wants each of his riders to be in peak condition.

Nicolas was proving the worth of periodization. With a well-focused approach to training, he was now able to predict a fitness peak to within about fifteen minutes on a particular Sunday morning, three months in the future. But I now had the sense of having been at a high simmer for too long, which also implied that when the time came to go for the boil, to apply full gas, I would no longer have much in reserve. I had also started berating and abusing my teammates during races. In my defence, some of the abuse was justified, as some came from mountain biking or triathlon backgrounds and the idea of a team strategy for any given event – other than agreeing to wear the same-coloured jerseys – was an alien concept. But when you are only racing for trophies or toffees, bawling out your friends is never acceptable.

An incident from the somewhat misnamed Tour of Friendship a few years earlier remained fresh in my mind. Into the melting pot of the race's final stage had been tossed too many combustible ingredients: a pair of excitable Frenchmen; a feisty Australian called Billy the Greek; and a working majority from the Excellent Noodles racing team, none of whom was much over 1.5m (5ft) tall, but whose owner was rumoured to have powerful Mafia connections in the Philippines. We were all fatigued and overheating, and the stage had been dull: a flat section of motorway circling the outskirts of Bangkok. At some point words were exchanged, then elbows, then half the peloton was on the deck, including a police motorbike outrider. No one was seriously hurt, but thousands of pounds worth of top-end bike had been summarily crumpled. It really wasn't worth it. When a section of the pro peloton goes down *en masse*, it's appalling enough – if grimly compelling TV viewing – but when we MAMILs inflict it upon ourselves, it's plain ridiculous and you begin to wish you had spent the week lounging on a beach instead.

In my final outing of the year, a mountain-bike race sponsored by Thai brewery Singha, I triumphed by accident in the masters event. I'd lined up for the race in a sulky mood, weary in anticipation of the suffering to follow and irritated first by the blazing-hot mid-afternoon start time, then by an unexpected cloudburst a few minutes earlier that had transformed a section of the course into a quagmire of muddy superglue. The gun went off and the field swarmed forward, jockeying for position ahead of a section of narrow single track. I hazarded a guess that Aesop's Fables had not been translated into Thai, or at least that the Thais – bounding hares each one of them – had not got around to reading them, thus remaining unwary of potential tortoises lurking in their midst. Suffice to say that Thais are not good at pacing themselves during a race. Possibly this relates to the Buddhist mindset and the emphasis on the present moment over an uncertain, unknowable future. In any case, I was content to drift to the back, resolving to complete at least a lap or two before quitting and driving home. Halfway through the first lap, my steely resolve to throw in the towel stiffened when my only water bottle catapulted out of its cage on a descent and disappeared into some thick undergrowth.

By the end of the second lap, though, I had caught up with several exhausted hares and it felt appropriate at least to complete another lap or two, to honour a well-managed event and to add a veneer of respectability to my efforts. Likewise, on the third and fourth laps, with the flagging hares now dropping more like flies in front of me, it suddenly seemed a singularly churlish, childish act to climb off my bike mid-race. And so it continued, until the final lap and to the finish line, which I crossed without at first realizing that I'd gone and tortoised the whole field. The legs were still willing, even if the spirit was weak. It was a classic beige-jersey performance, one for the archives.

CHAPTER 17

Bahamontes' Ghost

'*One of the symptoms of an approaching nervous breakdown is the belief that one's work is terribly important.*'

Bertrand Russell[234]

The 2,565m (8,415ft) Doi Inthanon is Thailand's tallest mountain. It's one of numerous high peaks in the Shan Hills, which extend all the way through Burma and Yunnan Province in south-western China up towards the Himalayas. Set yourself on a north-western trajectory from the Shan Hills and with sufficient gusto in your walking boots, you will find yourself eventually in the shadow of the world's highest mountains. Inthanon, while twice as high as anything on offer in the Scottish Highlands, is still only a little over half the height of Mont Blanc, Europe's most commanding peak. But anyone who has ever ridden a bike up to the summit of Inthanon tends to concede that it's high enough.

Several years ago, the cycling community of Chomtong, the small town that sits a few clicks from the base of Inthanon, decided that it might be fun to host an annual bike event, which would start at the town's main Buddhist temple and finish, 47km (29 miles) and 2,200 vertical metres (7,218ft) later, on top of the mountain. Although classified as a race, with the usual tableful of beribboned trophies on offer for the quickest finishers, the event was more realistically a *sportive*, with the vast majority of entrants simply looking for a fun yet challenging day out on the bike. The first event attracted a few hundred riders and was deemed a resounding success. The following year saw twice as many riders again lining up to tackle the mountain's vertiginous slopes. In February 2014, around 2,000 cyclists descended upon downtown Chomtong for what had evolved rapidly into a northern Thai one-day classic: an alternative 'Hell of the North' if you like, albeit one shifted half a dozen time zones to the east and tilted skywards.

The original 'Hell of the North', this most classic of cycling's one-day classics, has of course inspired numerous breathless documentaries over the years. It was Dutchman Theo de Rooij who perhaps best described the conflicted emotions of a man who submits himself each year to cobblestoned purgatory in the Paris–Roubaix slugfest: 'You're working like an animal, you don't have time to piss, you wet your pants,' a mud-splattered de Rooij vented from the back of his team car after abandoning the 1985 edition of the race. 'You're riding in mud like this, you're slipping; it's a piece of shit.'[235] A journalist then asked de Rooij if he would consider ever riding it again. 'Sure,' he said. 'It's the most beautiful race in the world!' The sentiments of the predominantly amateur field that attempts to climb Inthanon each year are not so different. Several hours of pain and misery are seen as a fair exchange for the sense of accomplishment that awaits them at the summit. Plus the views are exceptional and the absence of mud and rain is all but guaranteed.

At my first attempt on Inthanon, I managed a fourth place, edging up to third the following year. By 2012, however, this high-altitude *sportive* was definitively on the map, drawing not only a much larger field, but also a higher quality one. Riders travelled from Europe to take part. A Singapore-based professional squad was in town for a training camp and was also on the start list. And there was Peter Pouly, the former French mountain-bike champion and current holder of the amateur world record on the iconic climb of L'Alpe d'Huez. Pouly, who had taken a lengthy sabbatical from the sport, was back in the saddle after relocating to Thailand a few years earlier. In his first event on the comeback trail, the week-long Tour of North Thailand, Pouly had not achieved anything too special on the bike, but instead focused his efforts on one of the prettier podium girls, a local lass who soon after was to be unveiled as the next Mrs Pouly. So with the higher calibre of the field and the fact that my training hadn't yielded the same improvements as previous years, I doubted I could get near the 'toffee table' this time up the hill.

Pouly, the overwhelming favourite for the Inthanon winner's trophy, had started riding mountain bikes at the age of fifteen and turned professional two years later. He spent a total of eleven years in the pro ranks, winning two national mountain-bike championships and several junior French titles. He came out of early retirement in 2010 and has since won the Haute Route *sportive* – a punishing eight-day slog across the Alps – three times in a row. But during his build-up for the Athens Olympics in 2002, a twenty-five year-old Peter had been handed a two-year suspension from the French authorities after testing positive for corticosteroids. Recall that when American Jonathan Vaughters was refused a steroid treatment for a nasty wasp string, he was forced to abandon the Tour de France. But Pouly, who likewise took a bug sting to the eye during a race, was prescribed an anti-inflammatory that later showed up in a urine test. 'The Federation turned their back on me right away,' claimed Pouly, who never tested positive at any other time during his career. 'It made me realize that in competition there are no friends,' he added. 'At that time I hated cycling. I hated the whole world but what could I do? I left cycling because I got tired of people but finally I realized that it's the same everywhere.'

Pouly, in addition to continuing to compete at elite level, also runs regular training camps for aspiring racers. By supervising so many amateur bikers and seeing how they train, he knows exactly where so many of us make elementary mistakes. 'We all think that to be better we must suffer in training,' he explains. 'It is at that moment that we take the wrong road. We must learn to train without wanting to test or reassure ourselves and to store that energy for the race.'

A month before the gruelling Haute Route event, one of Pouly's protégés sent him an email: 'I want to train hard, I am ready to suffer,' he wrote. Pouly's simple reply was a request for patience – and reassurance there would be more than enough suffering during the event itself. As Peter explained, 'the last three weeks before the Haute Route were really hard because I was already feeling really great and I tried to restrain myself from pushing it – and that was truly difficult.' Pouly also oversees the training of another up and coming local rider, a rider who sometimes fails to heed the wisdom of his elders. 'He is young and won't train at a slower speed than me. He always wants to do the same intensity as me. At the end of the Haute Route he wasn't as strong as when he was training.'

When I caught up with Peter recently, I asked what had made him want to race again after his years away from the circuit. 'I don't really know,' he confessed. 'Maybe I realized how I lucky am to have these gifts: two strong legs and one big heart.' Peter is much enjoying his new lease of life as one of the top riders on the Asian circuit and of course holds the current record for the Inthanon climb – a record he's been chipping modest chunks off every year. But I was curious to know whether he thought his supernatural climbing speed was sourced from anywhere other than his legs and his heart. 'Truly I think I never feel suffering,' he told me. 'How much we're able to push comes from how we control our mind. On race day you can push yourself more than you expect.' Well, of course: the head and the legs, *la tête et les jambes*. Pouly's compatriot Henri Desgrange would have no issue with this.

But to *never* feel any suffering? Mr Eddy Merckx for one might disagree. I asked Peter how he prepared himself mentally when he knew in advance that a race would be especially hard. He replied:

> I learned from experience and it takes time. To win the race you have to make yourself *available to suffering*, you have to want to win more than the others. It feels like a big bullet inside you – a bullet to fire at the right time. It gets hard to control the bullet when we're super fit, but you can't show your power to other riders. Let everyone fire their bullets and when you decide to go, your mind must be 100 per cent in the moment. But when you win you don't feel the pain.

The vast majority of local riders at the Inthanon race were not intending to fire any bullets on their way up the mountain. They were only there for the *craic*, as they like to say in Irish pubs throughout Thailand. Maintaining a safe distance from us sixty or so swivel-eyed, leg-shaven serious racers, these local *randonneurs*, almost all of them on mountain bikes, would enjoy a far more leisurely pedal up to the summit, hopping off the bike whenever the urge struck, for a coffee, a meal, a photograph or two, or even a roadside nap. If they had to push their machines uphill for the excruciating last 6km (3.7 miles), then *mai pen rai* as they would say: 'never mind'. They had the whole day to do it.

It is debatable how even a bicycle tourist's tempo might qualify as leisurely on gradients that often register in excess of 20 per cent. Six kilometres from the summit, the road exits a forested section and arrives at a narrow ridge. A pair of pagodas, built in honour of Thailand's reigning king and queen, ease into view further along the ridge. With the legs deadened from at least a couple of hours of relentless climbing and the lower-oxygen air rattling in the lungs, the gold-tipped pagodas portend a 1km (0.6-mile) stretch of road that climbs 200m (656ft) vertically – and most likely a heartfelt desire to avoid biking up mountains ever again. European road engineers would no doubt construct a more sensible series of hairpin bends to snake their way up any similarly extreme chunk of topography, indeed the kind of hairpins shown on postcards of L'Alpe d'Huez and other Alpine passes. But in Thailand, with its more restricted budgets and its more *ad hoc* approach to motoring safety, the road simply forges straight ahead, ramping up relentlessly towards the heavens. There's usually a distinct smell of burning in the air: either the singed brake pads of vehicles creeping back down the mountain, or the seared lungs of cyclists painfully grinding their way up.

After a nominal round of early morning speeches, the race got under way. With several flattish and even downhill runs on Inthanon's lower slopes, staying in contact with the leaders – and the drafting bonus this offered – was paramount. Near to the head of the pack, Peter Pouly twiddled away on a low gear, possibly stifling the occasional yawn. It rarely took long for the lead group to be whittled down to a dozen or so riders, and so it was this time.

The decisive, deadly missile was launched as we reached a wooded section of false flat, close to the halfway point. Captain Lex, the missile launcher, was up out of his saddle, his long cranks and even longer Dutch legs combining into a lethal windmill of pedalling force. Lex had started racing in his early teens and had simply carried on racing, in classic Forrest Gump fashion, for the next thirty-five years. Periodization plans didn't appear to be part of Lex's armoury, unless of course he was working with periods of roughly half a century. 'One per cent a day,' Lex had told me when we first met. This was what a cyclist loses in performance for each day he doesn't train, he explained. It sounded a reasonable enough number. Stay off the bike for an entire week and you're a whole

7 per cent slower – well in excess of any race-deciding margin. Ignore the bike for a whole month and you might as well sell the damn thing and take up lawn bowls instead. And it's only to be expected that this process of deterioration seems to exacerbate with advancing age. It's the fickleness of fitness: another example of the impermanence of all things. For many objects of great worth, we've long since learnt how to conserve their value, how to safely store their benefits over the longer term, but for the moment at least, there is no way of doing this for physical fitness.

During the 2014 Tour of Langkawi, *Cycling Weekly* magazine ran a feature on Lex, then a few months shy of his forty-eighth birthday and undisputed holder of the title of the oldest rider in the pro peloton. 'I'm still riding and they are in the car,' Lex boasted to his interviewer.'[236] He went on to note how many of his contemporaries – for a while he'd been a teammate of Bjarne Riis – were now team managers. In addition to his trademark killer attack, the so-called 'Lexocet' missile, Lex featured elsewhere in cycling's glossary of terms. To get 'lexxed' on a tough climb was to have Lex ride up alongside you, invariably a casual, unruffled Lex who had already ridden to the top and had freewheeled back down before U-turning to repeat the climb. Getting 'lexxed' was usually demoralizing enough; a 'double-lexxing' might cause you to question your entire future in the sport. On flatter training rides, Lex sometimes went by his alternative moniker, the 'Lexington Avenue Express'. Lex was indeed part of the cycling lexicon.

As fine an example of racing longevity as he is, even Captain Lex himself would concede that he's now a year or two past his sell-by date, now exhibiting some of the inevitable, unmistakable signs of temporal wear and tear. And yet for as long as I've known him, Lex has always been exactly five days younger than me. One hundred and twenty hours to be precise. During the two seasons that we were teammates, I naturally did what I could to use this to my advantage. If my team captain ever had reason to question my performance or commitment on the bike, my invariable response would be: 'Ah, yes, but wait till you get to my age.'

Lex's Inthanon missile strike had wreaked destruction upon the lead group and I was one of the early casualties. Ten or so riders had survived the initial blast and were now receding into the middle distance, leaving behind a handful of stragglers, myself included. If Nicarus's legs had been unable to withstand a direct hit from the Taliban, I reflected ruefully, then my legs had proved less than shatterproof when a Flying Dutchman exploded right in front of me. The remnants of the lead group rounded a sharp bend and vanished from sight. I was now on my own all the way to the finish, assuming of course that I even made it to the finish. While there were still the minor placings to contest, was there really any point? I'd forfeited any chance of trading blows at the sharp end of the race. I may as well have not started, I told myself, or instead turned up on a bike fitted with panniers, a bell and a picnic hamper. Yet this was hardly the first time I'd been dropped in a race, and of course the only known remedy for getting dropped on a climb, as Phil Liggett famously stated, is to dig deeper into your suitcase of courage. But my own suitcase had been left unattended and was now gathering dust in a back room in lost luggage.

I pedalled on half-heartedly, unwilling to commit to the decisive U-turn that would take me back down the mountain and to a deserted car park in downtown Chomtong. After a few minutes at this reduced pace, another rider, an Italian, caught up to me.

'Ah. What a beautiful climb,' he emoted. '*Bellisimo.*'

'Yes, it certainly is,' I replied through my teeth.

Right on cue, the granite cliff face to our left dropped away sharply, revealing an unobstructed view into the wooded valley below. A ravine! If not quite yet overcome by bad morale, I was surely headed in that general direction. Neither was my internal affective state all it might be and my suitcase was still waiting to be reclaimed. Was this my Federico Bahamontes moment? One bike, one ravine: one quick, simple solution to that which was ailing me. But maybe not so simple, I reminded myself, and really not so sensible, given that I'd recently shelled out a large sum to replace the expensive bike frame on to which I'd carelessly dropped a pickup truck several months earlier. My fleeting fantasy of a bicycle in freefall soon passed and I continued to ride, just as Bahamontes, the Eagle of Toledo, had done many years earlier and I gradually eased my way back into some pedalling rhythm. A few kilometres further up the road, Andrew – the erstwhile owner of the ditched pickup truck and who had wisely opted to enjoy his Inthanon Sunday from the comfort of a large motorbike – appeared noisily alongside us. 'Several riders up just ahead,' he shouted over the engine drone. 'They're all over the place.'

It may well be true, as the late Lou Reed once said, that you need a busload of faith to get by. And in these troubled times, one bus may not even be enough. Two-thousand metres up a mountain, I had no particular means of accessing a busload of anything, but I felt a twinge of something – maybe a small hatchback of faith – urging me onwards. I clicked up a couple of gears and bade farewell to the annoyingly cheery Italian. I could make out the twin pagodas in the distance and, beneath them, several riders inching their way up the steep incline, like a group of Everest climbers approaching the Hillary Step. Within minutes, I'd overhauled two backmarkers and had others in my sights: The Return of the Tortoise. The final few kilometres of the Inthanon climb always struck me – in so far as I could imagine such a thing – as an experience similar to childbirth, namely the utter conviction that you will never, ever again, willingly put yourself through such acute discomfort. But in each instance the pain soon enough turns to relief, a relief felt amidst copious tears, strange gurgling sounds and a warm, satisfied afterglow.

Peter Pouly, who had again demolished the course record to win the event by almost ten minutes, was strolling serenely around the finish area as I wobbled wearily over the line. My eventual sixth place was a respectable effort, good enough even for a minor trophy, albeit one I'd earned under the guise of a disgruntled, hare-chasing tortoise. The greater part of any Inthanon afterglow always stems from the knowledge that it's all over for another twelve months, but this time I lacked any sense of a job well done.

CHAPTER 18

Hamster's High

'*Health and fitness are not synonymous. Unfortunately, many athletes are fit but unhealthy.*'

Joe Friel[237]

Overtraining syndrome (OTS) is less a specific condition than a ragtag of physical and emotional symptoms, of which decreased motivation, mild depression and insomnia are some of the more commonly cited. Failure to recover sufficiently between workouts on a repeated basis is the standard pathway into OTS. While specific types of workouts and training can make an athlete more susceptible to OTS, the underlying cause is almost always a lack of recovery. While all committed athletes are prone to pushing too far occasionally – while only partly recovered from previous efforts – the manner in which some approach their daily training places them at higher risk.

Multi-sportsman Scott Saifer, head coach at Wenzel Coaching in California, has witnessed countless cases of OTS in the two decades he's been working with clients. 'Most racers will say they train to improve performance,' he notes, 'but many ride in ways that do not support that goal. Sometimes from ignorance and sometimes for more insidious reasons, they undertake excessive volume or intensity for their current experience, fitness, or point in the annual training and racing cycle.'[238] He goes on to explain that most riders do learn sooner or later how to train more effectively, whether from a coach, from books and other media, or simply from other cyclists. Yet, as Saifer readily concedes, many others fail to make progress: 'They repeatedly train themselves into deep fatigue, injury or illness despite having access to the same information as the riders who do finally learn to train and rest more effectively.'[239]

Fitness coaches tend to draw a clear distinction between overtraining and 'overreaching' – here defined as the initial stages of overtraining and typically viewed as a necessary step on the path to competitive fitness. As Joe Friel, the unofficial godfather of bike coaching explains, 'It's not usually difficult at all to get serious athletes to train hard'.[240] All athletes have to accept occasional fatigue as a precursor of peak fitness and a few days of moderate tiredness is an acceptable response to a period of heavy training stress, of what Friel likes to call 'functional overreaching'. But any fatigue of a more persistent nature is often a warning sign, heralding the onset of the more insidious 'non-functional overreaching'. In the words of Scott Saifer: 'If periods of overreaching are interspersed with periods of recuperation, the rider continues to develop. The more quickly the athlete recognizes and corrects the overreaching, the more rapid the development.' But as he then explains:

> Training hard for an extended period after one is already overreached leads to a decrease in performance that is not correctable by a few days of recovery. This is called overtraining. Overtraining is not brought on by a single excessively long or hard training session. Rather, it is brought on by repeatedly training when already tired or injured, making the fatigue or injury worse. It is brought on by failing to rest when the body needs rest.[241]

Unfortunately for any athletes who suspect they might be overtrained, there is no clearly defined benchmark or diagnostic test. As Dr Mark Jenkins, NCAA team physician at Rice University and seven-time Ironman finisher observes, 'it is possible to have the overtraining syndrome, but have completely normal physical findings and biochemical tests. At this point, there is no single test that will confirm the presence of overtraining.'[242]

In the meantime, I'd self-diagnosed a chronic case of *Weltschmerz*, plus one or two other unspecified Teutonic maladies for good measure. My overall motivation – for the bike, for the world at large – was certainly nothing to write home about and my sleep patterns were worsening. Once overtraining has been identified in an athlete, Jenkins adds, 'the normal fine balance in the interaction between the autonomic nervous system and the hormonal system is disturbed ... Heaping more workouts onto this unbalanced system only worsens the situation. Additional stress in the form of difficulties at work or personal life also contributes.'[243]

The true litmus test was always how I felt on the bike. In times past, the bike was a natural pick-me-up, the daily go-to mood-lifter. But a few spins up and down the local mountain of choice, Doi Suthep, had failed to achieve the desired effect. Overtraining, *Weltschmerz*, the midlife U-bend and other maladies of the modern world: to what extent each of these was attributable to my current state of mind was hard to say. If the bike itself was part of the problem, then excessive volume of training probably was not to blame. Racking up huge distances in the saddle never held much appeal for me. After three or four solid hours of pedalling I could always think of something else I'd rather be doing, something like eating or sleeping, preferably in that order. A typical four hours on the bike works out at roughly 20,000 pedal strokes, so a heavy training week for me would equate to 100,000 or so revolutions. Which in turn translates to a million pedal strokes every three months, give or take, and a million of anything is an indecently large number. Punishment by a million strokes could have been one of the more obscure ancient Chinese tortures. Of course, the Contadors, Nibalis and Froomes of this world will rack up close to ten million pedal strokes in a typical year. But any amateur cyclist – any amateur masters cyclist, more the point – should be able to reach and maintain race fitness on considerably less.

On the other hand, 'repeatedly training when already tired': now this was right up my alley. I had an impressive track record at this specific discipline. Consider for example that final burst in a session of high-power intervals – the final one being the one that you really didn't want to do. To be fair, I usually didn't want to do any of them, but 'want' isn't the main issue here. And so the already disgruntled legs and lungs are tasked to complete one more maximal, out of the saddle effort – let's say for the sake of argument one that requires several minutes up-hill, through a series of steep switchbacks. And for the non-cyclist or non-athlete this might be better understood diagrammatically: for switchbacks please visualize instead a camel's back and for that ultimate interval, think straw. But I had to do it, or so I told myself, since I assumed that the others – my MAMILian rivals – would be doing much the same.

And through the infernal machine of social media, I saw that indeed they were – in fact, in some cases were doing even more. I saw that the Scotsman who had beaten me in the great Gelgate disaster had posted a single training ride totalling 4,000m (13,120ft) of climbing. This was impressive stuff, roughly on a par with the vertical requirements of an ultra-tough mountain stage in the Tour or the Giro. Except that this maniac had done it in Singapore of all places, where the loftiest peak is a massive 80m. He'd climbed it no less than *fifty* times in a row: up and down; up and down. In a sign that he wasn't taking his training all that seriously, he had stopped for a celebratory beer after the final ascent.

When a few weeks later I saw that he'd succumbed to a broken collar-bone after coming off second best in a bike versus van altercation, I allowed myself a shiver of *schadenfreude*. This surely was going to disrupt his training no end and several races were scheduled for the coming months. But barely a week later he cheerfully posted online a gruelling three-hour session on his indoor trainer. What kind of inhu-man beast rides indoors for three whole hours? Certainly not me. Less than one hour of this type of repetitive, hamster-wheel training was usually enough to bore me off the bike. And by a fairly wide margin, the oddest, most outlying MAMIL of all on the Chiang Mai scene (German, ex-military, certifiably insane) could be found on most days somewhere in the environs of the city attempting his usual series of excruciating hill repeats, either hefting a heavily weighted backpack, or at other times with a two-wheeled *trailer* – presumably one also loaded with rocks or bricks – shackled to the back of his bike.

Just as cyclists of a racing persuasion – to a greater or lesser degree – can be highly motivated to ride on their indoor trainers, so running along a ridged wheel for long periods of time appears to be a pleasurable, self-rewarding activity for the typical hamster. While of course getting nowhere fast, scientific experiments have shown that a seriously committed hamster can cover up to 10km (6 miles) a day, thereby stimulating release of various endorphins and endocannibinoids and producing what might be termed a 'hamster's high'. Yet medical research of this nature is more typically conducted on rats, the hamsters' second cousins from the extended family of Rodentia. While *Rattus rattus* and *Rattus norvegicus* – black and brown rats to you and me – are the most common subspecies, it's the male Wistar rat, an albino breed developed especially for lab research, that makes up the bulk of the numbers in these sample groups of rodential overreaching. But a number of experiments also reveal that male rats, in contrast to male humans, are not much given to overtraining themselves voluntarily. The miniature motorized treadmill that functions as the rats' training ground therefore also provides a mild electric shock to any rat whose pace falls below a pre-calibrated rate. And since these rats – in the absence of any electrified prompting – are clearly less prone to overreaching, there is some evidence here perhaps for the superior evolutionary development of rodents versus MAMILs.

One such study from Mashhad University in Iran analysed blood samples from a group of under-recovered rats after zapping them into a rodent-sized suffersphere for an hour each day over a two-month period. The study then compared them to a control group of their moderately trained, better-rested peers. The results showed that 'in contrast to moderate or intermittent physical activity, prolonged and overtraining exercise causes numerous changes in immunity that possibly reflect physiological stress and immune suppression'.[244] A similar study from the University of São Paulo found that their rats showed 'increases in pro-inflammatory cytokines in the adipose tissue after an overtraining protocol'.[245] Cytokines are a category of small proteins that play an important role in cell signalling and which help to regulate the immune system. While cytokines can be anti-inflammatory as well as pro-inflammatory, it's hypothesized that certain cytokines are involved in not only the initiation, but also the persistence of pathological pain. The general state of our cytokines is probably not something that keeps most of us awake at night – or at least not as far as we know. A study from the University of Western Australia, possibly running low on its supply of Wistar rats, monitored eight human elite rowers in the run-up to the 2007 world championships. 'Consistent with previous findings, pro-inflammatory cytokines were significantly associated with measures of depressed mood, sleep disturbances, and stress,' the study noted. 'These results are consistent with previous hypotheses describing how overtraining may be caused by excessive cytokine release, and lend further support for a cytokine hypothesis of overtraining.'[246]

While the lack of agreed diagnostic criteria for OTS remains a major issue for researchers, some have highlighted the importance of the hypothalamic-pituitary-adrenal (HPA) axis, a key element of the neuroendecrine system that controls our reaction to stress and regulates our immune systems and which itself is primarily modulated by cytokines. According to an Italian study:

> Athletes undergoing a strenuous training schedule can develop a significant decrease in performance associated with systemic symptoms or signs: the overtraining syndrome. This is a stress-related condition that consists of alteration of physiological functions and adaptation to performance, impairment of psychological processing, immunological dysfunction and biochemical abnormalities.[247]

As Joe Friel might say, it's not pretty. 'Physical training can produce muscle and skeletal trauma, thus generating a local inflammatory reaction,' the study continued. 'With the excessive repetition of the training stimulus the local inflammation can generate a systemic inflammatory response.'[248]

To prove that cyclists are fundamentally no different from rowers or rats, another Iranian study put a sample of elite bike racers through two months of prolonged, intense training. While significantly elevated plasma levels of pro-inflammatory cytokines were observed, the study found that a taper period of one to three weeks before competition essentially reversed the trend, providing the riders with a timely performance boost: 'Continuation of the more intense training for three more weeks will not result in improved cycling performances, nor will it attenuate pro-inflammatory cytokine levels in the blood as was seen in the taper group.'[249] The study concluded: 'Coaches should seek to optimise rest between training sessions and apply approximately three-week tapering periods prior to important competitions in order to properly prepare endurance cyclists for optimal performance and recovery.'

I was still trying to work out if I was overtrained, and this despite various, not so subtle clues. For a start, I certainly looked overtrained. After anything more demanding than a short spin on the bike, my face would flush red, a reaction, I strongly suspected, of overexposure to sun, sweat and stress. I sat down to scour the Internet for information on inflammation. Of the many possible cures offered therein, I seized upon turmeric, a strong anti-inflammatory and a staple of the sages of Ayurvedic medicine since the year dot. Topical applications of turmeric did help, but only at the cost of yet more unsightly, ingrained yellowness that refused to scrub off. After a few more failed home remedies, I threw caution to the wind and made an appointment to see a dermatologist. She prescribed an ointment and recommended I avoid all outdoor exercise for the next few months. Under normal circumstances such a course of action would be laughable, absurd even, but this time round it held a certain appeal.

A blood test might at least provide some pointers, I decided. Perhaps a simple vitamin deficiency was responsible, or a fickle imbalance of minerals that could be corrected with a quick trip to the pharmacy. At a smart new clinic in town, I duly submitted to the needle, which, I couldn't help noticing, was a rather large one. The young woman wielding the javelin-like weapon may or may not have carried out other blood tests during the course of her career. It was certainly hard to tell. I'd asked beforehand if she could also test my blood for elevated cytokines; she'd smiled and nodded in the uniquely Thai way that signalled she had no idea what I meant. The supersized needle then made its way into my arm, where it remained lodged for what seemed an unusually long time and I had to avert my eyes to avoid witnessing how many pints or gallons of blood were being drawn. At a certain point my brain unilaterally decided it could no longer rely on sufficient blood flow and placed itself into a self-protective shutdown mode. I came around a while later, foggy headed, a little unsure how much time had passed. Another woman, presumably a colleague of the needle fiend, offered me a glass of iced water and I sat there for a while, waiting for the appropriate moment to check whether the legs still worked. The test results came through a week later. It turned out I was in fine fettle, at least physically. Vitamins and minerals were all spot on. Cholesterol was superb. Testosterone was best in class and my haematocrit was a whopping, barely legal 48 per cent. With numbers like that, I should have been on the start list for the Tour de France.

Elevated levels of cortisone, the body's principal stress hormone, are another frequent marker of overtrained athletes and are often implicated in cases of insomnia. And sleeplessness had become a mainstay of my daily routine. What had started as a quick dabble, just a night or two to see what all the fuss was about, now had me enrolled as a fully paid-up member of the wideawake club. Quitting insomnia is no laughing matter either. Drugs and alcohol may get their own peer-supported twelve-step programmes, but when it comes to sleeplessness, you're very much out on your own. You're very much up on your own.

When I'd first moved to Chiang Mai some years earlier – and some years before I started waking up involuntarily at 3am – I would set the alarm before dawn a couple of times a week to ride up Doi Suthep, the perfectly pitched 10km (6-mile) climb on the town's western edge. The early start was a means of cheating both the heat and the diesel-emitting stream of tourist-bus traffic that grunts and burps up and down the mountain for much of the day. Despite believing myself largely immune to all matters spiritual, I still felt some sort of a frisson – of sanctity, maybe, who knows – as I'd start my climb, past the saffron-clad monks out collecting alms, then up into the forest, with the sun cresting the horizon and with only the sounds of the mountain's birdlife and my own steady breathing for company. I'd be out the front door and on the bike minutes after waking, fortified only by a quick shot of coffee. Solid sustenance could wait.

But one morning, running behind schedule, I skipped the coffee too. I was less than a couple of kilometres into the climb when I almost ground to a halt. What on earth was I doing? It was 6am, for God's sake. What exactly was the point of this? I struggled on as far as the halfway viewpoint, then headed glumly back down the mountain. Back in town, I stopped for a coffee and within minutes I felt better. I wanted to try the climb again. After this, I never again attempted the mountain – or any other training for that matter – without properly pre-caffeinating myself. Calibrating my intake became something of an art form. Too much, and I'd be buzzing around like a trapped housefly. Not enough, and I'd be morose and listless. But as I gradually increased my intensity on the bike, I was also logging more weekly cups of caffeine. 'I would rather suffer with coffee than be senseless,' opined Napoleon Bonaparte. While I largely agreed with the late emperor, if coffee was starting to infringe on my fundamental human right to a decent night's sleep, then I was in a serious quandary. After another week of nocturnal insurrections, I had no choice but to bite the caffeine bullet.

With less than ideal timing, I was invited to join a new racing team. Hans, a Belgian cyclo-cross specialist who had arrived in Thailand the previous year – and who had soon found a willing sponsor in the local Bianchi distributor – was now forming a new squad. Hans had started late in life, picking up bicycle racing only a few years earlier, but in the process also picking up seven-times world cyclo-cross champion Erik de Vlaeminck as his personal coach. In his first outing at the World Masters Championships, Hans had placed just outside the top ten. And like so many Belgians before him, Hans seemed to revel, to take uncommon delight, in suffering. During one of his first competitions in Thailand, a mountain-bike race held in the usual fearsomely hot conditions, Hans was cruising to an easy win in the masters event when his chain snapped: a truly chain-free moment of the non-Hincapie variety. Mildly peeved, Hans retreated to the team bus to get it repaired. Shortly afterwards, he ventured back into the blast furnace of the afternoon to contest the (longer, faster) elite race, where he finished a close second. He then missed the entirety of the prize ceremony, which he spent propped up and inert under a large tree, his anxious girlfriend dropping large ice cubes, one after the other, down the back of his sweat-sodden jersey.

I went to meet Hans and our new team sponsor, this time a Bangkok-based importer of high-end bicycle equipment. After a brief meeting, the company's head honcho – who bore an uncanny resemblance to an Asian Eddy Merckx, right down to the bushy eyebrows – reappeared from a storeroom clutching a team-issue carbon bike frame. 'I think this one is your size,' he said to me. This felt like an encouraging if possibly misplaced show of faith from our sponsors.

Chronic inflammation may play a significant role in many cases of OTS and it's also finding itself increasingly implicated as the common denominator in a wide variety of other pathologies, from hay fever to arthritis and even certain forms of cancer. To further compound matters, both cytokine levels and inflammation have been shown to rocket during depressive episodes. Several new theories even speculate that the condition of depression in fact may have as much to do with the body as the mind. 'Is depression a kind of allergic reaction?' queried a recent *Guardian* headline.[250] 'I don't even talk about it [depression] as a psychiatric condition any more,' said George Slavich, a clinical psychologist at UCLA. 'It does involve psychology, but it also involves equal parts of biology and physical health.'[251]

The logic of this approach is as follows: we all tend to feel tired and miserable when we're unwell and this so-called 'sickness behaviour' also happens to look a lot like depression, at least to outside observers. If people with depression show symptoms of classic sickness behaviour and sick people often feel a lot like people suffering from depression, might there be a common cause that accounts for both? The implied common cause here is of course cytokine-fuelled inflammation. In a similar vein, a 2009 study found that healthy males could be put into a depressed, anxious state when given a typhoid vaccine that caused a temporary spike in inflammation. And as the *Guardian* noted, there are a number of other clues: 'People with inflammatory diseases such as rheumatoid arthritis tend to suffer more than average with depression; cancer patients given a drug called interferon alpha, which boosts their inflammatory response to help fight the cancer, often become depressed as a side-effect.'[252] Lending further support to this theory is a handful of recent clinical trials that show an improved response to anti-depressant drugs when anti-inflammatory medicines are also added to the mix.

This highly interdependent axis of overtraining, inflammation and depression appears to complicate the situation for any underperforming, under-motivated athlete. But how to separate cause and effect? Might we be feeling depressed because we're overtrained? Or are we feeling overtrained as a result of depression-led inflammation? Or both. It's enough to drive anyone round the flaming bend, or at least make it difficult to know where to start on the road to recovery. It's no simple matter either to locate a start point on what is effectively a loop: a dangerous feedback loop, where each individual condition tends to exacerbate the other. As a 2002 *Sports Medicine* study of overtraining syndrome concluded, 'OTS and clinical depression involve remarkably similar signs and symptoms, brain structures, neurotransmitters, endocrine pathways and immune responses.'[253]

There's also evidence to suggest that certain athletes will show more resilience to the effects of overtraining than others. It's demonstrably not the case that all athletes exposed to severe physical or emotional stress will become overtrained or depressed. Studies have shown that during times of acute stress, an anti-anxiety neurotransmitter known as neuropeptide Y (NPY) is released into the brain's limbic system. A 2008 study reported in *Nature* journal found that 'genetic variation in human NPY expression has a measurable effect on stress response and emotion' and also helps to explain 'inter-individual variation in resiliency to stress'.[254] A study in *Biological Psychiatry* meanwhile reported that a group of combat-hardened war veterans free from symptoms of post-traumatic stress disorder (PTSD) displayed significantly higher NPY levels than another group suffering with PTSD who had not been exposed to combat situations. In plain English, an individual's innate supply of stress-fighting molecules is a better predictor of their ability to remain trauma-free than the extent to which they've been exposed to lethal harm. The study concluded: 'Plasma NPY levels may represent a biologic correlate of resilience to or recovery from the adverse effects of stress.'[255]

Countless studies have also shown that physical exercise can be at least as effective as any medication in relieving symptoms of depression. But such studies usually start from the assumption that their subjects are of a sedentary nature and a high proportion of those who suffer from depression do fit into this couch-potato category. A 1990 study found that 'exercise is associated with an anti-depressive effect in patients with mild to moderate forms of non-bipolar depressive disorders. An increase in aerobic fitness does not seem to be essential for the anti-depressive effect, because similar results are obtained with non-aerobic forms of exercise.'[256]

But for the trained athlete, especially those for whom intensive training – and in many cases a tendency towards overtraining – may have played a role in any emotional or physical decline, the relationship between exercise and depression is vastly more complex.

That excessive physical stress can lead to an abnormal immune response is now widely accepted in the medical community. Although doctors are yet to reach any consensus on a precise definition of chronic fatigue syndrome (CFS), a high proportion believe that it is caused by a disruption of the body's natural defences and variants of CFS are unusually prevalent among competitive cyclists and other athletes. Indeed, the distinction between CFS and OTS is also far from clear. Yet as Harvard Medical School specialists Andrew Nierenberg and Michael Ostacher (both cyclists) have suggested, a sudden *reduction* in training workload could also trigger a depressive episode.[257] Those elite cyclists who have returned home with bouts of the post-Olympic blues would almost definitely agree with this.

My initial response to my growing sense of the 'unsatisfactoriness of all things' – to arriving at the clogged apex of the U-bend – was to ramp up my efforts on the bike, adopting as best I could the Marxist doctrine of physical pain as the antidote to mental suffering. As ultra-marathon man Dean Karnazes wrote in his memoir, 'Pain is the body's way of ridding itself of weakness.'[258] This particular line of thinking suggests that when life starts to weigh too heavily upon our shoulders, when it becomes annoying, tiresome or painful, we then need to turn up our hurt dials to maximum. We want the legs to scream blue murder at us rather than shut up, which in turn will usher in the 'cleansing curtain' of suffering. But there's a fallacy here too. If mental suffering chooses to hold steady under a barrage of elective physical pain, it is then easy to conclude that you might not be training hard enough and that the ante must be upped once again.

In his 1987 novel *More Die of Heartbreak*, Saul Bellow observes that by a certain point in our lives, we all get to carry around our own individual 'pain schedule': 'A long schedule like a federal document, only it's your pain schedule.'[259] One that takes into account not only our physical pains, but also 'injured vanity, betrayal, swindle, injustice'. Our elective pains on the bike can function as a counterpoint to various other sufferings, a means of dampening the radio interference from our generalized pain schedules. But this type of pain schedule is supposed to last us a lifetime, designed essentially to accommodate only the occasional upswing in our levels of background suffering, our Geiger-clicks of *dukkha*. But when almost everything becomes painful and unsatisfactory – and this is essentially the experience of finding oneself lodged inside a midlife U-bend – additional elective pain starts to feel like more pain in aggregate. At this tricky inflection point, the nature of the relationship suddenly changes: suffering becomes additive rather than substitutional. And if there's still no consensus amongst the medical profession over a clear diagnosis for such cases of dysfunctional overreaching, then they're at least agreed on the recommended course of treatment: a period of complete rest until the symptoms subside.

For my first competitive outing with the new team, I travelled down with Nicarus to a place called Phichit, a front-running contender for the title of Thailand's least visit-worthy province. Nic had just taken delivery of a new car and I was more than happy to let him do the driving. In light of recent events, he refused in any case to allow me anywhere near the driver's seat. The following morning after breakfast we went to sign on at the start, only to discover our races were scheduled for mid-afternoon.

We'd already checked out of our hotel, so we had little choice but to loiter in the simmering cauldron of the race car park, watching the thermometer climb steadily. By midday, the heat was fierce and we still had two hours before our races.

'What on earth are we doing?' demanded Nic. 'Why are we even here?' He was lying on the grass in a patch of shade, droplets of sweat collecting on his brow. I was reasonably confident that what Nic meant by 'here' was, well, right here: Thailand's back of beyond in high summer, waiting for an inconsequential race that was still hours away. But my mind had been rambling; it had been monkeying around. It's surely not a bad idea to take stock of one's circumstances from time to time. And whatever curious chain of events had led me to a scorched, dusty car park deep inside Thailand's nether regions, this same question (what exactly was I doing?) had sidled up to me from a fundamentally more cosmic perspective.

Nic's race finally kicked off at 2pm. Twenty minutes later, he rolled back into the car park, ruefully shaking his head. 'Too damn hot,' he said. 'It's crazy out there.' As close to the surface of the sun as he'd flown these past few months, he knew well enough when to stop racing directly underneath its unflinching gaze. The masters race got under way soon after. On the second lap, my new teammate Super Hans decided to go superfast, initiating a breakaway and taking several other riders with him. This effectively signalled the end of my race. I dawdled around in the middle of the bunch for another handful of laps. After crossing the finish line, I soft-pedalled back through the heat-haze of the car park, where first my front and then my rear tyres suddenly deflated within seconds of each other.

CHAPTER 19

The Middle Way

'A good Tour takes one year off your life, and when you finish in a bad state, they reckon three years.'

Robert Millar[260]

Bike racing, according to many who do it for a living, can be bad for your health. Maybe not the weekly legs shave, if undertaken with due care and attention, or the regular massages, if not too vigorous, but much else about the sport seems to be inherently damaging. Eddy Merckx claimed his successful 1972 attempt on the hour record in Mexico City was the hardest ride he'd ever done and speculated it would take years off his life. Australian Jack Bobridge echoed similar sentiments after narrowly failing to beat the hour record early in 2015. 'I can't even describe how much pain my glutes and quads are in,' he said after his attempt, while team helpers held him up like a ventriloquist's dummy to stop him from falling flat on his face. 'It's by far the hardest thing I've ever done, and the hardest thing I'll ever do.'[261]

Merckx, now into his eighth decade and apparently in good health, may have overstated the dangers, but bear in mind that the great man opted for early retirement at the age of thirty-two. That Merckx's longevity as a pro cyclist was curtailed by such humungous efforts seems highly plausible.

Playing the ravenous cannibal on the one hand and on the other racing defiantly into your forties *à la* Chris Horner or Jens Voigt would seem to be mutually exclusive options. As Scottish climber Robert Millar once claimed: 'The riders reckon that a good Tour takes one year off your life, and when you finish in a bad state, they reckon three years.'[262] If we assume for the sake of convenience that Jens Voigt's record seventeen Tours were neither especially good nor bad, but mostly just okay, then Millar's maths implies that Jensie, at age forty-three, is staring down the barrel of a penalty of thirty-four years. Or, to put it another way, Voigt is already in his late-seventies and should now be claiming his pension. Merckx himself rode a total of seven Tours, of which only two he might consider to be *bad* Tours – the two he failed to win. But this still does not address the question of whether it's even possible for anyone to finish the race in a 'good' state. It's all relative.

The mantra of 'no pain, no gain' may have held sway over the past few decades, but there are now signs of a shift in the prevailing wisdom. The *Journal of the American College of Cardiology* recently drew attention to a Danish study that suggests intensive training may be as bad for you as no training at all. The study, which sampled 1,000 healthy joggers and non-joggers over a twelve-year period, concluded that 'light and moderate jogging was found to be more beneficial than being inactive or undertaking strenuous jogging, possibly adding years to your life'.[263] Building on previous research, the paper also suggested long-term strenuous endurance exercise can damage the heart. 'You don't actually have to do that much to have a good impact on your health,' claimed one of the Danish researchers, Jacob Marott. 'And perhaps you shouldn't actually do too much. No exercise recommendations across the globe mention an upper limit for safe exercise, but perhaps there is one.'[264]

There are, of course, those who contend that riding a bike doesn't have to be inherently harmful; that our reaching, our striving and our self-overcoming are in fact worthy attributes when practised in moderation, within sensible limits. They allude vaguely to the possibility of some form of compromise, perhaps even a bicycling analogue of the Buddhist Middle Way. It was, after all, a freshly enlightened Lord Buddha who announced his discovery of the Middle Way as the true path of wisdom: moderation in all things over the extremes of sensual indulgence and self-mortification. And having sampled so extensively from both extremes made the Buddha's conviction all the more unshakeable.

Born into royalty and heir to the throne, the pre-enlightened twenty-nine-year-old Buddha was by all accounts growing weary of daily life at the palace, 'trapped amidst the luxury like a bird in a golden cage', in the words of Buddhist scholar K. Sri Dhammananda.[265] Perhaps an early foreshadowing of modern-day *Weltschmerz* for the young prince, or even the fabled midlife U-bend, after adjusting for the lower life expectancies of circa 2,500BCE. We then have Gautama Buddha slinking quietly off into the night only hours after his wife Yasodhara had given birth to their first son. Not entirely honourable conduct this, certainly not in the eyes of the majority, but attaining complete insight into the true nature of human suffering is at least a better excuse than those typically proffered by absconding husbands. A forest-dwelling Buddha then devoted his next half a dozen years to numerous experiments in extreme self-mortification. 'He joined a band of ascetics and tortured his body so as to break its power and crush its interference, since it was believed that truth could be found this way,' writes K. Sri Dhammananda:

> A man of enormous energy and willpower, he outdid other ascetics in every austerity they proposed. While fasting, he ate so little that when he took hold of the skin of his stomach, he actually touched his spine. He pushed himself to

the extent that no man had done and yet lived. He, too, would have certainly died had he not realized the futility of self-mortification, and decided to practise moderation instead.[266]

Bodily torture. Austerity. Enormous energy and willpower. Old stone-face Henri Desgrange would have heartily approved of such antics. No great fan of moderation, he may have even wondered why his pampered Tour de France riders were being provided with beds and hotel rooms on stages where there happened to be some vacant caves nearby. But, as we now know, the Lord Buddha, after thoroughly exhausting all other options, chose the path of moderation.

For my part, I'd never given moderation much thought, but it seemed worth a try. A novel approach certainly, but a well-earned break from self-mortification could be just what the doctor ordered. I'd swung around meanwhile to the opposite extreme – a lay-off of several months from the bike, a hiatus from my regular diet of elective suffering. But now I was contemplating getting back in the saddle. Just a few restorative spins for now, nothing more. I'd progressed as far as resolving to clean, degrease and lube the bike – the still immaculate, barely used machine presented by my team sponsors – when I received a phone call from the latter requesting the bike's prompt return. Not unreasonable under the circumstances. I'd thus far failed to impress, mostly by failing to turn up at any races, let alone finish one or two, and the sponsors wanted their expensive bike back. I explained, less reasonably, that I'd rather hang on to it. After a little negotiation we arrived at the wisdom of the Middle Way. I agreed to reimburse my sponsors, but for a knock-down price, since the bike was after all no longer brand new. Moderation in all things.

For my first bike ride in several months I opted for a few laps of the local park. I had, though, underestimated the challenges I would face during the flat, ten-minute ride from my home to the park entrance. 'Whose legs were these?' I wondered aloud and somewhat expletively. What did these third-rate approximations of legs think they were playing at? Emerging from my bib shorts were a pair of pale, hairy, chicken drumsticks – slack, diminished versions of their previous selves. These were not my legs. They were possibly no longer even *the* legs. Not so much legs you would command to shut up, as legs you'd whisperingly urge to go and please cover up, to display a little decorum in a public place. Mine legs had seen the glory; now I was hoping no one would see my legs. Once inside the park, my morale improved and I completed the first 3km (2-mile) lap without too much fuss. The second lap had its moments, though. A light breeze had sprung up off the boating lake, retarding my progress on the outward leg. A kid on a mountain bike cruised past me. By the third – and last – lap I was back in my groove, in the flow zone, and I had no qualms about shifting out of bottom gear for the final, breeze-assisted stretch.

'Nothing compares to the simple pleasure of a bike ride,' said President John F. Kennedy, thereby setting a precedent (no pun intended) whereby each POTUS of recent times must be regularly photo-opped astride his mountain bike. Clinton, Bush and Obama, all photographed with this must-have presidential accessory. Plus, of course, David Cameron and Boris Johnson. (But not so much Tony Blair or Gordon Brown: discuss.) Yet with the convoluted question of pleasure placed to one side, my bike rides were no longer feeling even particularly simple. Almost impossible, I found, to get out of the front door without having first to perform a series of fiddly tweaks to the bike – oil, inflate, tighten, straighten, adjust, wipe, polish. Once out of the door, simplicity then had to contend with the usual procession of cars, trucks and buses, motorbikes, dogs, dogs on motorbikes (usually accompanied by a human guardian), nine-year-olds on motorbikes driving their grandmothers to the local market, mud and rain, sun and dust, and large swathes of the city's road system still under chaotic construction. Bypasses, underpasses and overpasses: all designed to greatly improve traffic flow, but for the moment at least creating the polar opposite of a flow state; a pronounced contraflow in both senses of the word.

Flow and simplicity were in short supply on the bike. The swimming pool, for the moment, seemed to offer more potential. Swimming, in a literal sense, is a process of flow and in comparison to the complex paraphernalia of cycling, making it down to the local pool with a full complement of trunks, goggles and a towel was plain sailing. The pool was undoubtedly a far simpler proposition: a pair of steamed-up goggles represented the worst possible suffering, the greatest unsatisfactoriness of swimming. But first the step to enlightenment for any road cyclist in the swimming pool is the discovery that he lacks any discernible upper-body strength. When former ski racer Tyler Hamilton first joined the ranks of professional cyclists, he became acutely aware of how he lacked the regular cyclist's physique. 'Their arms were toothpicks,' he noted of his peers at the Tour of Dupont.[267] But Hamilton would soon enough be seen sporting his own pair of impeccably tanned toothpicks, adept for lightly gripping handlebars and brake levers, but very little else. I found that my sorely neglected toothpicks were not of much assistance with the front crawl – which is, after all, supposed to be the quickest, most power-ful swim stroke. But mine really was a crawl.

A number of professional cyclists are now turning to the ancient prac-tice of yoga, hoping to boost race performance by building all-round strength and flexibility. While yoga also complements many other forms of exercise, for competitive cyclists it can work as a powerful antidote against the stiffening effects of long hours in the saddle. There are no quick fixes with any yoga practice, but in the words of ex-Garmin Slip-stream pro Will Frischkorn:

> Yoga has been a part of my life for a long time and such a fantastic way to balance the very unbalanced body that cycling creates. Opening up the body from the hunched over position where we spend so much time is critical and there is no better way than a balanced yoga practice.[268]

Yoga's burgeoning popularity in the west is a fairly recent phenomenon, although it turns out that the burly German track sprinter Rudy Altig was a convert as early as the 1960s: 'If a little relaxation was required, up he'd go, feet first, and he'd stay there until he felt ready to come back down again,' wrote Les Woodland, author of *Cycling's 50 Craziest Stories*. 'In La Rochelle he once walked out of a restaurant on his hands, a trick that others tried to copy but they succeeded only in crashing into other diners' tables.'[269]

Following Lance Armstrong's triumph in the 2005 Tour de France, a journalist asked the American if he'd altered his training programme in any way during the previous winter. Armstrong's answer was that he'd followed exactly the same routine on the bike, but had added an hour of post-ride yoga each day.

Accustomed to reasonably long hours of turning the pedals, my tight muscles were now struggling to reconfigure themselves for alternative forms of exercise such as swimming, or even less esoteric tasks like sitting. My hip and shoulder joints felt as if they'd been crudely bolted together and had seized from lack of maintenance. My hamstrings were no longer hamstrings exactly, but felt more like hamrods, similar to a pair of piston rods and with about the same degree of flexibility. And so it was to the yoga mat, where at least I found some pleasantly upgraded scenery versus the customary vistas of the peloton. No longer consigned to spending most mornings gazing from close quarters at other men's backsides, at least three-quarters of the hindquarters in a typical yoga class were under female ownership and were also youngish and shapely. No easy task, then, to 'clear your mind of all distractions' when surrounded by a brood of females in yoga pants. And yoga itself was demonstrably a process of flow. Perhaps one of the reasons for the current lack of empathy between the bike and myself was that we no longer appeared to have much to learn from each other. Or that with each passing year we both had to learn how to go a little more slowly: hardly an inspiring curriculum for either of us.

Nor was yoga lacking in opportunities to suffer. No need for hot yoga rooms in Thailand. They were already plenty hot enough. Thirty minutes into each class, small rivulets of sweat would start to trickle from the headwaters of my mat, pooling in becalmed estuaries on either side. The general idea in each pose is to locate your *edge*; that sweet spot of stretch just shy of acute discomfort or possible injury. But pushing a little beyond your edge, testing the boundaries of the yogic suffersphere, did not appear to infringe too seriously against the rules. If maintaining a challenging pose with the recommended placid smile might suggest that you have not yet toppled over your edge, then consider also that smiles and grimaces can be hard to tell apart, especially while upside-down. And to cycling friends who queried my absences from the morning group rides, I explained that yoga was not really all that different from cycling: yoga was basically cycling without a bike. They nodded blankly and wondered whether to stage an intervention on my behalf.

A local bike race was scheduled for the end of the month, timed to coincide with the cessation of the monsoon rains. A mountain time trial, a 10km (6-mile) thrash up Chiang Mai's Doi Suthep, an event that was each year gaining in popularity. The race would finish near the summit, close to the King's Palace – just one of an impressive array of King's palaces – with the finish line chalked on the tarmac adjacent to the Royal helicopter landing pad. I planned to be there, and to be there on my bike, but as a spectator. No reason to challenge myself this time, not when I'd be targeting a time several minutes slower than previous years. I would be there simply to channel the enduring spirit of Arthur Conan Doyle, 'to go out for a spin down the road, without thought on anything but the ride you are taking'. Apart from this being a spin *up* the road, I intended to follow the recommended prescription.

I started to suffer in earnest right after the 3km (2-mile) marker. Not quite maximum suffering, not the pop-eyed, zigzagging, cardio-mayhem of previous competition efforts on this hill, but it was definitely starting to hurt. Hurting a lot. The evening before the race, I'd ridden down to the start line, only a few minutes from home, to sign my name on the board and to collect my race number. I didn't have to race. But that didn't mean I couldn't race. Sure I could. I could race. I only needed to remain mindful of avoiding undue suffering. Fine. No problem at all. In fact, what could be simpler? I would race, but from the novel vantage point of an untainted, Conan Doyle-like frame of mind. Participation, not devastation: this was the key. This was healthy. This was the Middle Way.

But here was another race and here was me, against best-laid plans, striving, reaching, heaping more suffering upon myself. I could make out a rider 100m (328ft) or so ahead and he needed to be caught. Within minutes, I'd duly dispatched my minute man and was contemplating a drop in tempo to a more sustainable pace when I glanced back to see another rider, tucked in a few inches from my rear wheel. 'Hey, no drafting. It's against the rules!' I gasped, squandering valuable oxygen. The rider was a whippet-like young Frenchman. 'But I am not yet in ze race,' he offered, his breath controlled and even. 'I am only doing ze warm-up.'

He then stood on his pedals and in a marked lack of respect to one of his elders, sprinted straight past me. A little further up the road he made a neat U-turn, then swooped back down the mountain towards the start line. Continuing my dogged progress uphill, I clicked down into a lower gear, with the reproachful words of another Frenchman ringing in my ears: 'I still feel that variable gears are only for people over forty-five,' Henri Desgrange once claimed. 'Isn't it better to triumph by the strength of your muscles than by the artifice of a derailleur? We are getting soft.'[270]

I pedalled – softly – over the summit finish line as the rain began to fall. Not the cooling, refreshing shower of regular Thai rain, but a wind-chilled, high-altitude drizzle. 'I rode a perfect time trial for my abilities at the moment,' announced Australian Rohan Dennis, after placing a creditable fifth in the 2014 World Championships.[271] This is, of course, all that any of us can hope to do. Minutes later, Nicarus, in full aero facial-disappearance mode, blazed across the line. He'd finished second, just a few seconds off the quickest time of the day, which had been set by an Austrian who had competed in the Beijing Olympics and was a former runner-up at the World University Games. The disrespectful French whippet claimed the third spot on the podium. Home-grown Thai riders regularly used to get amongst the trophies at this quintessentially Thai event. But the times had changed.

My own collection of race trophies had been piled haphazardly into a cardboard box and stored in the back of a bedroom cupboard. I'd experimented with various display locations around my apartment, but somehow the trophies never looked right. Too glittery, too gilded, too garish: perched atop a bookshelf they'd resembled an agglomeration of miniature Buddhist temples. This, of course, begs the semantic question of whether a trophy undisplayed is still even a proper trophy – for instance, there can be no such thing as a trophy wife who prefers to stay home of an evening with her knitting. I eventually lost patience with this selfish hogging of my limited storage space and hauled the box of trophies over to the local children's home, whereupon a staff member offered her sincere thanks and explained that my trophies could be put to good use at the regular sports events they organized for the kids. I returned empty-handed to my car and – with the slightest of Proustian sighs – keyed the ignition and drove on up the road. My trophies were about to embark upon new and exciting lives, or so I hoped, and at least were no longer consigned to sit despondently in a cardboard box, destined to do nothing but collect dust for the rest of their days. The Germans even have a name for such pointlessly static objects: *Staubfänger*. Dust catcher. Oh, blessed are the Germans, for they shall inherit a word for everything.

If the simple, self-propelled, two-wheeled machine that we know to be a bicycle had been invented somewhat earlier – say around 4,400 years earlier – then the Lord Buddha might have even found it a useful analogy in his teachings of the Middle Way. Contemporary philosopher and theologian Alan Watts employed exactly this technique in his book *Eastern Wisdom, Modern Life: Collected Talks 1960–1980*. While the standard interpretation of the Middle Way is that of a compromise between extreme self-mortification and asceticism on the one hand, and intense, hedonistic pleasure seeking on the other, Watts suggests this is not entirely correct:

> It has a somewhat more profound sense than that. I think the easiest way of understanding what the Buddha meant by 'the Middle Way' would be to call it 'the balanced life' – avoiding falling into one extreme or another extreme. When you ride a bicycle, you do something that is very much like following the Middle Way because to stay upright as you go along you balance to avoid falling to either side. But the curious thing about riding a bicycle, which is so difficult for beginners to understand, is that when you start falling, say to the right, you have to turn the handlebars and the wheel to the right, to the direction in which you are falling. And as a result of this, surprisingly enough, you come upright.[272]

Whether I'd veered too far to the left or the right was hard to say. That I'd veered too far – not so much oversteered, but over-veered, over-strived – was an easier call. Children learning to ride a bike for the first time rely on a set of stabilizer wheels to keep their veering and wobbling under control. And for those who have an inbuilt tendency to veer off in the direction of self-mortification, prone to overcoming and overreaching, for those driven towards the pursuit of sporting excellence or even just a gleaming trophy, then perhaps a different kind of stabilizer – essentially a pair of training wheels for the monkey mind – may come in handy.

CHAPTER 20

Damage and Divinity

'I found the point where suffering on the bike became pleasure.'
Michael Barry[273]

'Bike racing,' according to veteran mountain-bike champion Ned Over-end, 'is about pain'.[274] A solid enough claim this, a testimony informed by years of suffering, and yet it's not the whole truth. If bike racing were only about pain, it's doubtful whether it would ever appeal to more than a handful of maladjusted masochists. The sport instead would be destined to skulk in relative obscurity, forever on the margins of the mainstream. For a more balanced assessment, it's reasonable to say that bike racing is about pain *and* passion. And we've seen plenty of confessionals over the years from the sport's elite competitors that reveal complicated – if not to say quasi-schizophrenic – relationships with these two closely inter-twined elements.

'When I was younger I loved racing. When I rode my bike it was for one reason alone: to train for races,' wrote David Millar. 'As I've grown older and matured in professional cycling I have fallen deeper in love with riding my bike.'[275] This, of course, is exactly the same David Millar who elsewhere railed against a 'bonkers' sport and its unflinching demands for 'suffering beyond what you thought possible'.[276] 'I will always be a pro cyclist,' Millar insists, 'but no longer is cycling just about training and racing. It is now something more profound and will forever be my passion.'[277]

In bicycle racing, pain and passion must trail each other around as dutifully as a pair of conjoined twins. 'In my teens, I found the point where suffering on the bike became pleasure,' revealed Canadian former pro Michael Barry in his book *Le Métier*, in which he details the daily routines of a hardworking *domestique*. 'Pushing myself to physical and mental extremes I arrived home elated. To find the sublime there is a balance where elements of pain and passion become equal: on a bike, pedalling in the environment, a human being can find divinity.'[278]

Whether you happen to be a Barry or a Buddha, finding the locus of this divine intersection remains the key. To lose balance – veering, wobbling – runs the risk that pushing to extremes no longer leads to the sublime, but merely to exhaustion, to dissatisfaction, to *dukkha*. Where passion subsides and pain intensifies. That which does not kill us can still make us exhausted and irritable – as old Nietzsche might have claimed, if only he'd been less caught up with the psyche and more attuned to matters *physikalisch*.

'There is nothing like racing your bike to make you feel alive,' announced my teammate Hamish, several hours after racing his bike. Earlier in the day and a few minutes after racing his bike, ostensibly alive and yet more resembling an extra from a *Living Dead* B movie, he'd been unable for a short while to exercise basic command of the English language, let alone offer any astute observations. But here lay the crux. To feel most tinglingly alive, to ping and vibrate with the simple joy of being, we first had to near crucify, near zombify ourselves.

It's this combined presence of passion and suffering that makes things memorable. We're each of us designed with an inbuilt tendency to remember the best and the worst of times, even if pain and pleasure are essentially present-moment phenomena – you can't record either for later playback. Our memories excel at extremes; they're calibrated for maximum contrast. It's not easy to recall an *okay* bike ride from twenty years ago; it's equally difficult to recall an *okay* day in your life from twenty years ago. But our greatest days – and our most awful days – are securely locked away in our minds. So it goes with the bike: tooth and nail race finishes, epically element-blasted training rides – all can be dredged up with ease from the deep sea of our memories. Yet those merely pleasant outings of yesteryear, rides in which we trundled along without incident for a couple of hours, these are most likely lost amongst the mental reeds and swirling sands. In cycling, the best and the worst often arrive bundled together.

An important adjunct of this essential bundling together of pain and passion is that both are more memorable when shared. While there's undeniable worthiness in the passion and suffering of any marathon solo training ride, or, *in extremis*, a solo circumnavigation of the globe, this worthiness can feel diminished, downgraded even, if there's no one else around to experience the pain and passion with you. What's it worth if there's no witness to such acts of self-sacrifice? Of course, we now get to post the intimate details of our striving on to social media, where we gauge our own worthiness from the tally of digital thumbs-ups received. But such kudos is necessarily diluted and devolved. There's still no substitute for genuine experience – shared experience. Most of our best days on the bike – and even the best of the worst days – are those spent in the company of friends, where the legs are spinning up a storm of *sukha* and the *dukkha*-prone head (our helmeted inner chimp) can disengage from all extraneous topics, from all non-cycling related distractions, except of course those distractions – perhaps football, beer, or philosophy – with which we actively wish to engage.

'On our bikes as we rode to extremes, we learned more about each other than in any other setting.'[279] This was how American Christian Vande Velde described his tough, trans-Rockies training rides in the company of former US Postal teammate Michael Barry. In the middle of one such ride, along a snow-covered gravel path 9,000ft up a Colorado peak, Barry commented on how they seemed to be riding through fresh tracks. 'Yeah, because we are the only ones stupid enough to be up here,' replied Vande Velde. 'But of course I loved every minute of it too,' he added in a foreword to Barry's autobiography. 'A decade later I still remember the ride.'[280]

Vande Velde went on to explain how he'd been 'coerced' by Barry into training rides that he would never have fathomed were even possible. 'We'll climb the extra mountain that puts us into snow and freezing digits,' he wrote. 'But every time I am happy to push my limits and experience what I thought was too much.'[281] And most cyclists – at least cyclists of a certain subtype – will relate to this kind of experience. There's a friend of mine whose innate curiosity ('I wonder where this trail leads?') transforms routine mountain-bike rides into legendary sagas of white-water crossings, endless portage through dense, snake-infested undergrowth and, just as the sun is dipping low, with our dehydration levels moderate if not life-threatening, reaching a natural conclusion in a place where the locals speak a different language from that spoken where we started. Ah, but what memories!

'Nature is an old lady with few friends these days, and those who wish to make use of her charms, she rewards passionately,' wrote Tim Krabbé in *The Rider*. 'Bicycle racing is boring, all of a sudden I remember thinking that last time too. So why do I do it? The greater the suffering, the greater the pleasure. That is nature's payback to riders for the homage they pay her by suffering.'[282] The theme continued:

> Velvet pillows, safari parks, sunglasses; people have become woolly. They still have bodies that can walk for five days and four nights through a desert of snow, without food, but they accept praise for having taken a one-hour bicycle ride. 'Good for you.' Instead of expressing their gratitude for the rain by getting wet, people walk around with umbrellas.[283]

Taking advantage of nature's charms while forging closer friendships; this certainly beats the modern alternative of going to the shopping mall. And as expensive a pastime as cycling often can be, unlike a day spent at the local mall, you don't have to spend much money while actually on the bike. This was my teammate Brian's well-conceived theory of comparative consumption, the one he'd often invoke to persuade his girlfriend that he needed a new bike. 'Cycling is such a fantastic sport,' said Brian, one morning. 'You wake up early on a lovely day. You get to go out and ride in the fresh air. And you get to spend some quality time with your best friends.'

This proclamation, several hours into our ride, felt a little over the top, coming as it did from the lips of the original beige-jersey holder. That Brian's short-sleeved jersey was actually black and green was irrelevant: beige is foremost a state of mind, not a state of dress. We were riding along *tranquillo* (as the Italians are fond of saying), on what was admittedly a gloriously sunny, late-spring Saturday morning. And while this was emphatically not a typical beige sentiment – frankly, it was no shade of beige at all – I surmised that Brian's endorphins must now be doing their thing, all those feel-good molecules buzzing around excitedly inside his skull. I nodded my agreement, while still giving my teammate a quick once-over for signs of dehydration or insufficient food intake. We were heading south along the Hudson River Palisades, the jagged peaks of the Manhattan skyline gradually easing into view ahead of us. 'Cycling's great, it really is. You go out and ride with your best friends,' Brian repeated. 'And then you try to kill them.'

This was also fair comment. Our *grupetto* of a dozen riders was now spread out over some distance. A couple of first-category bruisers were still in sight ahead of us, while a handful of frazzled stragglers brought up the rear. Our early morning journey outwards from the city was usually an easy-paced, sociable affair, either hugging close to the Hudson River, through the Palisades Park, or the hillier inland route that took us through the almost aptly named township of Suffern. But whether it was something explosive in the coffee at the regular rest stop in Nyack, or simply an unavoidable consequence of the Universal Accelerative Law of Group Rides, our speed on the return leg would progress all too predictably from fairly brisk, through several intermediate versions of quick, and on to downright murderous, leaving a trail of blown-up casualties strewn along the highway.

Of course, it feels great to be out there with your mates. And while feeling great is all well and good, *putting the hurt on* a bunch of your best friends has the potential to make you feel even better. For some reason, no word or phrase in the English language accurately describes this uniquely pleasurable sensation. Even the fastidious Germans don't appear to have yet coined a phrase. I suspect this is just an administrative oversight and they'll get round to it in due course. When they do, the correct term will be *schadenfreund*. English translation: 'friend damage'.

The excruciating and yet exquisite damage that we inflict upon ourselves must be always measured against the damage that we inflict upon others. Expressed most simply, a good day on the bike might be one where we finish with a positive balance in our damage accounts; where, like a victorious boxer, we've dished out more pain than we've taken.

'When at the end of his career, they asked Rudi Altig about his greatest race, he didn't mention his world championship of 1966 or his victory in the Spanish Vuelta in 1962,' wrote Tim Krabbé in *The Rider*. 'He spoke of Trofeo Baracchi in 1962. What Altig had always loved about that race (a time trial for two-man teams) was that he had ridden his brace-mate Anquetil, right into the ground.'[284] Krabbé depicts the scene at the velodrome finish where a shattered Anquetil is 'carried away between two strong men – not to the victor's scaffold, but to the catacombs, like an old man being pulled away from the wreckage of a hurricane.'[285] *Schadenfreund über alles.*

On a more prosaic level, while a third-category racer competing against stronger riders in a second-category race might risk running himself into a small damage deficit, the experience should prove challenging and useful: he'll learn the rudiments of damage limitation. But throw him in with the lions, into the elite race, and the only possible outcome is that of a crippling damage overdraft; and overdrafts are rarely instructive or fun. Similarly, too much time spent training alone may not be the best way for us to manage our damage. Solo rides are by definition all about withdrawals, not deposits.

Yet the spectacle of bike racing is usually at its most thrilling when there's some live-action damage on display. To sit through a complete broadcast of a six-hour Tour stage is to invite general ridicule and comments questioning your sanity from other family members. Many hours, many miles of nothing happening at all: men in Lycra, men on bikes. Yet we continue to watch, waiting patiently for that critical moment of *über*-damage: the launch of a blistering and potentially unanswerable attack. When the commentator's voice suddenly jumps an octave or two. When, if we're lucky, we're thrown a choice titbit from the Phil Liggett lexicon, something along the lines of 'it's as though someone dropped a bomb in the field!'

The question of damage is once again relative and not at all absolute. Crossing the finish line in many little pieces can still feel utterly fantastic if you arrive just ahead of the others – others in smaller, more jagged pieces. 'Truly I think I never feel suffering,' confessed former French champion Peter Pouly in an interview, a man with a lifelong habit of crossing finish lines with plenty of daylight behind him. 'Yes, it makes a big difference when you are in the front: you feel no pain, no suffering. And when you are in the back, it is pain everywhere.' Similarly, as Graeme Obree explained, 'there is no pain, only effort', although it must surely help if, like Obree in his heyday, you're about to shatter a world record with your current effort. This suggests that in our ongoing efforts to understand the true nature of pain, we come up against an uncertainty principle – a Heisenberg of Hurt, if you will. Put another way, in order to assess properly a rider's degree of real-time suffering, we must know not only his degree of exertion, but also his relative position in the race: the Quantum Theory of Pain.

While nearing the end of a draft version of this book – writing this final chapter, in fact – I heard that a British triathlete in his mid-thirties had died in his sleep at his home in Chiang Mai. I'd trained with him a number of times; we'd first met a few years earlier when he was an occasional, weekends-only competitor, always very enthusiastic and in decent shape, if carrying a little extra weight. But over the past couple of years the competitive bug had bitten him hard. He joined a sponsored team and ramped up his training accordingly. Initial reports suggested he'd been attempting intensive workouts while also undertaking periodic fasts in an effort to lose weight.

A terrible, isolated incident, the kind of tragedy that strikes once in a blue moon in sport, or indeed in any aspect of life – crossing the road, taking the train to work – and yet in those sports where testing one's physical limits is part of the intrinsic appeal, such incidents may not be so isolated. A similar tragedy took place in the Cape Epic MTB race I rode several years ago: a young rider went off to bed one night after a gruelling stage and never woke up again. I've witnessed over the years more than a few dramatic finish-line collapses, including one or two of my own. The question is whether we can ever be truly objective about our own striving. How candid and realistic are we in assessing our fitness levels, or a particular day's weather conditions – or, for many of us, our categorical middle-agedness?

Teammates of the stricken triathlete had urged him to ease off on his training routine. Some months earlier he'd complained of dizziness when standing up after a hard workout. This is another warning sign of over-training, formally known as postural hypertension. 'It's when you get up quickly and feel a little lightheaded,' personal trainer Dr Ken Kinakin explained to me. He went on:

> The adrenal glands can't produce enough epinephrine and norepinephrine – adrenal substances – to create actual vasoconstriction. So if you come up quickly, a lot of the blood rushes down out of the head and down further into the body. In the clinic, we take someone's blood pressure while they're sitting or lying down and then have them stand up. Technically, their blood pressure should go up when they stand. Vasoconstriction will cause an increase in blood pressure. But a lot of times, it will actually *decrease* because the adrenal glands are so overstressed from overtraining that they just can't produce enough.

I'd experienced this myself, on one occasion ending up face down in my soup at a smart London restaurant, a few hours after a race – and a dozen or so hours before heading off to another race the next morning. But in a country like Thailand, with its unforgiving climate, where typical midday temperatures would have even super-fit European pros staging a sit-down protest at the side of the road (in the shade), it's surprising that similarly awful incidents – the point where our elective suffering becomes dangerous, even lethal – are not more frequent.

Few of us start riding our bikes because it's an effective means of damaging ourselves. We do it because it's fun. Then we ride some more. And so it continues, until one day you find yourself on a dual-carriageway slip road in the middle of nowhere, awaiting the starter's countdown and watching fat raindrops slide off your handlebars. It's 6.30am, it's a few degrees above freezing, the stiff crosswind is morphing into a gale and you're staring down the barrel of an 80km (50-mile) time trial, close on two hours of uninterrupted pain and suffering – a sensation almost impossible to describe to anyone who's never attempted such a thing. But equally hard to convey is the sublime lightening of the spirit that supersedes the pain as soon as the race is over. For the lucky few who excel at this kind of thing, they're then offered a chance to do it for a living.

However, doing anything for a living isn't always the best way to preserve our passion. Crucially, the professional's routine of daily suffering becomes non-elective. During her first post-retirement bike ride, Olympic champion Victoria Pendleton experienced a minor epiphany. As she told the *Guardian*: 'We did about three hours and I really enjoyed it, just cruising around. It was a nice day, the sun was out, we stopped for a coffee. I was thinking, "I could turn round right now. I could go home. I could take a shortcut. I could have two pieces of cake." … It was really liberating. It was more like riding my bike in my childhood.'[286]

A flurry of asterisks now despoils the roster of Tour de France winners; a flurry that easily could have grown into a blizzard if the rules used to depose Big Tex had been applied more even-handedly. A belated asterisking of confessed doper Jacques Anquetil's five victories, and perhaps also those of another five-times winner, Miguel Indurain (whose stealthy domination of the early EPO era was largely swept under the performance-enhancing carpet), at least might satisfy those who now decry the witch-hunting of Lance. The Tour de France winners (or, more correctly, those riders who reached Paris in yellow) either side of the Armstrong years were Bjarne Riis, Jan Ullrich, Marco Pantani, Floyd Landis and Alberto Contador. All have either confessed to doping, or received bans for doping. The first four in this list also battled periods of depression during and after their careers – a battle tragically lost in Pantani's case. When 2012 Tour winner Bradley Wiggins remarked that he sometimes wished he hadn't won the Tour de France, he was trying to communicate the sense of unease he felt during his brief stint as 'the most famous man in the country'.[287] But Wiggins, a keen student of the sport's chequered history, might have also looked at the list of recent winners and wondered what might be in store for him.

The pain of bike racing can be transcendent, but the question is whether this particular brand of alchemy requires as its source material a minimum of background pain, a sufficient quantity of base suffering, to then transmute into superlative, golden efforts on the road or the track. Maybe not in each and every case, and yet so many of the toughest competitors on a bike have appeared fuelled by some form of inner angst. It's still no simple matter to deconstruct why Eddy Merckx drove himself as hard as he did. 'Why did Merckx tolerate such relentless suffering? Is there nobility in it? Is there beauty in its futility?' asked Henry Sheen in the *New Statesman*.[288] At the very least, a desire not only to win the race – every race – but also to destroy completely your rivals each time does take a certain mindset.

To start a race feeling more or less at peace with the world or with yourself is probably not ideal in this context. Instead, stewing up decent amounts of hurt, rage and injustice can make you a more destructive force on the bike. The Eddy Merckx who annihilated the rest of the field in the 1969 Tour de France, winning by over seventeen minutes and picking up the overall, points and mountain classifications, had been evicted from the Giro a few months earlier after testing positive for a banned stimulant. According to *L'Équipe*, Merckx arrived at the Tour 'an inaccessible and surly man ... and it's an angry champion, in a quest to be rehabilitated, who has crushed the Tour under the heavy weight of his bitterness'.[289] Recounting Merckx's equally impressive victory in the 1969 Tour of Flanders, where he unleashed similar havoc on the peloton, Suze Clemenson writes of how 'anger drives him as it so often will in his career ... Merckx is determined to show ... his rivals and *directeur sportif* – who's boss. For 25km he battles the wind alone, stiffening over the drops like a chilled cadaver, refusing to sit up or give up.'[290]

'For as long as I can remember, I've had this problem,' Tyler Hamilton revealed in his autobiography:

> The closest I can come to describing it is to say that it's a darkness that lives on the edge of my mind, a painful heaviness that comes and goes unexpectedly. When it comes on it's like a black wave, pushing on me until it feels like I'm a thousand feet down at the bottom of a cold dark ocean.[291]

Hamilton was also more adept than most at finishing Grand Tours nursing a broken bone or two. When he finished fourth in the 2003 Tour de France after snapping his collarbone in a spill on the first stage, race doctor Gérard Porte called it 'the finest example of courage I've come across'.[292] But if the painful heaviness in Hamilton's mind had somehow abated, might he have lost a degree of his uncommon ability to endure suffering in the saddle?

In a well-known 1980s survey, a number of elite athletes were asked what they would be willing to sacrifice in exchange for success. The results showed more than half of those polled would take a drug that guaranteed them an Olympic gold medal but would also kill them within five years – the so-called 'Goldman Dilemma' named after the survey's lead researcher. Subsequent surveys over the next decade yielded consistently similar results: roughly half of all pro athletes in the poll claimed that they would willingly accept such a Faustian bargain. Pro cycling may be slowly emerging from the dark ages of overstocked fridges and blood bags in hotel rooms, but too many elite racers still meet premature ends under what might be described at best as unusual circumstances. From the old 1920s staples of strychnine, cocaine, chloroform and horse ointment – as favoured by the long-suffering Pélissier brothers – the substances of choice have changed over the years, but they have never disappeared. They have instead become ever more sophisticated, more effective and more difficult to detect, bringing us to the point where the genetic make-up of athletes can now be artificially altered to 'manufacture' stronger and faster competitors – tweaking cyclists' genomes to allow them to produce more natural erythropoietin, for example. This prospect of laboratory-designed robo-athletes, custom-built to suffer harder and further, is no longer confined to the realm of science fiction. According to H. Lee Sweeney, a professor at the University of Pennsylvania School of Medicine, 'The world may be about to watch one of its last Olympic Games without genetically enhanced athletes.'[293] A chilling prediction, but also one made over a decade ago in 2004 – with four sets of Summer and Winter Olympics having taken place by September 2016.

In 2013, a number of elite cyclists tested positive for a drug known as GW1516, a synthetic substance that works on a muscle-building gene. Commercial development of the compound was abandoned almost a decade ago after clinical trials found it to be highly carcinogenic and yet today GW1516 can be easily ordered from any number of Internet sites. While the World Anti-Doping Authority has taken the unusual step of issuing an explicit caution against its use, the medical profession remains doubtful whether those with the most incentive to cheat will ever pay much attention to such warnings. An overarching desire to win is a defining characteristic of the elite athlete, according to Dr James McNair Connor of the University of New South Wales. Yet in Dr Connor's 2009 follow-up study of the Goldman Dilemma, this 'win at all costs' trait was virtually non-existent amongst the general population: less than 1 per cent of non-athletes said they would take a drug that ensured both athletic success and an early death.[294]

'*Vous etes des assassins! Oui, des assassins!*' bawled Frenchman Octave Lapize on his way to victory in stage ten of the 1910 Tour de

France, a 326km (203-mile) jaunt across several of the highest Pyrenean peaks.[295] Lapize, the eventual overall winner – and beyond all doubt the best mountain climber in the race – took over fourteen hours to complete the stage, approximately four hours fewer than the peloton's exhausted laggards, who wouldn't reach the finish until late that night.

'Tell Desgrange you cannot ask human beings to do a thing like this!' Lapize screamed at a roadside journalist.[296] This was while pushing his single-gear bike up the final climb of the day, the ungraded Col d'Aubisque. The 1910 Tour was the first edition of the race to include a detour to the Pyrenees, with press reports labelling many of the new routes 'bizarre' and 'dangerous' and later coining the phrase 'The Circle of Death' for the four brutal ascents of the Col de Peyresourde, the Col d'Aspin, the Col du Tourmalet and the Col d'Aubisque. Henri Desgrange would later pronounce the 1910 Tour de France a resounding success: sales of L'Auto newspapers were doing very nicely indeed. The experimental Pyrenean detour soon became a Tour standard and the race has since visited the Tourmalet no fewer than eighty-two times, more than any other major climb.

The uncompromising slopes of the Pyrenees were also where Eddie Merckx chose to write the opening pages of his personal Tour de France history. Climbing the Tourmalet during his first Grand Boucle in 1969, the young Belgian sprinted away from the lead group just before the summit to claim maximum bonus points. He waited on the descent for a regrouping, but after glancing back to see a decent gap, he attacked again and rode the next 140km (87 miles) alone. He won the stage by eight minutes. Where other, mortal riders might have chosen to coast home, grandly savouring the moment with waves and smiles to the crowd, Eddy Merckx instead drove a relentless pace all the way to the finish.

'Merckx – a mystery of the human condition – was greater than the Tour, greater than men,' trumpeted L'Équipe the next day.[297] The world, the newspaper claimed, had just witnessed 'the birth of Merckxism'. And for those L'Équipe readers unclear on the precise meaning of this, the newspaper duly obliged with a clarification. Merckxism was simply about winning for the sake of winning. Winning just for the hell of it. Merckxism, they explained, was 'the conquest of futility'.[298]

The Holy Trinity of bike racing – Damage, Divinity, Futility – and the conquest thereof. Naturally, this overcoming of futility usually carries distinctive French overtones. 'Always go too far, because that's where you'll find the truth,' said Albert Camus. And the hallmark of winners has always been to overreach, to boldly go too far. 'Winning isn't everything, it's the only thing,' is today's oft-quoted inversion of the original Olympic ideal. Yet the current tawdry realpolitik of world sports – seemingly endless corruption and doping scandals – is not quite what Baron de Coubertin had in mind.

'It might be lonely up here, but I sure like the view,' said actor Charlie Sheen, after famously claiming the #*winning* Twitter hashtag as his own. But as Eddy Merckx and Lance Armstrong (and Mr Sheen) know too well, the view can't last forever. A despondent Merckx finished sixth in his final Tour; a suddenly crash-prone Armstrong finished twenty-third (pre-DQ) in his last attempt. The clogged, chaotic vista from mid-peloton is far less appealing, the suffering feels more damaging and a sense of creeping futility may be harder to ignore. In a spectacularly rapid descent, Charlie Sheen went from being Hollywood's top earner to telling TV audiences he had tiger blood coursing through his veins. Which, if true, could be a significant improvement over EPO.

For athletes of the non-elite variety and, in particular, those making up the unwashed ranks of MAMILs, there's no obligation to forgo all of our elective suffering, our pain and damage. Without these, we would also forfeit our more humdrum conquests of futility and our occasional brushes with divinity – or, if you prefer, our ongoing personal growth and development. But navigating the smoothly paved path of the Middle Way, not so much as a bicycling Buddhist, but as more of a freewheeling agnostic, may in the end prove more satisfying than a devout existence as a two-wheeled fundamentalist. To keep our damage accounts in healthy credit, to ensure that the *sukha* in our spokes helps counterbalance the ever-present *dukkha* and to delve into the deeper suffersphere only sparingly. An Indian prince who seemed to know his onions emphatically ruled out bodily torture as a means of discovering inner truth well over 2,500 years ago. An oddly similar form of bodily torture, revived as grand sporting theatre in the early years of the twentieth century by eccentric newspaper proprietor Henri Desgrange, was initially dreamed up only as a ruse to increase his daily circulation numbers.

Notes

[1] Weber, E., 'Foreword' in 'Dauncey, H., and Hare, G., *The Tour de France 1903–2003* (London: Frank Cass, 2003; 2nd ed. Oxford: Routledge, 2012)

[2] *Tom Fordyce's Blog*, BBC Sport, http://www.bbc.co.uk/blogs/tomfordyce/2012/06/stephen_roche_remembers_one_sp.html, 26 June 2012

[3] YouTube, '1987 Tour de France – La Plagne', https://www.youtube.com/watch?v=sQojh-wqL04

[4] Hutchinson, M., *Faster: The Obsession, Science and Luck Behind the World's Fastest Cyclists* (London: Bloomsbury, 2014)

[5] *Ibid.*

[6] Fotheringham, W., *Merckx: Half Man, Half Bike* (London: Yellow Jersey Press, 2013)

[7] http://www.theguardian.com/sport/2014/jul/24/bradley-wiggins-commonwealth-games-tour-de-france

[8] http://www.theguardian.com/sport/2015/apr/05/bradley-wiggins-hated-being-tour-de-france-winner

[9] http://www.theguardian.com/sport/2013/sep/12/bradley-wiggins-almost-quit-2012-tour-de-france

[10] http://velonews.competitor.com/2013/07/news/must-read-wiggins-couldnt-bear-to-watch-tour_297330, 29 July 2013

[11] *The Autobiography of John Stuart Mill*

[12] Macmahon, D., *The Pursuit of Happiness* (London: Penguin, 2007)

[13] http://www.theguardian.com/sport/2014/jul/24/bradley-wiggins-commonwealth-games-tour-de-france

[14] http://www.theguardian.com/sport/2014/jul/24/bradley-wiggins-commonwealth-games-tour-de-france

[15] http://www.bbc.com/sport/0/cycling/30523006, 18 December 2014

[16] Syed, M., *Bounce* (London: Harper Collins, 2010)

[17] http://www.bbc.com/news/magazine-10965608, 14 August 2010

[18] http://www.theguardian.com/commentisfree/2012/sep/11/mamil-middle-aged-men-in-lycra

[19] http://bjsm.bmj.com/content/39/2/120.full, *British Journal of Sports Medicine*, Vol. 39, No. 2, 2005

[20] *Ibid.*

[21] http://www.bicycling.com/training/fitness/transcendent-pain, 5 July 2012

[22] Extract from Kundera, M., *Immortality*. Copyright © 1990, Milan Kundera, used by permission of The Wylie Agency (UK) Ltd

[23] http://www.bbc.com/sport/0/cycling/30523006, 18 December 2014

[24] Hamilton, T., and Coyle, D., *The Secret Race: Inside the Hidden World of the Tour de France* (London: Bantam Press, 2012)

[25] http://www.independent.co.uk/sport/general/others/federico-bahamontes-the-fiery-eagle-who-flew-up-the-mountains-1737770.html, 23 October 2011

[26] http://coachrobmuller.blogspot.com/2011/10/eddy-merckxthe-cannibal.html, 2 October 2011

[27] Kress, J.L., *Journal of Sport Behavior*, Vol. 30, No. 4 (Califomia State University)

[28] http://www.ncbi.nlm.nih.gov/pubmed/12595695, *Science*, 21 February 2003

[29] http://www.theguardian.com/sport/2009/jun/28/tour-de-france-mont-ventoux-1972

[30] Jarry, A., *The Selected Works of Alfred Jarry* (New York: Grove Press, 1965)

[31] http://jamesshelley.net/2011/03/passion-over-pleasure/

[32] https://100tours100tales.wordpress.com/2014/04/01/1969-the-birth-of-merckxissimo-at-the-tour-of-flanders/

[33] Karnazes, D., *Ultramarathon Man: Confessions of an All-Night Runner* (New York: Tarcher 2006)

[34] http://content.time.com/time/magazine/article/0,9171,333838,00.html

[35] Jarry, A., *The Selected Works of Alfred Jarry* (New York: Grove Press, 1965)

[36] http://www.outsideonline.com/1912501/how-strava-changing-way-we-ride, 8 January 2013

[37] *Ibid.*

[38] *Ibid.*

[39] *Ibid.*

[40] *Ibid.*

[41] http://www.newstatesman.com/culture/culture/2012/05/review-merckx-half-man-half-bike-william-fotheringham

[42] http://velonews.competitor.com/2014/04/news/fall-heard-round-liege-dan-martin-rues-bit-bad-poetry_325571, 27 April 2014

[43] Armstrong, L. with Jenkins, S., *Every Second Counts* (New York: Doubleday, 2003)

[44] http://www.theguardian.com/lifeandstyle/2011/jun/26/this-much-i-know-david-millar

[45] http://velonews.competitor.com/2014/07/news/must-read-ted-king-writes-early-exit-tour_336548, 15 July 2014

[46] http://velonews.competitor.com/2014/04/news/fall-heard-round-liege-dan-martin-rues-bit-bad-poetry_325571, 27 April 2014

[47] http://velonews.competitor.com/2014/05/news/tuft-dons-pink-orica-wins-stage-1-giro-ditalia_326920, 9 May 2014

[48] http://velonews.competitor.com/2012/07/news/hoogerland-and-flecha-looking-for-justice-in-2011-tour-car-crash_227194, 3 July 2012

[49] http://velonews.competitor.com/2014/10/news/taylor-phinney-qa-recovery-tour-crash_350454, 24 October 2014

[50] http://velonews.competitor.com/2012/10/analysis/from-the-pages-of-velo-remembering-hardman-fiorenzo-magni_262015, 19 October 2012

[51] Hamilton, T., and Coyle, D., *The Secret Race: Inside the Hidden World of the Tour de France* (London: Bantam Press, 2012)

[52] Ibid.

[53] Berstein, L., et al., Psychosomatics, Vol. 36, No. 3, May/June 1995

[54] Bergland, C., The Athlete's Way: Sweat and the Biology of Bliss (New York: St Martin's Press, 2007)

[55] https://www.psychologytoday.com/blog/the-athletes-way/201301/cortisol-why-the-stress-hormone-is-public-enemy-no-1, 22 January 2013

[56] Ralston, A., *Between a Rock and a Hard Place* (New York: Atria Books, 2004)

[57] http://velonews.competitor.com/2001/07/news/frustrating-end-for-vaughters_1265, 24 July 2001

[58] *Ibid.*

[59] Peppiatt, M., *Anatomy of an Enigma* (London: Weidenfeld & Nicolson 1996)

[60] Coelho, P., *The Alchemist* (London: HarperCollins 2006)

[61] http://www.theguardian.com/football/2014/jun/10/lionel-messi-vomits-argentina-alejandro-sabella-world-cup, 10 June 2014

[62] https://100tours100tales.wordpress.com/2014/04/01/1969-the-birth-of-merckxissimo-at-the-tour-of-flanders/, 1 April 2014

[63] http://jewishcurrents.org/jews-in-american-sports-7402, 3 October 2011

[64] http://mentalfloss.com/article/61140/15-unique-illnesses-you-can-only-come-down-german, 15 January 2015

[65] http://www.bbc.co.uk/news/magazine-15987082, 3 December 2011

[66] http://www.bbc.com/sport/0/cycling/30523006, 18 December 2014

[67] *Ibid.*

[68] https://twitter.com/greghenderson1/status/12691462660

[69] Agassi, A., *Open* (London: HarperCollins, 2009)

[70] *Ibid.*

[71] http://www.spiegel.de/international/world/spiegel-interview-with-andre-agassi-i-really-hated-tennis-a-660148-4.html, 10 November 2009

[72] Pendleton, V. *Between the Lines* (London: HarperSport, 2013)

[73] *Ibid.*

[74] http://www.theguardian.com/sport/2008/sep/30/bradleywiggins.cycling

[75] *Ibid.*

[76] http://www.independent.co.uk/sport/general/others/cycling-summer-fun-leaves-kenny-depressed-at-getting-back-on-track-8317159.html, 15 November 2012

[77] 'The Graham Jones Story', http://www.classiclightweights.co.uk/graham-jones-riders.html, 2010

[78] http://www.independent.co.uk/sport/football/news-and-comment/dr-steve-peters-the-psychiatrist-charged-with-ridding-anfield-of-the-fear-factor-8554166.html, 29 March 2013

[79] http://www.dailymail.co.uk/sport/othersports/article-2453191/Ronnie-OSullivan-exclusive-interview-Martin-Samuel.html, 10 October 2013

[80] Pendleton, V. *Between the Lines* (London: HarperSport, 2013)

[81] http://www.telegraph.co.uk/sport/othersports/cycling/bradley-wiggins/9420889/Bradley-Wiggins-The-hero-who-did-it-without-his-dad.html, 23 July 2012

[82] Pendleton, V. *Between the Lines* (London: HarperSport, 2013)

[83] http://www.independent.co.uk/news/business/comment/steve-peters-making-money-by-managing-the-inner-chimp-9503369.html, 7 June 2014

[84] http://www.bbc.com/sport/0/cycling/30523006, 18 December 2014

[85] http://www.theguardian.com/sport/2015/feb/16/laura-trott-weird-idol-world-championships, 16 February 2015

[86] Watson, D., 'Review: Howard Jones – *Human's Lib'*, *NME*, 17 March 1984 (London: IPC Media © NME/Time Inc. (UK) Ltd)

[87] Pendleton, V. *Between the Lines* (London: HarperSport, 2013)

[88] *Ibid.*

[89] http://www.theglobeandmail.com/sports/more-sports/german-cyclist-jens-voigt-rides-off-into-the-sunshine/article20182708/?page=1, 22 August 2014

[90] http://www.theguardian.com/sport/2009/sep/12/saracens-brendan-venter-premiership-wembley, 12 September 2009

[91] *Ibid.*

[92] http://www.theguardian.com/society/2014/aug/15/suicide-silence-depressed-men

[93] http://www.philosophyforlife.org/socrates-among-the-saracens/, 12 July 2013

[94] http://www.philosophyforlife.org/socrates-among-the-saracens/, 12 July 2013

[95] http://www.theguardian.com/sport/blog/2015/jan/11/saracens-x-patches-sean-ingle, 11 January 2015

[96] *Ibid.*

[97] http://www.philosophyforlife.org/socrates-among-the-saracens/, 12 July 2013

[98] Pendleton, V. *Between the Lines* (London: HarperSport, 2013)

[99] http://www.thepositivemind.com/poetry/aboutpainanddullnessarticle.html

[100] *Ibid.*

[101] http://www.heraldscotland.com/arts_ents/13099073.Graeme_Obree_smashes_the_myth_of_sporting_success/, 6 April 2013

[102] Obree, G., *The Flying Scotsman* (Edinburgh: Birlinn, 2004)

[103] http://www.dailyrecord.co.uk/sport/other-sports/cycling/graeme-obree-puts-beastie-up-2272927, 14 September 2013

[104] *Ibid.*

[105] http://www.parliament.uk/edm/2012-13/943

[106] Kimmage, P., *Rough Ride* (London: Yellow Jersey Press, 2008; first published 1990)

[107] *Ibid.*

[108] http://www.theguardian.com/sport/100-tours-100-tales/2015/jan/14/french-cartoons-charlie-hebdo-satirised-lance-armstrong-puerile-perfect, 14 January 2015

[109] Stockdale, J., Stockdale on Stoicism II: Master of My Fate, http://www.usna.edu/Ethics/_files/documents/Stoicism2.pdf

[110] *Ibid.*

[111] Collins, J., *Good to Great* (London: Random House, 2001)

[112] *Ibid.*

[113] *Ibid.*

[114] Krabbé, T., *The Rider* (London: Bloomsbury, 2002)

[115] *The Pursuit of Excellence: The Olympic Story* (London: Grolier Enterprises, 1979)

[116] *Ibid.*

[117] Kelly, S., *Hunger: The Autobiography* (Peloton Publishing, 2013)

[118] Macgowan, R., *Kings of the Road: A Portrait of Racers and Racing* (Champaign, IL: Human Kinetics, 1987)

[119] *Ibid.*

[120] *Ibid.*

[121] Velominati, *The Rules: The Way of the Cycling Disciple* (New York: W.W. Norton, 2013)

[122] http://www.thewashingmachinepost.net/sean_kelly/review.html, 1 July 2013

[123] http://www.theguardian.com/sport/2010/jul/22/tour-laurent-fignon-greg-lemond, 22 July 2010

[124] Fignon, L., *We Were Young and Carefree* (London: Yellow Jersey Press, 2010)

[125] *Ibid.*

[126] *Ibid.*

[127] *Ibid.*

[128] http://www.cyclingweekly.co.uk/news/laurent-fignon-a-tribute-to-an-icon-1425, 20 December 2010

[129] http://www.cyclingweekly.co.uk/news/latest-news/laurent-fignon-my-way-or-the-fairway-57955, 31 August 2010

[130] http://www.abc.net.au/worldtoday/content/2013/s3803336.htm, 15 July 2013

[131] Clemitson, S., *P is for Peloton: The A–Z of Cycling* (London: Bloomsbury, 2015)

[132] http://www.scotsman.com/lifestyle/interview-david-millar-cyclist-1-1701981, 19 June 2011

[133] http://autobus.cyclingnews.com/news/?id=2003/dec03/dec08news, 8 December 2003

[134] http://www.theguardian.com/news/2005/dec/08/guardianobituaries.cycling, 8 December 2005

[135] *Ibid.*

[136] *L'Équipe*, 12 July 2000

[137] http://www.independent.ie/sport/the-fatal-attraction-of-claveyrolat-26262128.html, 12 December 1999

[138] Ryckman, R.M., *Theories of Personality* (Belmont, CA: Wadsworth, 2012)

[139] http://www.cyclingnews.com/news/andy-schleck-retires-from-professional-cycling/, 9 October 2014

[140] http://www.cyclingnews.com/features/andy-schleck-im-still-here/, 1 July 2014

[141] *Ibid.*

[142] http://velonews.competitor.com/2014/10/news/andy-schleck-announces-retirement-from-bike-racing_348875, 9 October 2014

[143] Philip, R., *Scottish Sporting Legends* (London: Random House, 2011)

[144] Connor, J., *Wide-Eyed and Legless: Inside the Tour de France* (London: Random House, 1988)

[145] http://thesoftsaddle.com/stories/2013/7/22/the-curse-of-the-climbers, 22 July 2013

[146] http://www.theguardian.com/sport/2007/jul/06/cycling.tourdefrance

[147] Cale, J.J., 'Cocaine' (Shelter Records, 1976)

[148] Ullrich, J. with Bossdorf, H. *Ganz oder gar nicht: Meine Geschichte* (Berlin: Econ Verlag, 2004

[149] http://www.cyclingnews.com/news/ullrich-doubt-depression-and-physical-problems-after-doping-case/, 11 May 2012

[150] http://velonews.competitor.com/2012/12/analysis/from-the-pages-of-velo-in-the-eye-of-the-tornado_268980/2, 29 December 2012

[151] http://www.dhnet.be/sports/cyclisme/vdb-j-aurais-du-etre-un-dieu-51b7bb28e4b0de6db98a7f77, 19 April 2008

[152] Gaumont, P., *Prisonnier du Dopage* (Paris, Grasset & Fasquelle, 2005)

[153] Millar, D., *Racing Through the Dark* (New York: Touchstone, 2012)

[154] *Ibid.*

[155] Hamilton, T., and Coyle, D., *The Secret Race: Inside the Hidden World of the Tour de France* (London: Bantam Press, 2012)

[156] http://m.theweek.com/articles/492310/cleaning-tour-de-france, 30 July 2010

[157] http://www.theguardian.com/sport/2006/jan/27/cycling.cycling, 27 January 2006

[158] Tilin, A., *The Doper Next Door* (Berkeley, CA: Counterpoint, 2012)

[159] *Ibid.*

[160] http://www.outsideonline.com/1924306/drug-test, 1 November 2003

[161] http://velonews.competitor.com/2007/06/news/road/thursdays-eurofile-valverde-denies-manzano-charges-cofidis-plans-to-leave_12375, 7 June 2007

[162] Brand, R., *et al.*, 'Psychological symptoms and chronic mood in representative samples of elite student-athletes, deselected student-athletes and comparison students', *School Mental Health* (Springer Journals), 1 September 2013

[163] http://www.cyclingnews.com/features/bjarne-riis-bearing-the-burden-of-truth-1/, 22 April 2009

[164] http://www.cyclingnews.com/features/philippe-gaumont-the-life-and-times-of-an-enfant-terrible/, 16 July 2013

[165] Kabat-Zinn, J., *Wherever You Go, There You Are: Mindfulness Meditation in Everyday Life* (New York, 1994)

[166] Gardner, F.L. and Moore, Z.E., http://www.researchgate.net/publication/223394474_A_MindfulnessAcceptanceCommitment_(MAC)_based_approach_to_athletic_performance_enhancement_Theoretical_considerations, *Behavior Therapy Journal*, September 2004

[167] *Ibid.*

[168] Csikszentmihalyi, M., Flow: *The Psychology of Optimal Experience* (New York: Harper Perennial Modern Classics, 2008)

[169] *Ibid.*

[170] *Ibid.*

[171] Williams, M., and Penman D., *Mindfulness: A practical guide to finding peace in a frantic world* (London: Hachette UK, 2011)

[172] http://www.cyclingweekly.co.uk/news/latest-news/tramadol-blame-classics-crashes-says-lotto-belisol-doctor-119652, 2 April 2014

[173] http://bikesnobnyc.blogspot.com/2010/05/high-road-of-missiles-and-missionaries.html, 17 May 2010

[174] http://velonews.competitor.com/2010/07/news/jens-voigt-shrugs-off-another-high-speed-crash_130284, 23 July 2010

[175] http://www.si.com/more-sports/2013/05/10/andy-hampsten-1988-giro-ditalia, 10 May 2013

[176] http://uk.reuters.com/article/2014/10/02/uk-cycling-tour-thailand-idUKKCN0HR0KR20141002, 2 October 2014

[177] *Ibid.*

[178] http://www.si.com/more-sports/2013/05/10/andy-hampsten-1988-giro-ditalia, 10 May 2013

[179] *Ibid.*

[180] http://www.independent.co.uk/sport/general/others/bradley-wiggins-and-his-love-hate-affair-with-the-giro-ditalia-8603430.html, 7 May 2013

[181] http://www.podiumcafe.com/2008/5/27/540213/a-fine-whine, 27 May 2008

[182] http://www.cyclingweekly.co.uk/racing/giro-ditalia/epic-days-the-passo-di-gavia-giro-ditalia-1988-170175, 7 May 2015

[183] http://www.si.com/more-sports/2013/05/10/andy-hampsten-1988-giro-ditalia, 10 May 2013

[184] http://velonews.competitor.com/2012/05/news/from-the-pages-of-velo-hampstens-giro-i-was-so-happy-to-survive_221346, 27 May 2012

[185] http://www.bbc.com/sport/0/cycling/30523006, 18 December 2014

[186] http://www.investopedia.com/terms/l/liars-poker.asp

[187] Lewis, M., *Liar's Poker: Rising Through the Wreckage on Wall Street* (New York: W.W. Norton, 1989)

[188] http://www.theguardian.com/sport/2001/dec/20/tourdefrance2001.williamfotheringham, 20 December 2001

[189] *Ibid.*

[190] http://www.bbc.com/sport/0/cycling/30523006, 18 December 2014

[191] *Ibid.*

[192] http://www.bbc.com/sport/0/cycling/18507575, 4 July 2014

[193] http://www.cyclingnews.com/news/race-radios-saved-horrillos-life-rabobank-teammate-claims/, 4 February 2011

[194] http://www.theguardian.com/sport/2015/jan/11/team-sky-dave-brailsford-cycling, 11 January 2015

[195] *Ibid.*

[196] Hamilton, T., and Coyle, D., *The Secret Race: Inside the Hidden World of the Tour de France* (London: Bantam Press, 2012)

[197] *Ibid.*

[198] Shepard, R.J., http://www.sportsci.org/encyc/

[199] http://www.joefrielsblog.com/2012/08/the-aging-athlete-getting-older-getting-faster.html, 14 August 2012

[200] *Ibid.*

[201] Nichols, J.F., and Rauh, M.J., 'Longitudinal Changes in Bone Mineral Density in Male Master Cyclists and Nonathletes', *The Journal of Strength and Conditioning Research*, 2011; http://journals.lww.com/nsca-jscr/Abstract/2011/03000/Longitudinal_Changes_in_Bone_Mineral_Density_in.21.aspx

[202] *Ibid.*

[203] Pratchett, T., *Moving Pictures* (London: Victor Gollancz/Corgi, 1990)

[204] Cardain, L., and Friel, J., *The Paleo Diet for Athletes* (New York: Rodale, 2012)

[205] *Ibid.*

[206] http://usatoday30.usatoday.com/sports/cycling/2011-06-30-chris-horner-tour-de-france_n.htm, 30 June 2011

[207] http://chrishornerracing.com/articles/?currentPage=3, 8 January 2010

[208] Carter, M., *Uneasy Rider: Travels Through a Mid-Life Crisis* (London: Ebury Press, 2009)

[209] http://www.cyclingweekly.co.uk/news/latest-news/eddy-merckx-interview-59823, 17 June 2010

[210] http://www.theage.com.au/victoria/unlit-cyclists-face-greater-injury-20120726-22vep.html, 27 July 2012

[211] http://www.economist.com/node/17722567, 16 December 2010

[212] http://www.ft.com/intl/cms/s/0/26a4fa58-47a3-11dc-9096-0000779fd2ac.html, 7 August 2011

[213] http://okrent2.rssing.com/browser.php?indx=24547481&item=160, 27 January 2015

[214] Adams, D., and Lloyd, J., *The Meaning of Liff* (London: Pan Books, 1983)

[215] http://www.cyclingnews.com/news/voigt-i-cant-ask-for-a-better-goodbye/, 19 September 2014

[216] http://www.cyclingnews.com/news/voigt-breaks-world-hour-record/, 18 September 2014

[217] http://velonews.competitor.com/2012/02/news/centenarian-claims-hour-record_206632, 17 February 2012

[218] *Ibid.*

[219] http://www.cyclingweekly.co.uk/news/latest-news/eddy-merckx-interview-59823, 17 June 2010

[220] Friebe, D., *Eddy Merckx: The Cannibal* (London: Ebury Press, 2012)

[221] *Ibid.*

[222] Fotheringham, W., *Merckx: Half Man, Half Bike* (London: Yellow Jersey Press, 2012)

[223] *Ibid.*

[224] *Ibid.*

[225] http://www.cyclingnews.com/news/armstrong-says-cycling-is-still-in-a-mess-after-his-doping-confession/, 5 November 2014

[226] *Ibid.*

[227] Duffy, C.A., *The World's Wife* (London: Picador, 2012)

[228] Gladwell, M., *Outliers* (New York: Little, Brown & Co., 2008)

[229] http://www.cyclingweekly.co.uk/blog/dr-hutch-using-power-meter-like-getting-tattoo-157357, 13 February 2015

[230] *Ibid.*

[231] *Ibid.*

[232] http://www.velominati.com/the-rules/, 1 June 2009

[233] http://www.joefrielsblog.com/2010/04/kiss-periodization.html, 3 April 2010

[234] Russell, B., *The Conquest of Happiness* (London: George Allen & Unwin, 1930)

[235] http://velonews.competitor.com/2013/04/news/paris-roubaix-welcome-to-hell_280292, 2 April 2013

[236] http://www.cyclingweekly.co.uk/news/latest-news/lex-nederlof-oldest-rider-pro-peloton-116873, 6 March 2014

[237] http://home.trainingpeaks.com/blog/article/a-quick-guide-to-the-paleo-diet-for-athletes, 31 October 2008

[238] http://wenzelcoaching.com/blog/cyclists-who-ride-too-much-exercise-addiction-as-a-cause-of-overtraining/, 5 May 2007

[239] *Ibid.*

[240] http://www.joefrielsblog.com/2010/09/how-to-recover.html, 6 September 2010

[241] http://wenzelcoaching.com/blog/cyclists-who-ride-too-much-exercise-addiction-as-a-cause-of-overtraining/, 5 May 2007

[242] http://www.rice.edu/~jenky/sports/overtraining.html, 1998

[243] *Ibid.*

[244] 'Evaluation of immune response after moderate and overtraining exercise in Wistar rats', *Iran J. Basic Med. Sci.*, http://www.ncbi.nlm.nih.gov/pmc/articles/PMC3938879/, 7 January 2014

[245] 'Inflammation and adipose tissue: effects of progressive load training in rats', *Lipids in Health and Disease*, http://www.ncbi.nlm.nih.gov/pubmed/20920329, 4 October 2010

[246] 'Relationship between inflammatory cytokines and self-report measures of training overload', *Research in Sports Medicine*, http://www.ncbi.nlm.nih.gov/pubmed/20397115, 18 April 2010

[247] 'The overtraining syndrome in athletes: a stress-related disorder', *Journal of Endocrinological Investigation*, http://www.ncbi.nlm.nih.gov/pubmed/15717662, 27 June 2004

[248] *Ibid.*

[249] 'The effect of tapering period on plasma pro-inflammatory cytokine levels and performance in elite male cyclists', *J Sports Sci. Med.*, http://www.ncbi.nlm.nih.gov/pmc/articles/PMC3761545/, 1 December 2009

[250] http://www.theguardian.com/lifeandstyle/2015/jan/04/depression-allergic-reaction-inflammation-immune-system, 4 January 2015

[251] http://www.psyweb.com/lifestyle/depression/depression-a-non-contagious-infectious-disease, 20 February 2015

[252] http://www.theguardian.com/lifeandstyle/2015/jan/04/depression-allergic-reaction-inflammation-immune-system, 4 January 2015

[253] 'The unknown mechanism of the overtraining syndrome: clues from depression and psychoneuroimmunology', Sports Medicine, http://www.ncbi.nlm.nih.gov/pubmed/11839081, 2002

[254] 'Genetic variation in human NPY expression affects stress response and emotion', *Nature*, http://www.ncbi.nlm.nih.gov/pubmed/18385673, 24 April 2008

[255] 'Plasma neuropeptide Y concentrations in combat exposed veterans: relationship to trauma exposure, recovery from PTSD, and coping', *Biological Psychiatry*, http://www.ncbi.nlm.nih.gov/pubmed/16325152, 1 April 2006

[256] 'Benefits of exercise for the treatment of depression', *Sports Medicine*, http://www.ncbi.nlm.nih.gov/pubmed/2192427, June 1990

[257] http://velonews.competitor.com/2004/02/training-center/sports-psychology/a-cyclists-guide-to-depression-2_5584, 19 February 2004

[258] Karnazes, D., *Ultramarathon Man: Confessions of an All-Night Runner* (London: Penguin, 2006)

[259] Bellow, S., *More Die of Heartbreak* (New York: William Morrow & Co., 1987)

[260] https://www.timeshighereducation.com/features/a-national-epic-on-two-wheels/176971.article, 23 May 2003

[261] http://www.cyclingnews.com/races/jack-bobridge-hour-record-attempt-2015/results/, 1 February 2015

[262] https://www.timeshighereducation.com/features/a-national-epic-on-two-wheels/176971.article, 23 May 2003

[263] http://www.bbc.com/news/health-31095384, 2 February 2015

[264] *Ibid.*

[265] Sri Dhammananda, K., *What Buddhists Believe* (Taiwan: The Corporate Body of the Buddha Educational Foundation, Fifth Edition, 1993); http://www.budaedu.org/en/

[266] *Ibid.*

[267] Hamilton, T., and Coyle, D., *The Secret Race: Inside the Hidden World of the Tour de France* (London: Bantam Press, 2012)

[268] http://www.mindbodygreen.com/0-7088/tour-de-france-rider-talks-about-yoga-lance-cheese-and-more.html, 10 December 2012

[269] Woodland, L., *Cycling's 50 Craziest Stories* (McMinnville, OR: McGann Publishing, 2010)

[270] Henry, R., 'Vélocio vs the Tour de France', *Bicycle Quarterly*, (5) 2006

[271] http://www.cyclingnews.com/news/dennis-i-rode-a-perfect-time-trial-for-my-ability-at-the-moment/, 25 September 2014

[272] Watts, A., *Eastern Wisdom, Modern Life* (Novato, CA: New World Library, 2006); © Alan Watts, reprinted with permission of New World Library

[273] McMillan, C.J., and Barry, M., *Le Métier: The Seasons of a Professional Cyclist* (London: Bloomsbury, 2013)

[274] http://www.bicycling.com/training/fitness/transcendent-pain, 5 July 2012

[275] McMillan, C.J., and Barry, M., 'Foreword', *Le Métier: The Seasons of a Professional Cyclist* (London: Bloomsbury, 2013)

[276] http://www.scotsman.com/news/interview-david-millar-cyclist-1-1701981, 19 June 2011

[277] McMillan, C.J., and Barry, M., 'Foreword', *Le Métier: The Seasons of a Professional Cyclist* (London: Bloomsbury, 2013)

[278] McMillan, C.J., and Barry, M., *Le Métier: The Seasons of a Professional Cyclist* (London: Bloomsbury, 2013)

[279] McMillan, C.J., and Barry, M., 'Foreword', *Le Métier: The Seasons of a Professional Cyclist* (London: Bloomsbury, 2013)

[280] *Ibid.*

[281] *Ibid.*

[282] Krabbé, T., *The Rider* (London: Bloomsbury Publishing, 2002)

[283] *Ibid.*

[284] *Ibid.*

[285] *Ibid.*

[286] http://www.theguardian.com/sport/2013/may/28/victoria-pendleton-enjoy-riding-bike, 28 May 2013

[287] http://www.theguardian.com/sport/2014/jul/24/bradley-wiggins-commonwealth-games-tour-de-france, 24 July 2014

[288] http://www.newstatesman.com/culture/culture/2012/05/review-merckx-half-man-half-bike-william-fotheringham, 3 May 2012

[289] https://100tours100tales.wordpress.com/2014/04/01/1969-the-birth-of-merckxissimo-at-the-tour-of-flanders/ , 1 April 2014

[290] http://www.theguardian.com/sport/100-tours-100-tales/2014/apr/04/cycling-eddy-merckx-1969-tour-flanders, 4 April 2014

[291] Hamilton, T., and Coyle, D., *The Secret Race: Inside the Hidden World of the Tour de France* (London: Bantam Press, 2012)

[292] http://www.theage.com.au/articles/2003/07/23/1058853136522.html, 23 July 2003

[293] http://www.businessinsider.com/gene-doping-at-the-olympics-2014-2, 19 February 2014

[294] 'Would you dope? A general population test of the Goldman dilemma', *British Journal of Sports Medicine*, http://bjsm.bmj.com/content/43/11/871.abstract, 2009

[295] http://www.theguardian.com/sport/2003/jun/01/cycling.features, 1 June 2003

[296] *Ibid.*

[297] *Ibid.*

[298] *Ibid.*

Index